Economics: Current and Future Developments

Volume 1

Interest Rate Modeling for Risk Management

Market Price of Interest Rate Risk

Authored By
Takashi Yasuoka

Graduate School of Engineering Management,
Shibaura Institute of Technology.
3-9-14 Shibaura, Minato-ku, Tokyo
Japan

Contents

The Cover Image has been provided by Takashi Yasuoka, the author of this book

SUMMARY

This book addresses interest rate modeling for risk management. The interest rate model is specified under the real-world measure, and the result is used as to generate scenarios for interest rates. This type of system is referred to as real-world modeling in this book. For use in real-world modeling, this book introduces a theoretical framework that allows estimating the market price of interest rate risk, and this framework follows the line of my recent work. Some additional topics are covered, such as properties of the real-world model, the negative price tendency of the market price of risk, and a positive market price of risk (with an example of this actually occurring).

PREFACE

Interest rate risk is one of the most important types of financial risk that must be considered by banks, insurers, and other financial institutions. Typically, an empirical scenario model of interest rates has been used to measure risk. However, interest rate models are a promising tool for generating the scenarios. To develop this topic, this book introduces advanced methods for employing interest rate models as scenario models.

An interest rate model describes the dynamical behavior of interest rates by a stochastic differential equation. Initially, this behavior is specified under the real-world measure, with the result called a real-world model. The market price of risk is mathematically defined so as to ensure the arbitrage-free property of the model. In practice, the model is represented under a risk-neutral measure to eliminate the market price of risk; we call the result a risk-neutral model. Interest rate models has been developed as risk-neutral models because of their convenience: the market price of risk does not need to be estimated for such models. Because of this, estimation of the market price of risk has not been theoretically studied for several decades.

On the one hand, if we are going to use interest rate models for risk management, then we should use real-world models. This means that we need to numerically obtain the market price of risk to work with real-world models. On the other hand, estimating the market price of risk has been, in practice, fraught with ambiguity. To address this, this book introduces a theory of real-world modeling based on recent results in my other works.

This book is intended primarily for practitioners in financial institutions. Additionally, this book presents a new perspective on the study of interest rate models because real-world modeling is an emerging subject for the future. This book contains a number of substantial and advanced subjects likely to be of interest to researchers and graduate students in financial engineering or econometrics.

This book consists of two main parts. The first part summarizes the fundamentals of interest rate models. Chapter 1 introduces the basic concepts of fixed income risk and interest rate risk. Chapter 2 introduces stochastic calculus and stochastic differential equations. Chapter 3 presents arbitrage pricing theory, adopting the martingale approach, and defines the market price of risk. Chapter 4 introduces interest rate modeling in the Heath–Jarrow–Morton (HJM) framework. As the last topic in the first part, the LIBOR market model is introduced in Chapter 5.

The second part introduces the theory of real-world models, methods of estimating the market price of risk, properties of the market price of risk, and numerical features of real-world simulation. I expect that the contents of this part will be helpful to those who need to use the real-world model in practice. Results in this second part are based mostly on my other works, to which this book serves as a complement, offering additional precision and more thorough explanations. Additionally, this book contains newly written content on topics including maximum likelihood estimation of the market price of risk, real-world modeling in the Hull–White model, and the negative price tendency of the market price of risk.

Chapter 6 develops the fundamental theory of the real-world model in the HJM model, and in Chapter 7 we give some remarks about the real-world model. Chapter 8 presents real-world modeling, focusing on the Hull–White model as an application of the results in the HJM model. Chapter 9 introduces the theory for the real-world model in the LIBOR market model, presenting the topics in parallel with the presentation in Chapter 6. The remarks given in Chapter 7 are also applicable to the real-world models in the Hull–White model and the LIBOR market model. As a conclusion, Chapter 10 shows some numerical examples that demonstrate results from Chapters 6 to 9. The Appendix presents some basic algorithms used in numerical analysis and the proofs of some of the results from Chapter 9.

Throughout this book, I have tried to describe the development of mathematical expression as straightforwardly as possible and have included figures to illustrate some points. Because of this, in some places strict mathematical style has been left aside to obtain practical implications.

So far, the real-world model has been only a dream with respect to practical use. My hope is that this book will help bring the model from dreams to the real world and provide worthwhile suggestions for reconsidering the current state of interest-rate-risk management.

Takashi Yasuoka
Graduate School of Engineering Management,
Shibaura Institute of Technology.
3-9-14 Shibaura, Minato-ku, Tokyo 108-0023
Japan
E-mail: yasuoka@shibaura-it.ac.jp

ACKNOWLEDGEMENTS

I am very grateful to Toshifumi Ikemori, Shisou Kataoka, Chihiro Magara, Koichi Matsumoto and Naoki Matsuyama for their helpful comments and suggestions. I thank Chad Musick for English proofreading. Also, I am very grateful to Bentham Science Publishers for the opportunity to publish this book. I thank Miwako for her support during the writing of this book.

I acknowledge the financial support of KAKENHI Grant Number 26380399, from the Japan Society for the Promotion of Science, as well as support from the Project Research of Shibaura Institute of Technology for a series of studies on real-world models.

CONFLICT OF INTEREST

The author confirms that this eBook content no conflict of interest.

BIOGRAPHY

Takashi Yasuoka is a Professor in the Graduate School of Engineering Management at Shibaura Institute of Technology, where he has been a faculty member since 2009, and was a part-time instructor during 2003–2008. His main interest is the implementation of interest rate models in theory and practice. In particular, his current interest is applying interest rate models to risk management. He is specifically interested in estimation of the market price of risk, properties of the real-world model, and numerical implementation of real-world models.

During 1986-2009, he worked at Fuyo Research Institute (which merged with Fuji Research Institute Corporation and is presently Mizuho Information & Research Institute), where he worked in the Financial Engineering Division from 1997 to 2009. His main jobs were implementation of interest rate models for pricing derivatives and structured products, and improvement of arbitrage trading in interest rate markets. He served as a general manager from 2003 to 2009.

He holds a B.S. in Mathematics from Osaka University, an M.S. in Mathematics from Kobe University, and a Ph.D. in Mathematical Science from Kyushu University.

Professor Yasuoka is also a modern artist, working in oil painting, mixed media, and copper plate printing, among others. He has exhibited his work on more than ten occasions, in Tokyo, Aizu-wakamatsu, Machida, and other places from 1997 to the present. He was born in Japan and lives in Yokohama, Japan.

CHAPTER 1

INTEREST RATE RISK

Abstract: This chapter introduces basic concepts of managing risk from interest rates. We summarize the fundamental concepts of interest rate theory, such as discount factors, bond pricing, forward rate, swap rate, and term structures of interest rates. Additionally, historical data on interest rates of markets are shown, and these data suggest to us that market uncertainty is an important factor in financial risk.

Next, we introduce several risk measures used to evaluate interest rate risk: sensitivity, convexity, and value at risk (VaR). And, we briefly explain three methods to measure the VaR: covariance VaR, historical VaR, and Monte Carlo VaR. Additionally, nested simulation is explained for risk assessment in a derivative portfolio. After considering the validity of VaR as a risk measure, we address coherent risk measures.

Keywords: Bond price, Bootstrapping, Coherent risk measure, Convexity, Covariance VaR, Discount factor, Discount rate, Expected shortfall, Fixed coupon bond, Forward LIBOR, Forward rate, Historical VaR, Implied forward rate, Interest rate risk, LIBOR, Monte Carlo simulation, Nested simulation, Real-world measure, Risk factors, Sensitivity, Value at risk (VaR), Swap rate, Yield curve, Tail risk, Term structure, Yield to maturity, Zero-coupon bond

Takashi Yasuoka

This chapter introduces basic concepts of managing risk from interest rates. We summarize the fundamental concepts of interest rate theory, such as discount factors, bond pricing, forward rate , swap rate, and term structures of interest rates, *etc.* With these, many books have been written about interest rate markets, aimed at both practitioners and academics. For details, readers are recommended to consult Choudhry (2004), Filipovic (2009), Geiger (2011), Hull (2000), Nawalkha *et al.* (2005), Sadr (2009), Jha (2011), and Tavella (2003) as representative examples. For measuring the VaR or other risk measures, in particular, readers are recommended to consult Alexander (2001), Glasserman (2004), Jorion (2007), and Kriele and Wolf (2012).

1.1 Interest Rate and Discount Factor

This section introduces some fundamentals of interest rate theory, including discount factors, bond pricing, yield, forward rates, swap rates, and so on.

Discount factor

Let r denote a simple interest rate for a period $[0, T]$. If we invest 1 unit of currency today, this investment will be worth $1 + rT$ at time T. Thus, a present value of 1 is economically equivalent to a value of $1+rT$ at time T. In other words, today's $1/(1+rT)$ has a future value of 1 at time T. Accordingly a present value of

$$\frac{C}{1+rT} \tag{1.1}$$

is equivalent to a future value of C at time T.

The factor $1/(1 + rT)$ is called the *discount factor*, and r is called the *discount rate*. The discount factor to time T is denoted by $D(T)$, hence

$$D(T) = \frac{1}{1+rT}. \tag{1.2}$$

Typically, the *present value* of a cash flow C at time T is defined as the result of discounting back the cash flow as $D(T)C$.

Next, let r denote an annually compounded interest rate. If we repeatedly invest 1 at this rate r for n years, then the value of the investment would be

$(1+r)^n$ at time n. The discount factor for n years is thus formulated as

$$D(n) = \frac{1}{(1+r)^n}. \tag{1.3}$$

Similarly, when r denotes the semi-annually compounded interest rate, the discount factor for n years is

$$D(n) = \frac{1}{(1+r/2)^{2n}}. \tag{1.4}$$

Bond price

Consider a fixed-coupon bond with that matures in n years with annual coupon rate c. For this book, we always assume that bonds are risk-free; in other words, bonds do not suffer from credit risk. For convenience, we assume that interest payments on the bond are made at times $t = 1, \cdots, n$ and that the face value $(= 1)$ is paid at $t = n$ along with the interest. The price B of this bond is given as the sum of the present values of each payment. That is,

$$B = D(1)c + \cdots + D(n)(1+c). \tag{1.5}$$

Note that when $c = 0$, we obtain $B = D(n)$. This means, as expected, that the price of a zero-coupon bond is equal to the discount factor to the maturity date.

When the annual discount rate is r, the price of the bond is given by

$$B = \frac{c}{(1+r)} + \frac{c}{(1+r)^2} + \cdots + \frac{1+c}{(1+r)^n}. \tag{1.6}$$

Similarly, when the semi-annual discount rate is r, the price is

$$B = \frac{c}{(1+r/2)} + \frac{c}{(1+r/2)^2} + \cdots + \frac{1+c}{(1+r/2)^{2n}}. \tag{1.7}$$

Yield to maturity

Let B denote the price of a bond with annual coupon rate c and maturity at n years. If there is an annual interest rate r such that

$$B = \frac{c}{(1+r)} + \frac{c}{(1+r)^2} + \cdots + \frac{1+c}{(1+r)^n}, \tag{1.8}$$

then r is referred to as the *yield to maturity*. For a semi-annual coupon bond with price B, the yield to maturity is similarly defined, as the semi-annual interest rate r such that

$$FB = \frac{c}{(1+r/2)} + \frac{c}{(1+r/2)^2} + \cdots + \frac{1+c}{(1+r/2)^{2n}}. \tag{1.9}$$

In practice, the discount factor and the yield to maturity are calculated by taking account of the actual number of days for each payment. For the sake of simplicity, in this book we do not use the actual numbers. Instead, we make assumptions that simplify the details of computation, as shown in the above equations.

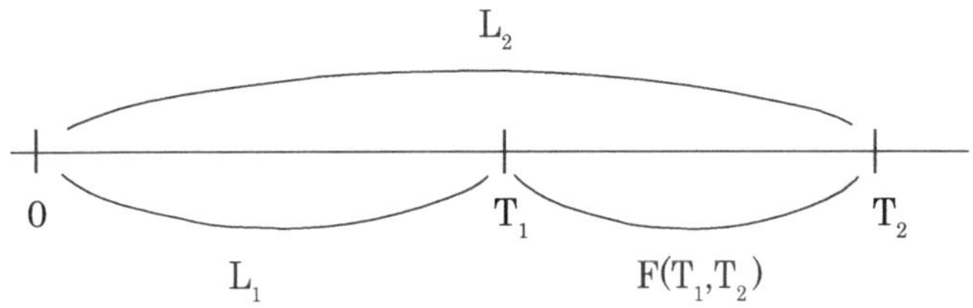

Figure 1.1: Two investment strategies to determine the forward rate $F(T_1, T_2)$

Forward rate

For future times $T_1 < T_2$, let r_1 and r_2 be simple interest rates for periods $[0, T_1]$ and $[0, T_2]$, respectively. We denote by $F(T_1, T_2)$ the *simple forward rate* (or forward rate, for short) over the future period $[T_1, T_2]$. To determine the forward rate $F(T_1, T_2)$, we consider two strategies.

A Lend 1 at time 0 for period $[0, T_2]$, and receive the principal at time T_2.

B Lend 1 at time 0 for period $[0, T_1]$, receive the principal at T_1, and lend it again for the period $[T_1, T_2]$.

In Fig. 1.1, the upper part shows strategy A, and the lower part shows strategy B.

In the absence of arbitrage opportunity between the two strategies, the terminal values should be equivalent; that is,

$$1 + r_2 T_2 = (1 + r_1 T_1)\{1 + F(T_1, T_2)(T_2 - T_1)\}. \tag{1.10}$$

From this equation, the forward rate $F(T_1, T_2)$ can be formulated as

$$F(T_1, T_2) = \frac{1}{T_2 - T_1}\left(\frac{1 + r_2 T_2}{1 + r_1 T_1} - 1\right). \tag{1.11}$$

Furthermore, the forward rate can be represented in a more general form. Let $D(T_1)$ and $D(T_2)$ denote the discount factors to T_1 and T_2, respectively. Then, the forward rate is given by

$$F(T_1, T_2) = \frac{1}{T_2 - T_1}\left(\frac{D(T_1)}{D(T_2)} - 1\right). \tag{1.12}$$

This equation will be used often in the theory of interest rate modeling.

Instantaneous forward rate

If we regarding the discount factor $D(T)$ as a function of T, and if $D(T)$ is differentiable on $[0, T]$, then the *instantaneous forward rate* $f(T)$ at maturity T is defined as

$$\begin{aligned} f(T) &= \lim_{\Delta T \to 0} F(T, T + \Delta T) \\ &= \lim_{\Delta T \to 0} \frac{-1}{\Delta T}\left(\frac{D(T + \Delta T) - D(T)}{D(T + \Delta T)}\right) \\ &= -\frac{1}{D(T + \Delta T)} \frac{dD(T + \Delta T)}{dT} \\ &= -\frac{d \log D(T)}{dT}. \end{aligned} \tag{1.13}$$

Integrating the above, we have

$$D(T) = \exp\left\{-\int_0^T f(s)ds\right\}. \tag{1.14}$$

The theory of interest rate models for the instantaneous forward rate will be introduced in Chapter 4.

1.2 Swap Rate and Forward Libor

This section introduces the fundamentals of the London Interbank Offered Rate (LIBOR) and swap rates, which are the most important interest rates in derivatives trading.

Interest rate swap

The most common example of a swap contract is a fixed-for-floating rate swap in a single currency. The floating rate is usually determined from the LIBOR, and the fixed rate is referred to as the swap rate. For example in a semi-annual swap, the six-month LIBOR rate is converted to a fixed rate.

Let $T_i, i = 1, \cdots, n$ be a sequence of future days, and let T_n be the maturity date of the swap. For simplicity, we assume that the notional principal is equal to 1. In the swap contract, the payer of the fixed rate pays the swap rate and receives the forward LIBOR at every T_i. The receiver of the fixed rate pays the forward LIBOR and receives the swap rate at every T_i.

We denote by $S(n)$ a swap rate with maturity T_n, and by $L(i)$ a forward LIBOR for the period $[T_i, T_{i+1}]$. $D(i)$ denotes the discount factor to time T_i. For simplicity, we assume that each interval of the period $[T_i, T_{i+1}]$ is the same length, $\delta > 0$. That is, $T_{i+1} - T_i = \delta$ for all $i < n$. Note that the floating payment $\delta L(i)$ takes place at time T_{i+1}, and so its present value is given by $L(i)D(i+1)$. Since the present value of the fixed cash flows should be equal to that of the floating cash flows, we obtain

$$S(n) \sum_{i=0}^{n-1} \delta D(i+1) = \sum_{i=0}^{n-1} \delta D(i+1) L(i). \tag{1.15}$$

From (1.12), it holds that

$$\delta D(i+1) L(i) = D(i) - D(i+1). \tag{1.16}$$

Taking the sum of (1.16) over $i = 0, \cdots, n-1$, the right side of (1.15) becomes

$$\begin{aligned} \delta \sum_{i=0}^{n-1} D(i+1) L(i) &= \sum_{i=0}^{n-1} D(i) - D(i+1) \\ &= 1 - D(n). \end{aligned} \tag{1.17}$$

Substituting the above into (1.15), the swap rate can be represented by the discount factors as

$$S(n) = \frac{1 - D(n)}{\sum_{i=1}^{n-1} \delta D(i+1)}. \tag{1.18}$$

Forward rate building

From (1.18), we have a system of linear equations such that

$$\begin{aligned} 1 &= S(m) \sum_{i=1}^{m-1} \delta D(i+1) + D(m) \\ &= S(m) \sum_{i=1}^{m-2} \delta D(i+1) + (1 + \delta S(m)) D(m), \end{aligned} \tag{1.19}$$

for $m = 1, \cdots, n/\delta$. Alternatively, this can be represented by the following equation.

$$\begin{pmatrix} 1+\delta S(1) & 0 & \cdots & 0 \\ \delta S(2) & 1+\delta S(2) & \ddots & \vdots \\ \vdots & \vdots & \ddots & 0 \\ \delta S(n) & \delta S(n) & \cdots & 1+\delta S(n) \end{pmatrix} \begin{pmatrix} D(1) \\ D(2) \\ \vdots \\ D(n) \end{pmatrix} = \begin{pmatrix} 1 \\ 1 \\ \vdots \\ 1 \end{pmatrix} \tag{1.20}$$

Then, from all swap rates $S(m), m = 1, \cdots, n$, we can obtain all discount factors $D(m), m = 1, \cdots, n$ by solving the above equation. Fortunately, the coefficient matrix of (1.20) is lower-triangle, and so the above equation is readily solved by forward substitution as follows.

1) $D(1)$ is directly solved from the first row in (1.20) by $D(1) = 1/(1 + \delta S(1))$.

2) Substituting $D(1)$ into the second equation, we have

$$(1 + \delta S(2)) D(2) = 1 - \delta S(2) D(1). \tag{1.21}$$

Solving $D(2)$ from this equation, it follows that

$$D(2) = \frac{1 - \delta S(2) D(1)}{1 + \delta S(2)}. \tag{1.22}$$

3) Substituting $D(1)$ and $D(2)$ into the third equation, we obtain

$$(1+\delta S(3))D(3) = 1-\delta S(3)(D(1)+D(2)). \tag{1.23}$$

Then,

$$D(3) = \frac{1-\delta S(3)(D(1)+D(2))}{1+\delta S(3)}. \tag{1.24}$$

4) Inductively, we have

$$D(m) = \frac{1-\delta S(m)(\sum_{i=1}^{m-1} D(i))}{1+\delta S(m)}. \tag{1.25}$$

for all $m \leq n$.

This algorithm is known as *bootstrapping* (cf. Nawalkha *et al.* (2005)). The discount factors are computed with respect to all m by solving the above equation. Finally, the forward LIBOR is determined from the discount factors by using (1.16) as

$$L(i) = \frac{D(i)-D(i+1)}{\delta D(i+1)} \tag{1.26}$$

for all i.

We remark that it is not possible to observe all swap rates for $S(m), m = 1, \cdots, n$ in an actual market. In the practice, some values of $S(m)$ are computed by interpolation.

1.3 Term Structure of Interest Rates

The yield to maturity of bonds can be observed in the bond market. The yield curve is a graph that plots time to maturity on the horizontal axis and the yield to maturity on the vertical axis, which visually exhibits the term structure of interest rates. The swap rate curve and the forward LIBOR curve are similarly exhibited.

For example, from (1.15) the swap rate $S(n)$ is represented by a series of forward LIBORs $L(i), i = 1, \cdots, n-1$ as

$$S(n) = \frac{\sum_{i=0}^{n-1} \delta D(i+1)L(i)}{\sum_{i=0}^{n-1} \delta D(i+1)}. \tag{1.27}$$

(a) Yield curve

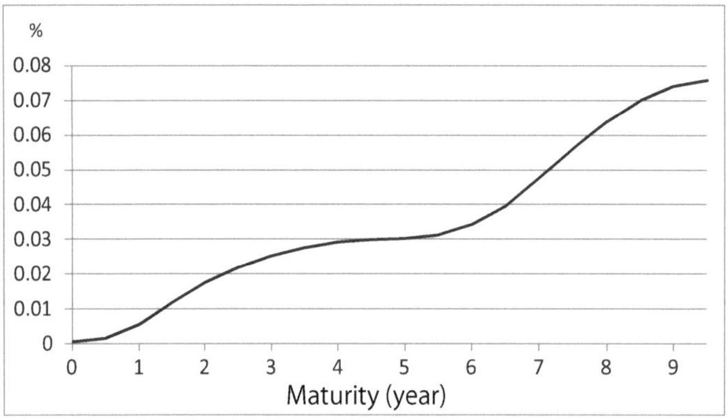

(b) Six-month implied forward rate

Figure 1.2: Yield curve and the implied forward rate. U.S. Treasury market on 25 July 2014. Yield data were retrieved from the Bloomberg site. The author calculated the implied forward rates and created the figure.

This means that the swap rate consists of several forward LIBORs $L(i)$ for $i < n$. This property is the same when considering the yield to maturity.

In contrast, the forward rate is the obtained interest rate of the corresponding future period. Therefore, the forward rate curve shows us the term structure of interest rates more clearly than the yield curve and the swap rate curve can. For this reason, the forward rate curve is often used to analyze the interest rate market. In particular, the forward rates derived from a term structure of interest rates are called the *implied forward rate*. For example, the "implied" forward rate can be practically observed in a government bond market or a swap market.

Example 1.3.1: Yield curve and forward rate curve
Fig. 1.2(a) exhibits the yield curve for U.S. Treasury bills on 25 July 2014. From this data, the six-month forward rates are implied; these are shown in Fig. 1.2(b). The graph shows that the forward rate curve dips at around five years. That is, the forward rates for the periods [5, 5.5] and [5.5, 6] (years) are relatively lower than those of other periods. This is typical of how the forward rate curve is usually observed by market participants, including bond investors and derivatives traders.

Example 1.3.2: Historical data on interest rates
Market interest rates are continuously fluctuating. As an example, Fig. 1.3 shows a monthly historical chart of six-month forward rates in the U.S. Treasury market. This chart suggests that movements in forward rates are uncertain and unpredictable. Therefore, the evolution of the forward rates can reasonably be mathematically modeled as a stochastic process. For this, the term structure model of interest rate is constructed so that it simulates the forward-rate dynamics, which will be introduced in Chapters 3 and 5.

1.4 Interest Rate Risk of Bonds

This section summarizes a basic risk measure for the interest rate risk of bonds. First, we examine the relation between bond price and bond yield by calculating some simple examples. Then, we introduce sensitivity risk and convexity risk by referring to the example calculations.

Bond price and yield

Let us consider an n-year bond with annual coupon rate c. We denote by r the annual yield to maturity at n years, which is supposed to be the market yield. This yield is used as the discount rate, and the present price p of the bond is obtained from (1.6) as

$$p = \frac{c}{(1+r)} + \frac{c}{(1+r)^2} + \cdots + \frac{1+c}{(1+r)^n}. \tag{1.28}$$

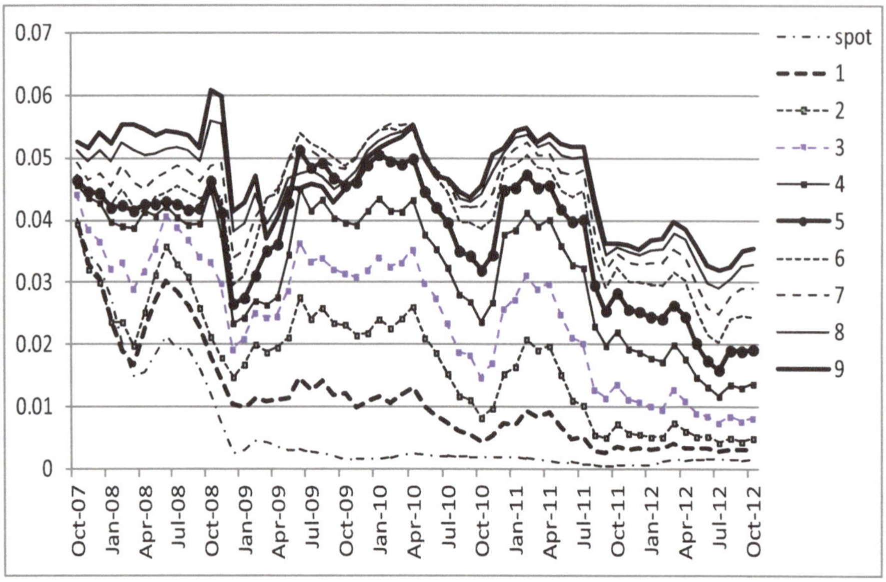

Figure 1.3: Historical chart of implied forward rates. U.S. Treasury market from Oct 2007 to Oct 2012. In the graph, a number such as "3" indicates the forward rate over the period [3, 3.5] (years). Yield data were retrieved from the Board of Governors of the Federal Reserve System (http://www.federalreserve.gov/releases/h15/data.htm) Implied forward rates were calculated by the author.

Example 1.4.1

As an example, let us consider a five-year bond with annual coupon rate of 5%. From (1.28), the present price of this bond is calculated as

$$\begin{aligned} p &= \frac{0.05}{1.05} + \frac{0.05}{(1.05)^2} + \frac{0.05}{(1.05)^3} + \frac{0.05}{(1.05)^4} + \frac{1.05}{(1.05)^5} \\ &= \frac{0.05}{1.05} + \frac{0.05}{1.1025} + \frac{0.05}{1.157625} + \frac{0.05}{1.215506} + \frac{1.05}{1.276282} \\ &= 0.04762 + 0.04535 + 0.04319 + 0.04114 + 0.82270 \\ &= 1.00. \end{aligned} \tag{1.29}$$

Thus, we can buy this bond at face value.

Next, we consider a three-year bond with annual coupon rate of 5%. The price is obtained by

$$\begin{aligned} p &= \frac{0.05}{1.05} + \frac{0.05}{(1.05)^2} + \frac{1.05}{(1.05)^3} \\ &= \frac{0.05}{1.05} + \frac{0.05}{1.1025} + \frac{1.05}{1.157625} \\ &= 0.04762 + 0.04535 + 0.90703 \\ &= 1.00. \end{aligned} \tag{1.30}$$

As with the five-year bond, we can buy the three-year bond at face value. Generally, the bond price is par (i.e., face value) when the market yield coincides with the coupon rate.

Interest rate sensitivity

We define the *interest rate sensitivity* of bonds with respect to yield by

$$\frac{\partial p}{\partial r} = -\frac{c}{(1+r)^2} - \frac{2c}{(1+r)^3} - \cdots - \frac{n(1+c)}{(1+r)^{n+1}} < 0. \tag{1.31}$$

This represents the degree of change in the price of bonds in response to fluctuations in market interest rates. For business, the basis point value (BPV) corresponds to the interest rate sensitivity. Traditionally, duration is also used as a measure of interest rate sensitivity.

From the right side of (1.31), it obviously holds that $\partial p/\partial r < 0$. Thus, interest rate sensitivity is always negative, that is, a rise in interest rates will cause bond prices to fall. If we assume that $c \approx 0$ and $r \approx 0$, then we have the approximation

$$\frac{\partial p}{\partial r} \approx -n. \tag{1.32}$$

Thus, bonds with longer time to maturity show larger changes in price than those with shorter time to maturity. This suggest that the longer a bond has until maturity, the larger the interest rate risk is.

Example 1.4.2: Interest rate sensitivity

Consider the three-year bond in Example 1.4.1. The interest rate sensitivity is calculated by (1.31) as follows.

$$\begin{aligned}\frac{\partial p}{\partial y} &= -\frac{0.05}{(1.05)^2} - \frac{2 \times 0.05}{(1.05)^3} - \frac{3 \times 1.05}{(1.05)^4} \\ &= -\frac{0.05}{1.1025} - \frac{0.1}{1.157625} - \frac{3.15}{1.215520} \\ &= -0.04535 - 0.08639 - 2.59151 \\ &= -2.72325 \end{aligned} \tag{1.33}$$

From this, (1.32) implies that $\partial p/\partial r \approx -3$. Hence, we may consider that (1.32) roughly approximates $\partial p/\partial r$.

Convexity

If the three-year yield falls to 4%, then the price of the three-year bond will become

$$\begin{aligned} p &= \frac{0.05}{1.04} + \frac{0.05}{(1.04)^2} + \frac{1.05}{(1.04)^3} \\ &= \frac{0.05}{1.04} + \frac{0.05}{1.0816} + \frac{1.05}{1.124864} \\ &= 0.04808 + 0.04623 + 0.93344 \\ &= 1.02775. \end{aligned} \tag{1.34}$$

Then, a 1% yield rise causes a 2.775% price fall, which is somewhat different from the result of (1.33). The difference here is caused by interest rate sensitivity that is not constant with respect to the level of the interest rate. Indeed, (1.31) is a nonlinear function of r.

The second derivative of the price p is represented by

$$\frac{\partial^2 p}{\partial r^2} = \frac{2c}{(1+r)^3} + \frac{6c}{(1+r)^4} + \cdots + \frac{n(n-1)c}{(1+r)^{n+2}}. \tag{1.35}$$

We see that the right hand is always positive, and from this the price function of (1.31) is strictly convex.

If, instead, the three-year yield rises to 6%, then the price of the above three-year bond will be

$$\begin{aligned} p &= \frac{0.05}{1.06} + \frac{0.05}{(1.06)^2} + \frac{1.05}{(1.06)^3} \\ &= \frac{0.05}{1.06} + \frac{0.05}{1.1236} + \frac{1.05}{1.191016} \\ &= 0.04717 + 0.04450 + 0.88160 \\ &= 0.97327. \end{aligned} \tag{1.36}$$

Here, a price fall of 2.673% results in a 1% yield rise. The percentage increase in price is greater than the percentage decrease in price. This difference represents the degree of convexity of (1.28).

Convexity risk

Assume that we hold a three-year bond when the three-year yield is 5%. Let us consider the interest rate future, whose interest rate sensitivity is 1% to a 1% change in three-year yield. Here, we may assume that the interest rate future has convexity of 0. If we sell the future for 2.723 units, then our interest rate risk becomes 0 today. If the yield falls to 4%, then we lose 2.775% from the bond and gain 2.723% from the future. We lose from this trade, by a hedge error of $-2.775 + 2.723 = -0.052 \quad (\%)$. This hedge error represents the risk caused by convexity, which is referred to as *convexity risk.*

Fig. 1.4 contains graphs of the bond price relative to the yield for three-, five-, and ten-year bonds with a coupon rate of 5%. This shows that the slope of the curve is larger for longer maturity bonds, and all the curves seem to be slightly convex.

1.5 Value at Risk

This section studies risk measures for portfolios. For the sake of simplifying descriptions, we assume that the portfolio has only assets, with liabilities regarded as negative assets. We additionally regard a single asset as a portfolio.

There are two kinds of risk measures to assess the portfolio risk. One is sensitivity, which is the price change in a portfolio resulting from changes in the risk factor. Another is VaR. We begin by addressing the risk factors.

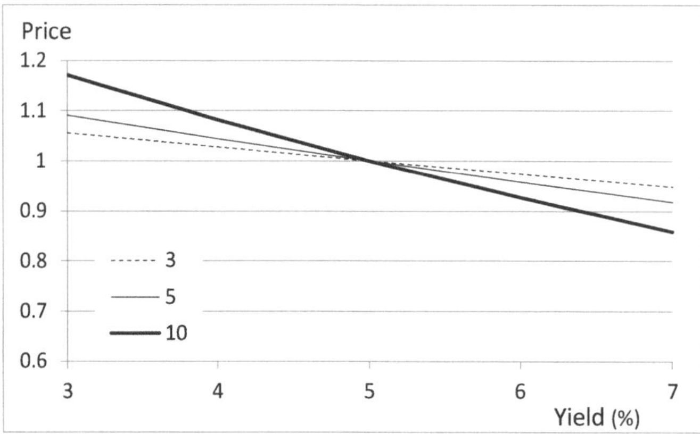

Figure 1.4: Bond price to yield for 3-, 5-, and 10-year bonds.

Risk factors of portfolio

The value of a portfolio is affected by changes in *risk factors*. The basic risk factors for financial assets consist of market risk, credit risk, liquidity risk, and so on. The market risk is generally classified into interest rate risk, exchange rate risk (also called currency risk), and stock price risk. The interest rate risk of bonds was discussed in Section 1.4 of this chapter. Credit risk is the risk of default by the counterparty, such as the risk that a bond issuer will default on payments. Liquidity risk is the risk that arises from the difficulty of selling an asset; sometimes it is reflected in widening of the bid–ask spread.

$$\text{risk factors} = \begin{cases} \text{market risk} & (\text{market risk, exchange rate, stock price}) \\ \text{credit risk} & \\ \text{liquidity risk} & \\ \textit{etc.} & \end{cases} \tag{1.37}$$

Basically, the risk factor of government bonds is the interest rate risk only. The risk factors of foreign government bonds are exchange rate risk and foreign interest rate risk. Sometimes, sovereign credit risk is non-negligible.

Risk measures: Sensitivity

Let $x_1, \cdots$ denote factors with risk, such as yield, forward rate, and exchange rate. We assume that the price of a portfolio is represented by $p(x_1, x_2, \cdots)$.

Then, the x_i-*sensitivity* of a portfolio is defined by $\partial p(x_i)/\partial x_i$, for $i = 1, 2, \cdots$.

For example, the bond price p is represented in (1.28) by a function of yield r, as

$$p = \frac{c}{(1+r)} + \frac{c}{(1+r)^2} + \cdots + \frac{1+c}{(1+r)^n}. \tag{1.38}$$

The interest rate sensitivity is given in (1.31) by the partial derivative with respect to r, as

$$\frac{\partial p}{\partial r} = -\frac{c}{(1+r)^2} - \frac{2c}{(1+r)^3} - \cdots - \frac{n(1+c)}{(1+r)^{n+1}}. \tag{1.39}$$

In practice, there are several measures of interest rate sensitivity. The basis point value (BPV) is the sensitivity to a change of 0.01% (= 1 basis point) in the forward rates. The "delta" of an option is that option's sensitivity to the underlying risk factor. These sensitivities are significant measures for both assessing the risk of the portfolio and determining the hedge ratio of the portfolio. For details, see, among others, Hull (2000) and Sadr (2009).

Linearity of portfolio

If the value of a portfolio is represented by a linear combination of risk factors, such that

$$p(x_1, x_2, \cdots) = c_0 + c_1 x_1 + c_2 x_2 + \cdots, \tag{1.40}$$

then the portfolio is called linear to $x_1, x_2, \cdots$.

For example, consider a forward contract of some asset with a delivery date of T. We denote by r the simple interest rate to T and by p the present price of the asset. Then, the forward price is given by $F_p = p/(1 + rT)$. Therefore, when regarding the asset price as a risk factor, F_p is linear to p.

Similarly, regarding the underlying asset as a risk factor for futures implies that the future price is also linear to p. As an example, interest rate futures can be considered as linear to the forward LIBOR.

Convexity

It is more usual for a portfolio to be nonlinear. Indeed, we have already seen that the price of fixed-coupon bonds is not linear, as shown in (1.39).

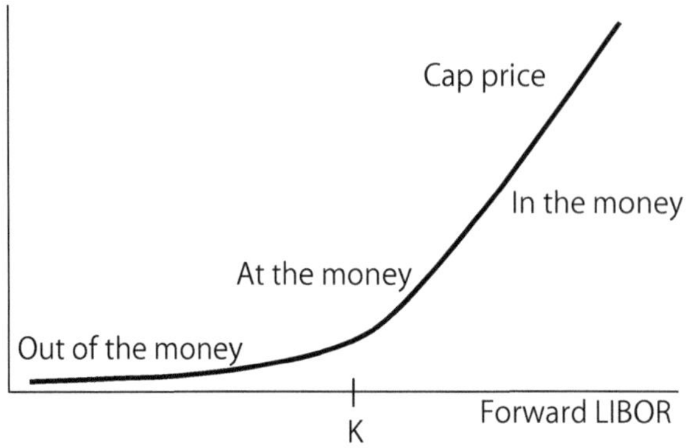

Figure 1.5: Convex property of cap price for the forward LIBOR

Furthermore, a call/put option written on some underlying risk factor has noteworthy nonlinearity. For example, let us consider a European (interest rate) cap with strike rate K and some expiry date $T > 0$. The price of the cap at $t = 0$ is conceptually illustrated in Fig. 1.5. The price is low and flat out of the money, but the slope of the price curve becomes steeper in the money. The convexity is at maximum near the point where the price is at the money. Thus, European cap/floor options written on the forward LIBOR are the most basic example that exhibits such convexity.

Additionally, it is well known that structured products involving derivatives exhibit strong convexity. Therefore, sensitivity is not sufficient to measure the risk from large changes in risk factors.

Value at risk

In financial risk management, "risk" means the downside risk of the portfolio, rather than sensitivity and convexity. In this context, VaR is a standard measure for financial risk management. Briefly, VaR is the maximum expected loss over a given holding period, calculated at a certain confidence level.

Next, we give the quantitative definition of VaR. Let p_t denote the value of a portfolio at time t, with p_0 as the current value of the portfolio. The value of p_t moves uncertainly according to time. The loss of this portfolio over a holding period T is given by a random variable L, where $L = p_0 - p_T$, with a

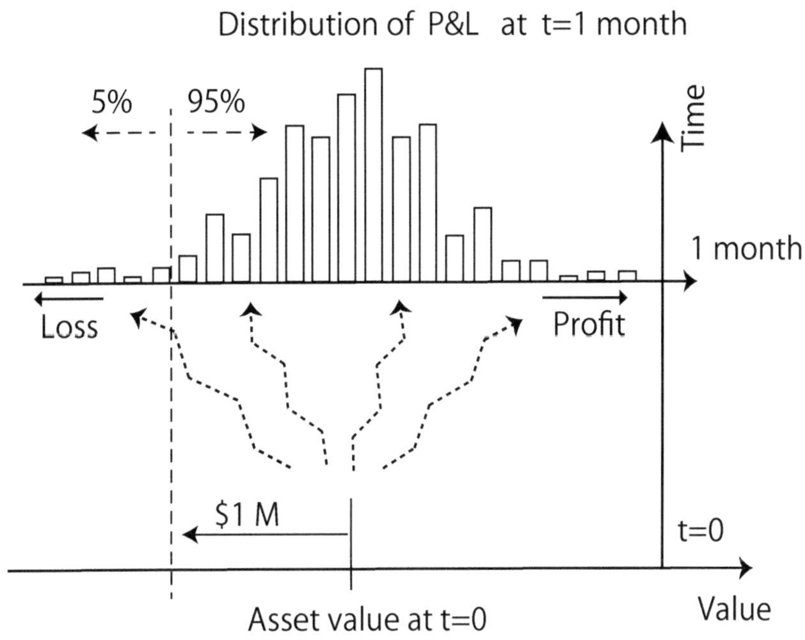

Figure 1.6: VaR and the distribution of asset value

loss represented by a positive value.

To measure the downside risk, we build the profit–loss (P&L) distribution of the portfolio at time T from historical data, as shown in Fig. 1.6. Let α be a constant with $0 < \alpha < 1$. Usually, we set α as a small value, taking, for example, $\alpha = 0.01$ or 0.05. The VaR at confidence level of $1 - \alpha$ over the holding period T is defined by the $100(1 - \alpha)$th centile, such that

$$VaR_\alpha = -\inf\{l : \mathbf{P}(L \leq l) > \alpha\}, \tag{1.41}$$

where $\mathbf{P}$ denotes the probability of the event $L \leq l$, as given by the P&L distribution. In practice, VaR_α is referred to as $100(1-\alpha)\%VaR$. For example, $99\%VaR$ denotes $VaR_{0.01}$.

Meaning of VaR

The definition of VaR formalizes the potential loss in value of the portfolio over a holding period T for a given confidence level $1 - \alpha$. For example, Fig. 1.6 illustrates that the 95% confidence level (95th centile) shows the loss of 1 million U.S. dollars over one month. For that case, the 1-month VaR of the portfolio is estimated as 1 million dollars; that is, there is a 5% chance that the loss in value will be more than 1 million dollars in any given month. As is customary in the literature, VaR is expressed as a positive value in this book.

1.6 Computing VaR

It is possible to theoretically evaluate sensitivity and convexity, which are deterministic, but not to evaluate VaR, because it contains stochastic characteristics. Three basic types of models are used to measure VaR:

1) covariance VaR models;

2) historical simulation models; and

3) Monte Carlo simulation models.

We briefly explain the concepts of these models below, and additionally introduce nested simulation for use with derivative portfolios.

1.6.1 Covariance VaR Models

One-factor model

The covariance VaR model assumes that the portfolio value is linear to the risk factor and normally distributed. Then, the key parameters are the mean and variance of the P&L distribution, which are measured from historical data.

Let us consider a portfolio with a single risk factor x, the value of which is denoted by $p(x)$. From the linearity assumption, we can model $p(x)$ as $p(x) = a+bx$ for some positive constants a and b. Let μ and σ^2 be, respectively, the mean and variance of x. For convenience, we assume that $p(\mu)$ is equal to the current value of the portfolio. It is known from the normality of the distribution that the 95% confidence level of x is $\mu - 1.645\sigma$, and the 99% confidence level is $\mu - 2.326\sigma$. From this, we can see that the 95%VaR is given by

$$\begin{aligned} 95\%VaR &= \{a + \mu b\} - \{a + b(\mu - 1.645\sigma)\} \\ &= 1.645\sigma b. \end{aligned} \tag{1.42}$$

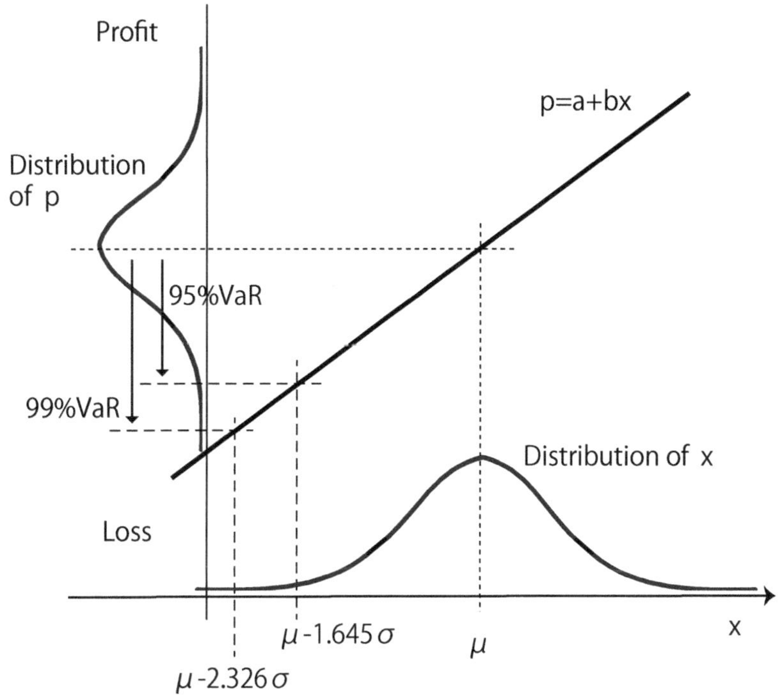

Figure 1.7: Covariance VaR in a one-factor model

Fig. 1.7 may help in understanding this scheme. Similarly, we have

$$99\% VaR = 2.326\sigma b. \tag{1.43}$$

When $p(x)$ is not linear but almost linear, that is, when $p(x) \approx a + bx$, we can approximate the VaR from (1.42) and (1.43).

Multi-factor model

Generally, portfolios have several risk factors. For a model with multiple risk factors, the covariance VaR is estimated by combining the individual means and variances of factors with the covariances among sets of factors.

Let us consider a two-factor model. We assume that the value of a portfolio is represented by two risk factors, x_1 and x_2, and that this portfolio is linear to x_1 and to x_2. Then, for some positive constants a, b_1, and b_2, we have

$$p(x) = a + b_1 x_1 + b_2 x_2. \tag{1.44}$$

Let μ_i and σ_i^2 be the mean and variance of factor x_i, with $i = 1, 2$. We denote by ρ the correlation coefficient between x_1 and x_2. From the assumption that x_1 and x_2 are normally distributed,

$$a + b_1 x_1 + b_2 x_2 \tag{1.45}$$

follows a normal distribution with mean $a + \mu_1 + \mu_2$ and variance σ^2, where

$$\sigma^2 = b_1^2 \sigma_1^2 + b_2^2 \sigma_2^2 + 2 b_1 b_2 \rho \sigma_1 \sigma_2. \tag{1.46a}$$

Equivalently,

$$\sigma^2 = b_1^2 \sigma_1^2 + b_2^2 \sigma_2^2 + 2Cov(x_1, x_2), \tag{1.46b}$$

since $Cov(x_1, x_2) = \rho \sigma_1 \sigma_2$.

We assume that the current value of the portfolio is equal to $p(\mu_1, \mu_2)$. As in the one-factor model, the 95%VaR is obtained by

$$\begin{aligned} 95\%VaR &= \{a + b_1\mu_1 + b_2\mu_2\} - \{a + b_1\mu_1 + b_2\mu_2 - 1.645\sigma\} \\ &= 1.645\sigma. \end{aligned} \tag{1.47}$$

Similarly, we have $99\%VaR = 2.326\sigma$.

The advantage of the covariance VaR is that it is simple and quick to calculate. The disadvantage is that the assumption of linearity restricts the portfolios to which it can be applied. Moreover, the covariance is known to be difficult to estimate because it depends strongly on the sampled period.

1.6.2 Historical Simulation Models

In historical simulation models, the empirical distribution of the P&L is directly constructed from historical data.

For simplicity, we consider a portfolio consisting of two assets, A and B. For a holding period ΔT, let $t_1, \cdots, t_{J+1}$ be a sequence of past days with $t_i - t_{i+1} = \Delta T$ and $t_1 = 0$. We let $p_A(i)$ and $p_B(i)$ denote the prices of A and B, respectively, at t_i. Let $r_A(i)$ and $r_B(i)$ be the rates of return for A and B, respectively. These are defined by

$$r_A(i) = \frac{p_A(i) - p_A(i+1)}{p_A(i+1)} \tag{1.48a}$$

$$r_B(i) = \frac{p_B(i) - p_B(i+1)}{p_B(i+1)} \tag{1.48b}$$

for $i = 1, \cdots, J$.

For the present values $p_A(0)$ and $p_B(0)$, the P&L distribution of the portfolio is built from the set

$$\{p_A(0)r_A(i) + p_B(0)r_B(i)\}_{i=1,\cdots,J}, \tag{1.49}$$

as shown in Fig. 1.6. From this distribution, we obtain the VaR, with the process working according to the idea shown in Fig. 1.6. Even for a very large portfolio, we can measure the VaR in the same way.

It is a point in favor of this model that it does not require assumptions about neither the distribution of prices nor the linearity of assets. However, it is difficult to collect the sufficient historical data for this method. Even when there are sufficiently many data points from a long period of observation, some data might be too old to reasonably reflect future risk, which is needed for measuring VaR.

1.6.3 Monte Carlo Simulation Models

A Monte Carlo method is a simulation technique that uses randomly generated numbers for simulation. Here, distribution functions of risk factors are created by using a sequence of random numbers.

Let T be a holding period. For simplicity, we assume a single risk factor and let $p(x)$ and x denote, respectively, the value of the portfolio and the value of the risk factor at T. We assume that x is normally distributed with mean μ and variance σ^2, and that the current value of the portfolio is equal to $p(\mu)$.

Let $z_i, i = 1, \cdots, J$ be a sequence of numbers generated randomly according to a standard normal distribution, where J is the number of simulation runs. Then, we can assign $x_i = \mu + \sigma z_i$. By regarding generated sequences $x_i, i = 1, \cdots, J$ as scenarios for the risk factor x, we can obtain a distribution $p(x_i)$, where the probability of each scenario is $1/J$. Next we rearrange $\{p(x_i)\}_{i=1,\cdots,J}$ to $\{q_k\}_{k=1,\cdots,J}$ such that

$$\{p(x_i); i = 1, \cdots, J\} = \{q_k; k = 1, \cdots, J\} \tag{1.50}$$

with $q_k \leq q_{k+1}$ for all k.

To obtain a confidence level $1-\alpha$, we set $k_\alpha = \alpha J$. Then, $(1-\alpha)100\%$VaR is given by

$$VaR_\alpha = \frac{-1}{2}(q_{k_\alpha} + q_{k_\alpha+1}). \tag{1.51}$$

It is advantageous that Monte Carlo simulation models are applicable to nonlinear assets and path-dependent assets. This makes it possible to consider a great many scenarios. Moreover, we can employ this technique to the arbitrage-free model, which we will introduce in Chapter 3. The disadvantages of Monte Carlo simulation are high computational time and increased model risk.

For a more advanced treatment of Monte Carlo simulation in financial engineering, interested readers are recommended to consult Glasserman (2004).

Remark

Monte Carlo simulation models should be built under the real-world measure, but it is not a trivial exercise to use the arbitrage-free model under that measure. The reasons for this difficulty are addressed in Section 4.2. A key purpose of this book is to study the theory of arbitrage-free models under the real-world measure, and we will work with these in the later part of this book.

1.6.4 Nested Simulation

There are many exotic options whose price depends on the path of an underlying asset. If a structured product involves an exotic derivative, then the price of the product is also path-dependent. Since the pricing of complex products is not trivial, recombining trees and Monte Carlo simulation are employed for pricing.

When a portfolio contains exotic products such as those described above, it is difficult to price them for a future date, which is necessary for measuring VaR. Nested simulation is a computing technique for measuring VaR of a derivatives portfolio, which we briefly introduce below.

Let T be a holding period for measuring VaR. We denote by x_t the value of the risk factor at time t, and by p_T the price of a derivative asset at T. As illustrated in Fig. 1.8, the distribution of the risk factor x_T at T is simulated

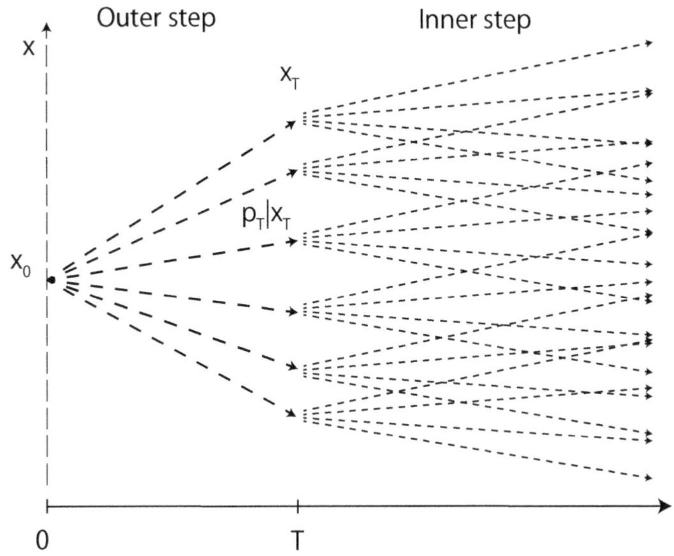

Figure 1.8: Nested simulation

by a Monte Carlo method in the outer step. Then, we consider x_T to represent a scenario in which VaR is to be measured. At each scenario x_T, the derivative is priced as $p_T|x_T$ by another Monte Carlo simulation starting at time T. This is the inner step. Once we obtain the distribution of $p_T|x_T$, we can compute the VaR in the manner described in Section 1.6.3 of this chapter.

A problem intrinsic to nested simulation is that the number of simulation becomes enormous. There are many studies on algorithms for accelerating nested simulation. As examples, see Devineau and Loisel (2009) and Gordy and Juneja (2010), among others.

1.7 Validity of VaR

VaR is widely used as a risk measure in regulatory guidelines in the banking sectors. However it is known that VaR at a particular confidence level does not tell us the loss beyond that level, although the validity of VaR has been studied mathematically and financially in many papers. In this section, we make some brief remarks about the properties of VaR as a downside risk measure and define expected shortfall as a coherent risk measure. We address these issues

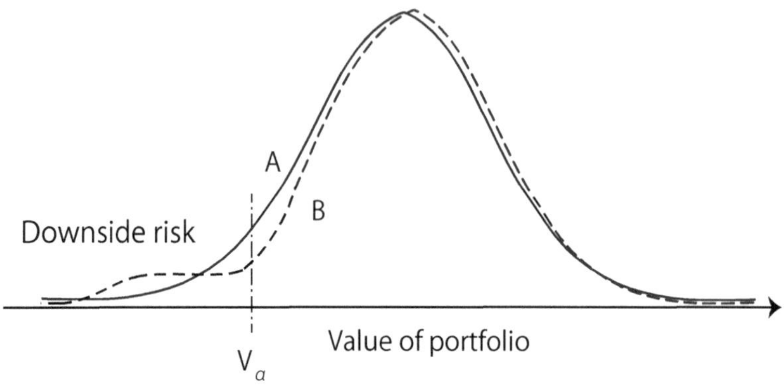

Figure 1.9: VaR and downside risk of two portfolios. Downside risk of B is larger than that of A.

basically according to the Bank for International Settlement (BIS, 2004b) for tail risk and according to Artzner *et al.* (1999) for coherent risk measures.

For this purpose, we denote by X the value of a portfolio at time T, and by ρ a risk measure for X. Then, $\rho(X)$ represents the size of the risk of X measured by ρ. Naturally, the portfolio is allowed to sell some options, which creates the possibility that X will take a negative value. To avoid confusion, we note that a large positive $\rho(X)$ represents a larger risk than a small positive or negative $\rho(X)$. We remark that up to the previous section, risk measures have been defined in terms of the profit–loss measures of a portfolio, such as sensitivity, convexity, and VaR. In this section, we work with a risk measure for X that does not represent profit or loss. In this context, we define a VaR of V_α at confidence level $1-\alpha$ over a holding period T as

$$V_\alpha(X) = -\inf\{x|\mathbf{P}(X \leq x) > \alpha\}. \tag{1.52}$$

Tail risk

To explain the tail risk, we consider two portfolios, whose prices at time T are denoted by A for one portfolio and B for the other. We use A and B as the names of these portfolios. We assume that A and B have the same VaR at confidence level $1-\alpha$, so that $V_\alpha(A) = V_\alpha(B)$. In Fig. 1.9, the solid line shows the distribution of future value of A, and the dashed line shows that of B. We see that the downside risk of portfolio B is larger than that of A. This shows that VaR_α does not capture the difference in downside risk between portfolios, as exemplified by A and B; this risk is noted in BIS (2004b) as *tail risk*.

Under VaR regulations, risk managers will choose portfolio B in preference to A because there is a larger opportunity for profit in B. Thus, VaR might mislead risk managers who optimally control their portfolios. For further argument along these lines, see Basak and Shapiro (2001) and Yamai and Yoshiba (2002), among others.

Coherent risk measure

Furthermore, other conceptual problems with VaR are claimed by Artzner *et al.* (1999) and others. To address this, we define four properties according to Artzner *et al.* (1999) as follows.

1) Translation invariance: For a real number c, it holds that $\rho(X+c) = \rho(X) - c$. Namely, if we add cash in the amount c to the portfolio, then the risk is reduced by c.

2) Subadditivity: $\rho(X_1 + X_2) = \rho(X_1) + \rho(X_2)$. This can be summarized as "a merger does not create extra risk."

3) Positive homogeneity: For positive values of λ, it holds that $\rho(\lambda X) = \lambda\rho(X)$.

4) Monotonicity: If $X_1 \leq X_2$, then $\rho(X_1) \geq \rho(X_2)$.

When a risk measure ρ satisfies these four properties, it is said to be *coherent*. Artzner *et al.* (1999) states that risk measures ought to be coherent for use in financial risk management.

Example 1.7.1: Subadditivity

Next, we present a famous example from Artzner *et al.* (1999), showing that percentile-based VaR does not satisfy subadditivity. Consider an investor who has two digital options a and b on a stock price with expiry T. The initial price of option a is $u > 0$, and the payoff at T is defined by the stock price S_T at T and the strike price U as follows.

- The investor pays 1000 if $S_T > U$.
- The investor pays nothing if $S_T \leq U$.

This scenario is equivalent to selling a digital call option with strike price U. The initial price of option b is $l > 0$, and the payoff at T is defined by S_T and the strike price L, with $L < U$, as follows.

- The investor pays nothing if $S_T \geq L$.
- The investor pays 1000 if $S_T < L$.

This is equivalent to selling a digital put option with strike price L.

We assume that

$$\mathbf{P}(S_T < L) = \mathbf{P}(S_T > U) = 0.008. \tag{1.53}$$

Then, the VaR at the 99% confidence level for each position is given by $V_{0.01}(a) = -u$ and $V_{0.01}(b) = -l$. Note that these negative values indicate a profit. Consider a portfolio $a + b$. Since

$$\mathbf{P}((S_T < L) \cup (S_T > U)) = 0.016, \tag{1.54}$$

the VaR of $a + b$ is

$$V_{0.01}(a + b) = 1000 - u - l. \tag{1.55}$$

We see that $V_{0.01}(a + b) > V_{0.01}(a) + V_{0.01}(b)$; that is, subadditivity is not satisfied. This is caused by the fact that both $V_{0.01}(a)$ and $V_{0.01}(b)$ fail to capture downside risk beyond the confidence level.

Expected shortfall

An *expected shortfall* (also called tail conditional expectation and conditional VaR) at a confidence level $1 - \alpha$ over the holding time T is defined by

$$ES_\alpha(X) = E[-X| - X \geq V_\alpha(X)]. \tag{1.56}$$

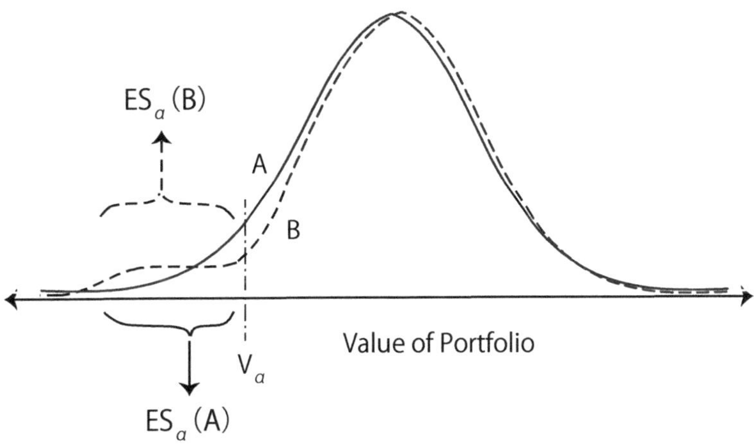

Figure 1.10: Expected shortfalls of two portfolios

Fig. 1.10 illustrates the value distributions of A and B, which are the as same as in Fig. 1.9. We additionally include $ES_\alpha(A)$ and $ES_\alpha(B)$ in the figure, which intuitively shows that $ES_\alpha(B)$ is larger than $ES_\alpha(A)$. This relation looks more reasonable for risk management than the percentile-based VaR does.

We remark that the expected shortfall is not always a better risk measure for financial risk management than the percentile VaR is, which is addressed in Yamai and Yoshiba (2002, 2005), and so on.

Dynamic risk measure

The VaR and expected shortfall are static measures. However, in financial institutions, the risk profile changes with time. With this change, a dynamic risk measure has been studied successfully. This subject is beyond the scope of this book. For details, readers are recommended to consult Hardy and Wirch (2004) or Kriele and Wolf (2012).

Remark

Although the investigation into the best measure to use is of practical importance, it is undisputed that these risk measures should be calculated under the real-world measure. And so, the problem of risk measure should be studied in connection with the problem of real-world modeling. Hence, the study of real-world modeling will remain a central subject of risk management. Additionally, if future financial regulations require a risk measure other than VaR to be used, the theory in this book will still be applicable.

CHAPTER 2

FUNDAMENTALS OF STOCHASTIC ANALYSIS

Abstract: This chapter briefly summarizes basic concepts of stochastic calculus, using intuitive examples. First, the fundamentals of probability spaces are introduced by working with a simple example of a stochastic process. Next, stochastic processes are introduced in connection with a natural filtration and a martingale. Then, we introduce a stochastic integral and Ito's formula, which is an important tool for solving stochastic differential equations. Finally, we address some fundamental examples of stochastic differential equations, which simply model the price process of a financial asset.

Although these subjects are applied in practice to interest rate modeling, the definitions are given for the one-dimensional case for the sake of simplicity. We complement this with some basic results for multi-dimensional cases in Section 2.7, at the end of this chapter.

Keywords: Abstract Bayes' rule, Augmented filtration, Brownian motion, Conditional expectation, Distribution function, Euler approximation, Equivalent measure, Exponential martingale, Filtered probability space, Girsanov theorem, Ito's formula, Market measure, Martingale, Measure change, Natural filtration, Probability space, Quadratic covariation, Random walk, Real-world measure, Risk-neutral measure, Radon–Nykodim derivative, Random variable, Sample space, Stochastic differential equation, Stochastic integral, Stochastic process

This chapter briefly summarizes basic concepts of stochastic calculus, using intuitive examples. We remark that the descriptions in this section are not as rigorously given as they would be in academic textbooks in this field. For readers who are more interested in theoretical aspects, there are many excellent works in the field of probability. Chung and Williams (1990), Karatzas and Shreve (1998), Öksendal (2003), Pliska (1997), and Shreve (2004) are particularly recommended. In connection with interest rate modeling, the reader may find it useful to consult Baxter and Rennie (1996), Björk (2004), Cairns (2004), Gatarek *et al.* (2007), Hull (2000), James and Webber (2000), Shreve (2004), and Tavella (2003), among others.

2.1 Probability Space

Probability space

We denote by Ω a set of all possible outcomes, called the *sample space*, and an element $w \in \Omega$, called a *sample*. The family $\mathcal{F}$ is a collection of subsets of Ω and is assumed to be a σ-algebra. A stochastic event A is represented as an element in $\mathcal{F}$.

The function $\mathbf{P}$ is a probability function defined on $\mathcal{F}$ such that $\mathbf{P}(\Omega) = 1$ and $\mathbf{P}(\phi) = 0$; this is also called a *probability measure*. For $A \in \mathcal{F}$, $\mathbf{P(A)}$ indicates probability of event A occurring. From these, we characterize a *probability space* by a triplet $(\Omega, \mathcal{F}, \mathbf{P})$.

Example 2.1: Sample space

In financial engineering, a sample $w \in \Omega$ is regarded as a history of up and down moves of a stock price observed in a fixed period. This makes Ω the set of up and down sequences of the stock price. If a period consists of two days $\{t_1, t_2\}$, then Ω will contain four samples and be given by

$$\Omega = \{uu, ud, du, dd\}, \tag{2.1}$$

where we represent by u and d the up and down movements, respectively, of the stock price. Accordingly, $\mathcal{F}$ consists of all subsets of Ω,

$$\mathcal{F} = \{\phi, \Omega, uu, ud, du, dd, \{uu, ud\}, \{uu, dd, \}, \cdots\}, \tag{2.2}$$

which means that $\mathcal{F}$ has 16 ($= 2^4$) events.

Real-world measure

In financial market analysis, the probability measure derived from observation of market prices is called the *market measure*, with many synonyms, such as historical measure, physical measure, actual measure, and *real-world measure*. We regard historical data as being observed under the real-world measure.

Recall the previous example. If our observation estimates that the probability of an up move is constant at 0.5 and the down-move probability is 0.5, then we have

$$\mathbf{P}(uu) = \mathbf{P}(ud) = \mathbf{P}(du) = \mathbf{P}(dd) = 0.25 \tag{2.3}$$

Accordingly, for an arbitrary event $A \in \mathcal{F}$, it is possible to give $\mathbf{P}(A)$. This probability measure $\mathbf{P}$ is an example of the real-world measure.

Risk-neutral measure

Another important measure is the risk-neutral measure, which is used in practice for derivatives pricing. Many financial engineers regard the risk-neutral measure as artificial or just a mathematical concept used in arbitrage pricing.

In economics, the risk-neutral measure is explained as occurring in a virtual world where risk-neutral investors are living and trading. This world is sometimes called the "risk-neutral world." To contrast with the risk-neutral world, the "world of the real-world measure" is called a "real world." In financial institutions, many practitioners work in the risk-neutral world, and they may be unaware of the real-world measure, or may not need to know the difference between the two measures.

This book focuses on interest rate modeling in the "real world." It is natural to assume the uniqueness of the real-world measure for working with the financial market as a mathematical model. The risk-neutral measure is artificially implied from the real-world measure, and so several kinds of risk-neutral measures exist and are applied for various objectives. These include the spot measure, spot LIBOR measure, forward measure, and terminal measure; after Chapter 4 these will be used often.

Equivalent measures

Let $\mathbf{P}$ and $\mathbf{Q}$ be probability measures defined on $\mathcal{F}$. The measure $\mathbf{Q}$ is said to be *absolutely continuous* with respect to $\mathbf{P}$ if $\mathbf{Q}(A) = 0$ holds for any $A \in \Omega$ for which $\mathbf{P}(A) = 0$. Additionally, $\mathbf{P}$ is said to be *equivalent* to $\mathbf{Q}$ if $\mathbf{P}$ and $\mathbf{Q}$ are mutually absolutely continuous. We sometimes denote by

$$\mathbf{P} \sim \mathbf{Q} \tag{2.4}$$

that $\mathbf{P}$ is equivalent to $\mathbf{Q}$.

In derivatives pricing, the risk-neutral measure is the most important example of a measure equivalent to the real-world measure.

2.2 Random Variables

Expectation and variance

A random variable X is defined as a real-valued measurable function on a sample space Ω. We regard interest rates, bond prices, and stock prices on future days as random variables throughout this book.

The expectation of a random variable X under measure $\mathbf{P}$ is defined as

$$E[X] = \int_{w \in \Omega} X(w)\mathbf{P}(dw). \tag{2.5}$$

The expectation is sometimes referred to as the *mean*. The variance of X is defined as

$$v(x) = \int_{w \in \Omega} X(w)^2\mathbf{P}(dw). \tag{2.6}$$

The variance $V(X)$ is a measure of how widely X varies from $E[X]$.

Expectation is linear on linear combinations of random variables. Let Y be another random variable. As an example, for constants a, b, and c, the expectation of the linear combination $a + bX + cY$ is given by

$$E[a + bX + cY] = a + bE[X] + c[Y]. \tag{2.7}$$

The variance of $a + bX + cY$ is given by

$$V(a + bX + cY) = b^2V(X) + c^2V(Y) + 2bc\ Cov(X,Y), \tag{2.8}$$

where Cov is the covariance between X and Y and is defined as

$$Cov(X,Y) = \int_{w\in\Omega} (X(w) - E[X])(Y(w) - E[Y])P(dw). \tag{2.9}$$

The *correlation coefficient* $\rho(X,Y)$ is defined as

$$\rho(X,Y) = \frac{Cov(X,Y)}{\sqrt{V(X)V(Y)}}. \tag{2.10}$$

For any constants a and b, it holds that

$$\begin{aligned}\rho(aX,bY) &= \frac{Cov(aX,bY)}{\sqrt{V(aX)V(bY)}} = \frac{ab\ Cov(X,Y)}{\sqrt{a^2b^2V(X)V(Y)}} \\ &= \rho(X,Y).\end{aligned} \tag{2.11}$$

Hence, the correlation coefficient is invariant to the magnitudes of a and b. The correlation coefficient can be used as a measure of the strength of the linear relationship between X and Y. Naturally, it holds that $-1 \leq \rho \leq 1$.

Distribution function

For a random variable X, we define a real-valued function $F(x)$ on $\mathbf{R}$ by

$$F(x) = \mathbf{P}(X < x). \tag{2.12}$$

F is called the *cumulative density function.* We assume in this book that $F(x)$ is always differentiable at x, and so the derivative with respect to x,

$$f(x) = \frac{dF(x)}{dx}, \tag{2.13}$$

is well defined on $\mathbf{R}$. The function $f(x)$ is called the *density function* or *distribution function* of X. That is, the distribution function $f(x)$ represents the probability that the random variable X takes the value x.

The most important distribution function in financial risk management is the normal distribution; for the definition of that distribution, see Appendix A.1. As examples, the forward rates in Heath *et al.* (1992) and the short rate in Hull and White (1994) have normal distributions. These are introduced in Chapter 4.

For a positive-valued random variable X, if $\log X$ has a normal distribution, then X is said to be *lognormally distributed.* For example, an asset price equation in Section 2.6 implies that the future asset price is lognormally distributed, which means that the price will take positive values. Similarly, the interest rate should be modeled so as to take positive interest. To give another example, the LIBOR market model, as introduced by Miltersen *et al.* (1997), Brace *et al.* (1997), Musiela and Rutkowski (1997), Jamshidian (1997), and others, assumes that the forward LIBOR has a lognormal distribution. This model is practically important as a positive interest rate model for derivatives pricing, which will be introduced in Chapter 5.

The Radon–Nikodym theorem

The relation between two measures $\mathbf{P}$ and $\mathbf{Q}$ can be represented by applying the Radon–Nikoym theorem, which asserts that there exists a measurable function $z \geq 0$ almost everywhere (a.e.), such that for arbitrary $A \in \Omega$ it holds that

$$\int_A \mathbf{Q}(dw) = \int_A z(w)\mathbf{P}(dw). \tag{2.14}$$

Here, $z(\omega)$ is called a *Radon–Nikodym derivative* and denotes

$$z = \frac{d\mathbf{Q}}{d\mathbf{P}}. \tag{2.15}$$

To distinguish the measure used when calculating the expectation, we denote by $E^{\mathbf{Q}}[\,]$ the expectation under $\mathbf{Q}$. Then, for a random variable X, the expectation under $\mathbf{Q}$ is represented by

$$\begin{aligned} E^{\mathbf{Q}}[X] &= \int_{w\in\Omega} X(w)\mathbf{Q}(dw) = \int_{w\in\Omega} X(w)z(w)\mathbf{P}(dw) \\ &= E[zX]. \end{aligned} \tag{2.16}$$

In this book, the Radon–Nikodym theorem will be applied often to construct another measure $\mathbf{Q}$ from the original measure $\mathbf{P}$ by using a measurable function that has $z(\omega) > 0$ a.e.

2.3 Stochastic Process

For arbitrage pricing, the dynamics of market price change is represented by a stochastic process. To introduce the concept of a stochastic process, we develop a probability space such that stochastic processes are well defined in the space, where the key is a filtration used to define a stochastic process.

Filtration

For a fixed time $\tau > 0$, let $\mathcal{F}_{t\in[0,\tau]}$ denote an increasing subset of $\mathcal{F}$; that is, $\mathcal{F}_s \subset \mathcal{F}_t$ for $0 \leq s < t \leq \tau$. We assume that each $\mathcal{F}_t$ is a σ-algebra. Under this definition, $\mathcal{F}_{t\in[0,\tau]}$ is called an *augmented filtration*, or a *filtration* for short. Along these lines, $(\Omega, \mathcal{F}, \mathcal{F}_{t\in[0,\tau]}, \mathbf{P})$ is called a *filtered probability space*, or a *probability space* for short.

Without loss of generality, we may set $\mathcal{F} = \mathcal{F}_\tau$, which means that $(\Omega, \mathcal{F}, \mathcal{F}_{t\in[0,\tau]}, \mathbf{P})$ can be represented by a triplet $(\Omega, \mathcal{F}_{t\in[0,\tau]}, \mathbf{P})$ for convenience.

In particular, we use a filtration chosen such that it represents a flow of information; namely, $\mathcal{F}_t$ comprises the information about all events observed up to time t. An example of such a filtration is given in Example 2.3.1.

Stochastic process

Recall the probability space introduced in Example 2.1.1, that is, the up and down moves of stock price. Stock price movement between days is uncertain and unpredictable, making it an example of a discrete-time stochastic process.

In a continuous-time setting, a stochastic process X_t is defined as a set of random variables indexed by time $t, t \geq 0$ and defined on a probability space $(\Omega, \mathcal{F}_{t\in[0,\tau]}, \mathbf{P})$. The process X_t is said to be *continuous* if almost all sample paths are continuous in t. Additionally, X_t is said to be *adapted* if X_t is $\mathcal{F}_t$-measurable at an arbitrary time $t \in [0, \tau]$. This is called $\mathcal{F}_t$-adapted for short. In this book, we work mostly with adapted processes.

Example 2.3.1: Adapted processes and natural filtration

Regarding the up and down moves of a stock price in Example 2.1.1 as a stochastic process, we construct a filtration. At time 0, we set $F_0 = \{\phi, \Omega\}$. This represents the absence of information about stock price moves at $t = 0$. The sets U and D are defined by

$$U = \{uu, ud\}, \qquad D = \{du, dd\}. \tag{2.17}$$

Set U shows a stock price rise up at time 1, but the movement direction at time 2 is not known. Similarly, D indicates that the stock price falls at time 1, but the movement direction at time 2 is not known.

Then, the information that we have at time 1 is denoted by F_1, and we write

$$F_1 = F_0 \cup \{U, D\}. \tag{2.18}$$

Next, UU, UD, DU, and DD are each defined by a one-sample path such that

$$UU = \{uu\}, \quad UD = \{ud\}, \quad DU = \{du\}, \quad DD = \{uu\}. \tag{2.19}$$

Accordingly, F_2 is defined as a σ-algebra such that

$$F_2 = F_0 \cup \{UU, UD, DU, DD, UU \cup UD, DU \cup DD \cdots\}. \tag{2.20}$$

In this way, a filtration is constructed from $F_{i\in\{0,1,2\}}$. We see that F_i represents the information on the stock price up to time i for $i = 0, 1, 2$. In this sense, $\mathcal{F}_t$ is explained as the flow of information observed up to time t.

The filtration $F_{i\in\{0,1,2\}}$ is generated by the stock price process; such a filtration is called a *natural filtration.* Then this is the adapted process corresponding to the natural filtration.

Random walks

A *random walk*, in this context, is a process of up/down movements (jumps); a random walk is a well-known example of a stochastic discrete-time process. For example, the stochastic process in Example 2.3.1 is a random walk.

Given an integer n, let us consider a random walk $w^n(t)$ such that

- the initial value $w^n(0) = 0$;
- the value jumps at time $i/n, i = 1, \cdots$;
- the probabilities of up and down jumps are always equal, at 0.5 each; and
- the size of jumps is fixed at $1/\sqrt{n}$.

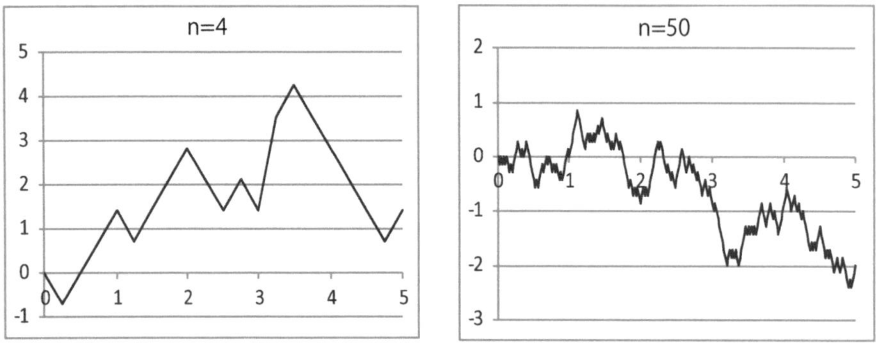

Figure 2.1: Random walks for $n = 4$ and $n = 50$

Fig. 2.1 exhibits examples of a random walk for $n = 4$ and $n = 50$. It is known that if we let n go to infinity, then $w^n(t)$ becomes a Brownian motion. Because of this, we may view the case of $n = 50$ in Fig. 2.1 as approximately exhibiting a path of Brownian motion.

Brownian motion

The *Wiener process* is the most important example of a stochastic process in financial engineering and is also referred to as a *Brownian motion.* A stochastic process $W_t, t \geq 0$ is called a Brownian motion when the following properties hold.

- $W_0 = 0$.
- For $0 \leq s < t$, W_t and $W_t - W_s$ are independent from each other.
- $W_t - W_s$ is normally distributed with mean 0 and variance $t - s$.

In this book, we always assume that $\mathcal{F}_{t\in[0,\tau]}$ is a natural filtration generated by Brownian motion.

2.4 Martingales and Conditional Expectation

Conditional expectation

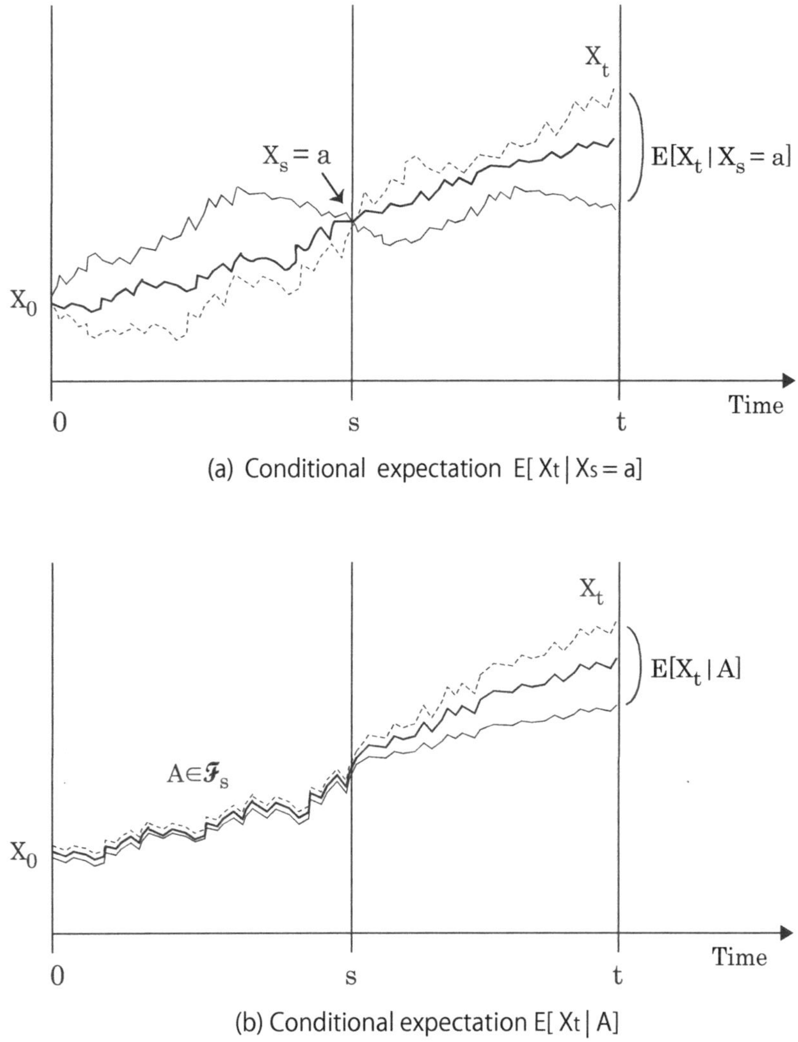

Figure 2.2: Two examples of conditional expectation

For an $\mathcal{F}_\tau$-measurable random variable X and $t \leq \tau$, $E[X|\mathcal{F}_t]$ is the expectation of X conditional on the information $\mathcal{F}_t$. Sometimes, $E[X|\mathcal{F}_t]$ is denoted by $E_t[X]$ for simplicity, and called *conditional expectation* for short. Intuitively, the conditional expectation $E_t[X]$ is the expectation of X implied from the information up to time t.

Let us consider the meaning of conditional expectation using Fig. 2.2, where Fig. 2.2(a) exhibits three sample paths, all taking the value a at time s. Under this condition, the expectation of X_t at time $t \geq s$ is denoted by

$$E[X_t|X_s = a], \tag{2.21}$$

which is shown in Fig. 2.2(a). The conditional expectation with respect to all values of X_s is defined by $E[X_t|X_s]$. We can see that $E[X_t|X_s]$ is a random variable with respect to the state X_s at time s.

Next, Fig. 2.2(b) exhibits three sample paths, all having the same path up to time s. According to Example 2.3.1, we may regard these paths as an event $A \in \mathcal{F}_s$. The expectation of X_t under the condition A is denoted by

$$E[X_t|A] \quad ; \quad A \in \mathcal{F}_s, \tag{2.22}$$

which is also written in Fig. 2.2(b). Then, $E[X_t|\mathcal{F}_s]$ represents the expectation, conditional on all events of $\mathcal{F}_s$. This is a random variable with respect to all event in $A \in \mathcal{F}_s$.

Fig. 2.2(b) suggests that the conditional expectation

$$E[X_t|\mathcal{F}_s] \quad ; \quad 0 \leq s \leq t \tag{2.23}$$

represents the expectation of X_t implied from the information up to time s, as previously mentioned.

Properties of conditional expectation

Here, we introduce three basic properties of conditional expectation that we will use repeatedly later.

1) The following equation is known as the *law of iterated expectations*:

$$E_s[E_t[X]] = E_s[X] \quad ; \quad 0 < s < t < \tau. \tag{2.24}$$

2) For an $\mathcal{F}_t$-measurable random variable Y, the following relation is sometimes employed.

$$E_t[XY] = Y E_t[X]. \tag{2.25}$$

3) Note that $E_t[X]$ is a random variables on $\mathcal{F}_t$ for $t > 0$. In particular, $E_0[X]$ is precisely the usual expectation of X, that is, $E_0[X] = E[X]$.

In particular, both relations (2.24) and (2.25) hold under more general conditions. For details, see, for example, Jacod and Protter (2003) or Shreve (2004).

Bayes' rule

Bayes' rule is a well-known formula that can be used to calculate conditional probability. This is generalized to conditional expectation as follows, with the result called the abstract Bayes' rule. For details, see, for example, Björk (2004), or Musiela and Rutkowski (2011).

Proposition 2.4.1 *For an arbitrary $t, 0 < t < \tau$, let X be an $\mathcal{F}_t$-measurable random variable. Set $z = d\mathbf{Q}/d\mathbf{P}$. Then, it holds that*

$$E_t^{\mathbf{Q}}[X] = \frac{E_t[Xz]}{E_t[z]}, \tag{2.26}$$

where $E^{\mathbf{Q}}[\ ]$ denotes the expectation under $\mathbf{Q}$.

Martingale

A stochastic process X_t is called a *martingale* if it holds for arbitrary $t > s > 0$ that $X_s = E_s[X_t]$. A martingale is a mathematical model of a fair game. Specifically, the averaged future value of X_t cannot be predicted at time s from the past trajectories. Next, we show two important examples of martingale processes.

Example 2.4.1

(1) Let X be an $\mathcal{F}_\tau$-measurable random variable. From the law of iterative expectation, it holds that

$$E_s[E_t[X]] = E_s[X], \quad s \le t \le \tau. \tag{2.27}$$

Then, regarding $E_t[X]$ as a stochastic process, $E_t[X]$ is a martingale.
(2) The Brownian motion W_t is known as a martingale. Then, it holds for $0 < s < t$ that $E_s[W_t] = W_s$.

Measure change and martingales

Arbitrage pricing theory is constructed by using the properties of martingales, which allow us to sometimes change measure from the real-world measure to a risk-neutral measure, or vice versa. In such a measure change, the following proposition is repeatedly applied so as to preserve the martingale structure.

Let $\mathbf{Q}$ be a measure equivalent to $\mathbf{P}$. We define a stochastic process z_t by

$$z_t = E_t\left[\frac{d\mathbf{Q}}{d\mathbf{P}}\right]. \tag{2.28}$$

It follows that $z_0 = 1$ and $z_t > 0$ almost surely (a.s.). Substituting $d\mathbf{Q}/d\mathbf{P}$ into X of (2.27), we have

$$E_s\left[E_t\left[\frac{d\mathbf{Q}}{d\mathbf{P}}\right]\right] = E_s\left[\frac{d\mathbf{Q}}{d\mathbf{P}}\right]. \tag{2.29}$$

Substituting (2.28) into the above equation, it follows that $E_s[z_t] = z_s$. Thus, z_t is a $\mathbf{P}$-martingale. The following proposition holds.

Proposition 2.4.2 *Let X_t be a stochastic process. Then, X_t is a $\mathbf{Q}$-martingale if and only if $X_t z_t$ is a $\mathbf{P}$-martingale.*

Proof We may set $z_\tau = d\mathbf{Q}/d\mathbf{P}$. If X_t is a $\mathbf{Q}$-martingale, then $X_t = E_t[X_s]$ for $0 \le t < s \le \tau$. From (2.24), (2.25), (2.28), and the abstract Bayes' rule, we have

$$\begin{aligned} X_t &= E_t^{\mathbf{Q}}[X_s] = \frac{E_t[X_s z_\tau]}{E_t[z_\tau]} \\ &= \frac{E_t[E_s[X_s z_\tau]]}{E_t[z_\tau]} = \frac{E_t[X_s E_s[z_\tau]]}{E_t[z_\tau]} \\ &= \frac{E_t[X_s z_s]}{z_t}. \end{aligned} \tag{2.30}$$

It holds that $X_t z_t = E_t[X_s z_s]$, and so $X_t z_t$ is a $\mathbf{P}$-martingale. The converse is shown in the same way as above. □

2.5 Stochastic Integral

This section summarizes basic definitions and results for stochastic differential equations but omits proofs. For details and a rigorous description see any of Chung and Williams (1990), Karatzas and Shreve (1998), Öksendal (2003), and Shreve (2004).

Stochastic integral

Let W_t be a Brownian motion under a measure $\mathbf{P}$. For a stochastic process X_t satisfying $\int_0^t |X_s|^2 ds < \infty \quad a.s.$, the stochastic integral of X_t with respect to W_t is defined by

$$\int_0^t X_s dW_s = \lim_{\Delta \to 0} \sum_{i=1}^{n-1} X_{t_i}\{W_{t_{i+1}} - W_{t_i}\}, \tag{2.31}$$

where $0 = t_0 < \cdots < t_n = t$ and $\Delta t = \max_{0 \leq i \leq n-1}(t_{i+1} - t_i)$.

The following properties are well known.

1) If X_t is a deterministic process, that is, generated by a deterministic function on t, then it holds that

$$E\left[\int_0^t X_s dW_s\right] = 0. \tag{2.32}$$

2) $\int_0^t X_s dW_s$ has normal distribution with mean 0 and variance

$$E\left[(\int_0^t X_s dW_s)^2\right] = \int_0^t |X_s|^2 \, ds. \tag{2.33}$$

Generally, for a function $\sigma(t, X_t)$ with inputs t and X_t, and regarding $\sigma(t, X_t)$ as a stochastic process, the stochastic integral is defined by

$$\int_0^t \sigma(s, X_s) dW_s. \tag{2.34}$$

Euler approximation

In practice, it is typically necessary to compute the stochastic integral numerically. Euler approximation (or integration) is a widely used technique for this problem, and furthermore plays an important role in theoretical studies of numerical analysis. Indeed, we shall apply the Euler approximation for investigating a real-world model after Chapter 4.

For a continuous stochastic process X_t, we denote the stochastic integral of X_t with respect to W by $\int_0^t X_s dW_s$. By the definition of the integral, we have, from (2.31),

$$\int_0^t X_s dW_s = \lim_{\Delta \to 0} \sum_{i=1}^{n-1} X(t_i)\{W(t_{i+1}) - W(t_i)\}. \tag{2.35}$$

Then, it follows for a sufficiently short period Δt that

$$\begin{aligned} \int_0^{\Delta t} X_s dW_s &\approx X_0\{W_{\Delta t} - W_0\} \\ &= X_0 W_{\Delta t} \\ &= \sqrt{\Delta t} X_0 W_1, \end{aligned} \tag{2.36}$$

where W_1 is identified as a random variable having a standard normal distribution. Hence, by substituting numbers generated according to a standard normal distribution into W_1, we approximately obtain the distribution of $\int_0^{\Delta t} X_s dW_s$.

Example 2.5: Martingale

For future time τ, let f_t be an $\mathcal{F}_t$-adapted process satisfying $E[\int_0^\tau f_s^2 ds] < \infty$. From this, it is known that $X_t = \int_0^t f_s dW_s$ is a martingale with respect to $\mathbf{P}$. Since $X_t = 0$, it holds for $t \le T$ that

$$E[\int_0^t f_s dW_s] = 0. \tag{2.37}$$

The difference of the above from (2.32) is that X_t in (2.32) is deterministic, but f_s in the above is a stochastic process.

2.6 Stochastic Differential Equation

Let us consider a stochastic differential equation of the form

$$dY_t = \mu(t, X_t)dt + \sigma(t, X_t)dW_t \tag{2.38}$$

with initial value Y_0. The solution of this equation is given by

$$Y_t = Y_0 + \int_0^t \mu(s, X_s)ds + \int_0^t \sigma(s, X_s)dW_s. \tag{2.39}$$

A stochastic process of the form (2.39) is called an *Ito process*, where $\mu(t, X_t)$ is called the *drift term* and $\sigma(t, X_t)$ is called the *diffusion term.*

For convenience, we denote $\mu(t, X_t)$ and $\sigma(t, X_t)$ by $\mu(t)$ and $\sigma(t)$, respectively. Sometimes, we will denote them by μ_t and σ_t or by μ and σ when the meaning is unambiguous. In the same way, we may denote a stochastic process X_t by $X(t)$ or X for simplicity and according to the situation.

Example 2.6: Constant drift and diffusion

For positive constants a and b, consider the following process:

$$dY_t = adt + bdW_t. \tag{2.40}$$

This is the most trivial example of a stochastic differential equation. From (2.39), the solution is given by

$$Y_t = Y_0 + at + bW_t. \tag{2.41}$$

Here, Y_t is a sum of the deterministic drift at and a Brownian motion bW_t with the diffusion term b.

Covariance process

For stochastic processes X and Y, the *quadratic covariation process* is denoted by $\langle X, Y \rangle_t$. In particular, if X and Y are Ito processes such that

$$dX_t = \mu_1(t)dt + \sigma_1(t)dW_t \tag{2.42a}$$

$$dY_t = \mu_2(t)dt + \sigma_2(t)dW_t, \tag{2.42b}$$

then $\langle X, Y \rangle$ is obtained by

$$\langle X, Y \rangle_t = \int_0^t \sigma_1(s)\sigma_2(s)ds. \tag{2.43}$$

In practice, we empirically estimate the covariance among several asset prices from historical observation. This covariance corresponds to a discrete-time version of the quadratic covariation process.

Ito's formula

Let X_t be an Ito process defined by $dX_t = \mu(t)dt + \sigma(t)dW_t$. For a C^2-function $g(t,x)$, $g(t,X)$ is also an Ito process and

$$dg(t,X_t) = \frac{\partial g}{\partial t}dt + \frac{\partial g}{\partial x}dX + \frac{1}{2}\frac{\partial^2 g}{\partial x^2}dXdX, \tag{2.44}$$

which is called the *Ito formula.*

We have

$$dXdX = \{\mu(t)dt + \sigma(t)dW_t\}^2. \tag{2.45}$$

Using the relations

$$dtdt = dtdW_t = dW_tdt = 0 \tag{2.46}$$

and $dW_tdW_t = dt$, we have $dXdX = \sigma^2(t)dt$. Then, the Ito formula can be represented as

$$\begin{aligned} dg(t,X_t) &= \frac{\partial g}{\partial t} + \frac{\partial g}{\partial x}\{\mu(t)dt + \sigma(t)dW_t\} + \frac{\sigma^2(t)}{2}\frac{\partial^2 g}{\partial x^2}dt \\ &= \left\{\frac{\partial g}{\partial t} + \mu(t)\frac{\partial g}{\partial x} + \frac{\sigma^2(t)}{2}\frac{\partial^2 g}{\partial x^2}\right\}dt + \sigma(t)\frac{\partial g}{\partial x}dW_t. \end{aligned} \tag{2.47}$$

It is a notable property of the Ito formula that the process $g(t,X_t)$ is also represented by another Ito process. Some stochastic differential equations can be solved by applying Ito's formula as in the following.

Asset price equation

Let μ and σ be positive constants. Consider the following equation with initial value X_0

$$\frac{dX_t}{X_t} = \mu dt + \sigma dW_t \tag{2.48a}$$

or

$$dX_t = \mu X_t dt + \sigma X_t dW_t. \tag{2.48b}$$

To solve this equation, we set $g(t,x) = \log x$, and then we have

$$\frac{\partial g}{\partial t} = 0, \quad \frac{\partial g}{\partial x} = \frac{1}{x}, \quad \frac{\partial^2 g}{\partial x^2} = -\frac{1}{x^2}. \tag{2.49}$$

Substituting these into (2.47), and σX_t and μX_t into $\sigma(t)$ and $\mu(t)$, respectively, in (2.47), we have

$$\begin{aligned} dg(t,X) &= d\log X_t \\ &= \left(0 + \frac{\mu X_t}{X_t} - \frac{\sigma^2 X_t^2}{2}\frac{1}{X_t^2}\right)dt + \frac{\sigma X_t}{X_t}dW_t \\ &= \left(\mu - \frac{\sigma^2}{2}\right)dt + \sigma dW_t. \end{aligned} \tag{2.50}$$

Hence,

$$\log\frac{X_t}{X_0} = \left(\mu - \frac{\sigma^2}{2}\right)t + \sigma W_t. \tag{2.51}$$

Thus, the solution of (2.48a) is obtained as

$$X_t = X_0 \exp\left\{\left(\mu - \frac{\sigma^2}{2}\right)t + \sigma W_t\right\}. \tag{2.52}$$

From (2.51), we see that X_t is lognormally distributed. A stochastic process represented as (2.52) is called a *geometric Brownian motion.*

The dynamics of asset price is sometimes represented by the equation (2.48a). As an example, the Black–Scholes model represents a stock price process in this form.

Next, we consider the more general case where $\mu(t)$ and $\sigma(t)$ are deterministic functions of t. Then, a stochastic differential equation can be described as

$$dX_t = \mu(t)X_t dt + \sigma(t)X_t dW_t. \tag{2.53}$$

By the same arguments as above, the solution is given by

$$X_t = X_0 \exp\left\{\int_0^t \left(\mu(s) - \frac{\sigma^2(s)}{2}\right)dt + \int_0^t \sigma(s)W_s\right\}. \tag{2.54}$$

Furthermore, this result is generalized for the equation with stochastic coefficients such that

$$dX_t = \mu_t X_t dt + \sigma_t X_t dW_t, \tag{2.55}$$

where μ_t and σ_t are adapted processes. Similarly to (2.54), the solution of (2.55) is given by

$$X_t = X_0 \exp\left\{\int_0^t \left(\mu_s - \frac{|\sigma_s|^2}{2}\right) ds + \int_0^t \sigma_s dW_s\right\}. \tag{2.56}$$

These results are applied for interest rate modeling in the multi-dimensional case and for bond price process equations. We will present analogous results for the multi-dimensional case in Section 2.7 of this chapter.

Exponential martingale

Let σ_t be an adapted process and consider an Ito process such that

$$dX_t = \sigma_t X_t dW_t. \tag{2.57}$$

Substituting $\mu_t = 0$ into (2.56), we have

$$X_t = X_0 \exp\left\{-\int_0^t \frac{|\sigma_s|^2}{2} ds + \int_0^t \sigma_s dW_s\right\}. \tag{2.58}$$

It is known that X_t is a martingale under $\mathbf{P}$; this type is referred to as an *exponential martingale.* For details, see Shreve (2004). We will apply this property for arbitrage theory in Chapter 3, where a relative bond price process will be represented in the above form.

The Girsanov theorem

Recall that we are working in the probability space $(\Omega, \mathcal{F}_{t\in[0,\mathcal{T}]}, \mathbf{P})$, where $\mathcal{F}_{t\in[0,\mathcal{T}]}$ is the natural filtration generated by the Brownian motion W_t. Let Y_t be an Ito process of the form $dY_t = \mu(t)dt + dW_t$. Let $\mathbf{Q}$ be another probability measure defined by the Radon–Nikodym derivative such that

$$\frac{d\mathbf{Q}}{d\mathbf{P}} = \exp\left\{-\int_0^{\mathcal{T}} \mu_s dW_s - \frac{1}{2}\int_0^{\mathcal{T}} \mu(s)^2 ds\right\}, \tag{2.59}$$

where $\mathbf{Q}$ is equivalent to $\mathbf{P}$. The Girsanov theorem states that Y_t is a Brownian motion with respect to $\mathbf{Q}$.

W_t is a martingale with respect to $\mathbf{P}$, and Y_t is also a martingale with respect to $\mathbf{Q}$. To distinguish the measure where a process is a martingale, we say that W_t is a **P**-*martingale* for short. From the same reason, a Brownian motion with respect to $\mathbf{P}$ is referred to as a **P**-*Brownian motion* for simplicity. The treatment of **Q**-*martingale* and **Q**-*Brownian motion* is analogous.

2.7 Multi-dimensional Stochastic Process

In the previous section, the definitions and results for the stochastic differential equation were given for the one-dimensional case. Naturally, most of these can be generalized to the multi-dimensional case, which is where we will work for arbitrage pricing in this book. We briefly introduce a multi-dimensional case of the Ito formula and the Girsanov theorem.

Stochastic integral

Let $(\Omega, \mathcal{F}_{t\in[0,\tau]}, \mathbf{P})$ be a probability space. Let $W_t = (W_t^1, \cdots, W_t^d)^T$ and $X_t = (X_t^1, \cdots, X_t^d)^T$ be a d-dimensional Brownian motion and a d-dimensional stochastic process, respectively. Here the superscript T denotes the transpose. We denote by $X_t dW_t$ the standard Euclidean inner product of X_t and dW_t in $\mathbf{R}^\mathbf{d}$.

The stochastic integral of X_t with respect to W is defined by

$$\int_0^t X_s dW_s = \sum_{i=1}^d \int_0^t X_s^i dW_s^i. \tag{2.60}$$

Ito's formula

Let X_t be an n-dimensional Ito process $dX_t = \mu_t dt + \sigma_t dW_t$, where μ_t is an n-dimensional process and σ_t is a process with $n \times d$ matrixes as entries. Let

$$g(t,x) = (g_1(t,x), \cdots, g_p(t,x)) \tag{2.61}$$

be a set of C^2-functions. With this, the Ito formula is described as

$$dg_k(t,X_t) = \frac{\partial g_k}{\partial t} dt + \sum_{i=1}^n \frac{\partial g_k}{\partial x_i} dX^i + \frac{1}{2} \sum_{i,j=1}^n \frac{\partial^2 g_k}{\partial x_i \partial x_j} dX^i dX^j, \tag{2.62}$$

for $k = 1, \cdots, p$.

Example 2.7: Multi-dimensional Ito's formula

Setting $p = 1$ for the above, we consider an Ito process

$$dY_t = \mu_t Y_t dt + \sigma_t Y_t dW_t, \tag{2.63}$$

where σ_t is a d-dimensional process and W_t is a d-dimensional Brownian motion. We set $g(t,x) = \log x$, and then it follows that

$$\frac{\partial g}{\partial t} = 0, \quad \frac{\partial g}{\partial x} = \frac{1}{x}, \quad \frac{\partial^2 g}{\partial x^2} = -\frac{1}{x^2}. \tag{2.64}$$

Substituting these into (2.62), we have

$$\begin{aligned} dg(t,Y) = d\log Y_t &= 0 + \frac{dY_t}{Y_t} - \frac{1}{2Y_t^2} dY_t dY_t \\ &= \mu_t dt + \sigma_t dW_t - \frac{1}{2Y_t^2}(\mu_t Y_t dt + \sigma_t Y_t dW_t)^2 \\ &= \mu_t dt + \sigma_t dW_t - \frac{|\sigma_t|^2}{2} dt \\ &= \left(\mu_t - \frac{|\sigma_t|^2}{2}\right) dt + \sigma_t dW_t, \end{aligned} \tag{2.65}$$

where we use (2.46) and $dW_t^i dW_t^j = \delta_{ij} dt$. Consequently, we have

$$Y_t = Y_0 \exp\left\{ \int_0^t \left(\mu_s - \frac{|\sigma_s|^2}{2}\right) ds + \int_0^t \sigma_s dW_s \right\}. \tag{2.66}$$

The difference of (2.66) from (2.56) is that $\sigma_s dW_s$ is the standard Euclidean inner product in $\mathbf{R^d}$. This result will be used frequently for multi-factor interest rate models later.

The multi-dimensional Girsanov theorem

The Girsanov theorem is also available for the measure change in a multi-dimensional case as follows. Let Y_t be a d-dimensional Ito process $dY_t = \mu(t)dt + dW_t$, where μ_t is a d-dimensional process and W_t is a d-dimensional Brownian motion. Let $\mathbf{Q}$ be a probability measure defined by

$$\frac{d\mathbf{Q}}{d\mathbf{P}} = \exp\left\{ -\sum_i \int_o^T \mu_i(s) dW_s^i - \frac{1}{2}\sum_i \int_0^T \mu_i(s)^2 ds \right\}. \tag{2.67a}$$

Then, $\mathbf{Q}$ is equivalent to $\mathbf{P}$, and Y_t is a Brownian motion under $\mathbf{Q}$.

For convenience, we represent the above in the following form:

$$\frac{d\mathbf{Q}}{d\mathbf{P}} = \exp\left\{ -\int_o^T \mu_s dW_s - \frac{1}{2}\int_0^T |\mu(s)|^2 ds \right\}. \tag{2.67b}$$

CHAPTER 3

ARBITRAGE THEORY

Abstract: This chapter summarizes arbitrage theory in the framework of martingale theory. First, we introduce an arbitrage-free market and arbitrage price for the general asset market, where the key concepts are the state price deflator and a martingale. Next, a numéraire and a numéraire measure are introduced to generalize arbitrage theory. Accordingly, we will see that the arbitrage price does not vary with the choice of numéraire.

Next, we work with a bond market where the bond prices are represented by Ito processes. For this, the market price of risk is introduced to ensure the arbitrage-free condition in the market. The market price of risk widely plays an important role in traditional interest-rate models, as an example, which will appear in the basic theory of the HJM model in Chapter 4. The estimation of the market price of risk is the most important subject of this book and is studied after Chapter 6.

Keywords: Accumulated contribution rate, Arbitrage opportunity, Arbitrage pricing, Bond market, Change of numéraire, Complete market, Contribution rate, Eigenvalue, Equivalent martingale measure, Numéraire, Numéraire measure, Market price of risk, Option pricing, Pricing kernel, Principal component, Relative price process, Risk-neutral measure, Risk-neutral pricing, Risk-neutral valuation, Self-financing trading strategy, State price deflator, Time-homogeneous short rate model

Takashi Yasuoka

This chapter briefly summarizes arbitrage theory in the framework of martingale theory. The arbitrage pricing theory has been mathematically constructed in Harrison and Kreps (1979) and Harrison and Pliska (1981). For details, refer to those works, or to others such as Pliska (1997) and Munk (2011). For interest-rate models, refer to Björk (2004), Cairns (2004), or Munk (2011), among others.

3.1 Arbitrage Pricing

Asset market

Let $\tau > 0$ be a time horizon, and let $(\Omega, \mathcal{F}_{t\in[0,\tau]}, \mathbf{P})$ be a probability space, where $\mathcal{F}_{t\in[0,\tau]}$ is the augmented filtration and $\mathbf{P}$ is a real-world measure.

Let $\mathcal{M} = \{S_{it}\}_{i\in\Lambda}$ denote a family of price processes of assets, where $\mathcal{M}$ may contain very wide classes of asset, for example, a stock market or a bonds market. We remark that each S_{it} is not assumed to be an Ito process. We denote by Λ a set of indices of assets. For example, a finite set of numbers $\{1, \cdots, n\}$ can be used for a finite asset market, and a time interval $[0, \tau]$ can be used for the family of bonds with maturity $T \leq \tau$. In this context, $\mathcal{M}$ is referred to as a market.

Self-financing trading strategy

For simplicity, we work with a finite asset market $\mathcal{M} = \{S_{it}\}_{i=1,\cdots,n}$. A *trading strategy* is an $\mathbf{R}^n$-valued process $\theta_t = (\theta_{1t}, \cdots, \theta_{nt})$, where each θ_{it} represents a volume of asset i. Then, the value of the portfolio $p(t)$ at t is given by

$$p(t) = \theta_t S_t = \sum_{i=1}^{n} \theta_{it} S_{it}. \tag{3.1}$$

θ is said to be a *self-financing trading strategy* if

$$dp(t) = \theta_t dS_t. \tag{3.2}$$

In the self-financing trading portfolio, we neither add nor withdraw money. The next example shows the meaning of (3.2).

Example 3.1

Let T be a fixed time in the future. Suppose a market that consists of only two assets: a risk-free asset and a risky asset. Let r be a risk-free rate for a period $[0, T]$. We use S_{1t} to denote an investment at this rate. Then, it holds that $S_{1t} = \exp(rt)$. We use S_{2t} to denote a price process of a risky asset with $S_{20} = 1$. We set a trading strategy as

$$\theta_{1t} = -1, \qquad \theta_{2t} = 1. \tag{3.3}$$

These indicate borrowing 1 at the rate r and buying the risky asset by paying 1, respectively. The initial value of this portfolio is equal to 0, and it holds that

$$dp(t) = -dS_{1t} + dS_{2t}. \tag{3.4}$$

This is an example of the form (3.2), and so it is a self-financing trading strategy.

Arbitrage opportunity

An *arbitrage opportunity* is a self-financing trading strategy in which the value of the initial portfolio is not greater than 0 but the value at time T is nonnegative with probability 1 and positive with nonzero probability.

In Example 3.1.1, the initial value of the portfolio is 0, where we neither pay nor borrow any money for the principal. If it holds that $p(T) \geq 0$ with probability 1, then we absolutely do not lose. Additionally, if $p(T) > 0$ with positive probability, then we have a chance for profit with no risk of loss. Such cases are arbitrage opportunities.

Arbitrage-free market

The market $\mathcal{M}$ is said to be *arbitrage-free* if no arbitrage opportunities exist. That is, if starting from no money allows no profitable choices. Therefore, the arbitrage-free condition is deeply related to the risk-free investment.

The arbitrage-free condition is mathematically represented as a stochastic process $\xi_t > 0$ (a.s.) with $\xi_0 = 1$ such that the processes $\xi_t S_{it}$ are $\mathbf{P}$-martingales for all $i \in \Lambda$. Typically, ξ is called the *state price deflator* (or the pricing kernel).

We remark here that the state price deflator might not exist as more than a theoretical concept, and it is not obvious how to numerically calculate it. Practically, the state price deflator roughly represents a kind of discount factor, as explained below.

Arbitrage pricing

To introduce arbitrage pricing in an arbitrage-free market, we consider a security whose payoff at time $T \le \tau$ is given by an $\mathcal{F}_T$-measurable random variable X. We denote by p_t the arbitrage price of this security at time $t, 0 \le t \le T$. Then, p_t is given by

$$p_t = \frac{1}{\xi_t} E_t[\xi_T X], \tag{3.5}$$

where ξ_t is the state price deflator.

The financial meaning of this price is that we can find no arbitrage opportunity in our market at this price. In particular, the time 0 price of this security can be represented as

$$p_0 = E[\xi_T X]. \tag{3.6}$$

If we regard ξ_T as the discount factor to the time T, then (3.6) suggests that the arbitrage price is equal to the expectation of the present value of the payoff at T. Although this interpretation seems intuitively to be comprehensive, we have no feasible information for determining the value of ξ_T explicitly, and we do not have a method to calculate it at time 0. Thus, (3.5) is not sufficiently practical for use in pricing; in the next section, we develop a version of (3.5) that is more usable.

3.2 Change of Numéraire

This section presents the most basic argument in arbitrage theory. We show that the arbitrage price is not affected by choice of numéraire, and make an arbitrage pricing system that is more practical. First, we present Theorem 3.2.1, which gives an arbitrage-free condition in a martingale approach. Theorem 3.2.1(2) will be applied to constructing the HJM model in Chapter 4. Additionally, Theorem 3.2.1(2) is generalized to Theorem 3.2.2, which will be used in constructing the LIBOR market model in Chapter 5.

Numéraire and numéraire measure

A *numéraire process* is a price process of a traded asset that takes positive value almost surely. For example, a risk-free bond can be used as a numéraire.

Consider the market $\mathcal{M} = \{S_{it}\}_{i \in \Lambda}$, which appeared in the previous section. Let an arbitrary $i \in \Lambda$ be fixed, and define z_t by

$$z_t = \xi_t \frac{S_{it}}{S_{i0}}. \tag{3.7}$$

From the assumption of an arbitrage-free market, z_t is a $\mathbf{P}$-martingale with $z_0 = 1$ and $z_t > 0$ a.s. Let $\mathbf{P_i}$ denote a measure defined by the Radon–Nikodym derivative such that

$$\frac{d\mathbf{P_i}}{d\mathbf{P}} = z_\tau \quad \left(= \xi_\tau \frac{S_{i\tau}}{S_{i0}} \right). \tag{3.8}$$

From (3.7), we have $z_t / S_{it} = \xi_t / S_{i0}$. For any arbitrary j, multiplying both sides of the above by S_{jt} gives

$$z_t \frac{S_{jt}}{S_{it}} = \frac{\xi_t S_{jt}}{S_{i0}}. \tag{3.9}$$

The arbitrage-free assumption implies that the right side is a $\mathbf{P}$-martingale. From Proposition 2.4.2, we see that S_{jt}/S_{it} is a $\mathbf{P_i}$-martingale for all j. Obviously, $\mathbf{P_i}$ is equivalent to $\mathbf{P}$. This is called the S_i *numéraire measure*.

Accordingly, we have the following theorem.

Theorem 3.2.1 *(1) If $\mathcal{M}$ is arbitrage-free, and it holds that $S_i > 0$ a.s. for some $i \in \Lambda$, then S_{jt}/S_{it} is a $\mathbf{P_i}$-martingale for all $j \in \Lambda$.*
(2) If there exists $S_{it} > 0$ a.s. for some $i \in \Lambda$ such that S_{jt}/S_{it} is a $\mathbf{P_i}$-martingale for all $j \in \Lambda$, then $\mathcal{M}$ is arbitrage-free.

Proof Case (1) has already been shown. It is sufficient to prove only case (2). From (3.7) and (3.8), we see that

$$z_t = E_t \left[\frac{d\mathbf{P_i}}{d\mathbf{P}} \right] = \frac{\xi_t S_{it}}{S_{i0}}. \tag{3.10}$$

Since S_{jt}/S_{it} is a $\mathbf{P_i}$-martingale for every j, Proposition 2.4.2 implies that $S_{jt}z_t/S_{it}$ is a $\mathbf{P}$-martingale. Accordingly, we have, from (3.10), that

$$\frac{S_{jt}z_t}{S_{it}} = \frac{S_{jt}}{S_{it}}\frac{\xi_t S_{it}}{S_{i0}} = \frac{S_{jt}\xi_t}{S_{i0}}. \tag{3.11}$$

Hence, $\xi_t S_{jt}$ is a $\mathbf{P_i}$-martingale for every j, and so $\mathcal{M}$ is arbitrage-free. This completes the proof. □

S_{jt}/S_{it} is referred to as a *relative price process*. The condition that the relative price process S_{jt}/S_{it} is a $\mathbf{P_i}$-martingale means that investment in asset j is a fair game when comparing with investment in asset i in the "world of $\mathbf{P_i}$." In this context, the numéraire is regarded as a kind of benchmark for investment in the world of $\mathbf{P_i}$.

Arbitrage pricing under $\mathbf{P_i}$

Recalling the security with payoff X at $T \leq \tau$, the price process of this security is given by (3.5). Taking S_i as a numéraire, we denote by $E^i[\,]$ the expectation under the S_i numéraire measure $\mathbf{P^i}$.

From (3.8), (3.10), and the abstract Bayes' rule, we have

$$\begin{aligned} S_{it}E_t^i\left[\frac{X}{S_{iT}}\right] &= S_{it}E_t\left[\frac{Xz_\tau}{S_{iT}}\right]\frac{1}{E_t[z_\tau]} = E_t\left[\frac{Xz_\tau}{S_{iT}}\right]\frac{S_{it}}{z_t} \\ &= E_t\left[\frac{Xz_\tau}{S_{iT}}\right]\frac{S_{i0}}{\xi_t}. \end{aligned} \tag{3.12}$$

From (3.7), it follows that

$$\begin{aligned} E_t\left[\frac{Xz_\tau}{S_{iT}}\right] &= E_t\left[\frac{X}{S_{iT}}\frac{\xi_\tau S_{i\tau}}{S_{i0}}\right] = E_t\left[E_T\left[\frac{X}{S_{iT}}\frac{\xi_\tau S_{i\tau}}{S_{i0}}\right]\right] \\ &= E_t\left[\frac{X}{S_{iT}}E_T\left[\frac{\xi_T S_{it}}{S_{i0}}\right]\right] = E_t\left[\frac{X}{S_{iT}}\frac{\xi_T S_{iT}}{S_{i0}}\right] \\ &= \frac{E_t[X\xi_T]}{S_{i0}}. \end{aligned} \tag{3.13}$$

Substituting (3.13) into (3.12), we have

$$\begin{aligned} S_{it}E_t^i\left[\frac{X}{S_{iT}}\right] &= \frac{E_t[X\xi_T]}{S_{i0}}\frac{S_{i0}}{\xi_t} = \frac{E_t[\xi_T X]}{\xi_t} \\ &= p_t. \end{aligned} \tag{3.14}$$

Consequently, the time t price of this security satisfies

$$p_t = S_{it} E_t^i \left[\frac{X}{S_{iT}} \right]. \tag{3.15}$$

If we take another S_k as the numéraire, it also holds that

$$p_t = S_{kt} E_t^k \left[\frac{X}{S_{kT}} \right]. \tag{3.16}$$

Therefore, the arbitrage price is not affected by the choice of the asset used as numéraire. The following theorem gives us a more general form of Theorem 3.2.1(2).

Theorem 3.2.2 *Let $S_{it}, i \in \Lambda$ be a price process of some asset in the market $\mathcal{M}$ with $S_{it} > 0$ (a.s.). If there exists a measure $\mathbf{Q}$ equivalent to $\mathbf{P}$ such that S_{jt}/S_{it} is a $\mathbf{Q}$-martingale for all $j \in \Lambda$, then $\mathcal{M}$ is arbitrage-free.*

Proof We set

$$z_\tau = \frac{d\mathbf{Q}}{d\mathbf{P}}, \qquad z_t = E_t \left[\frac{d\mathbf{Q}}{d\mathbf{P}} \right] \tag{3.17}$$

for $0 \le t \le \tau$. This means that z_t is well defined and a $\mathbf{P}$-martingale. We define ξ_t by

$$\xi_t = z_t \frac{S_{i0}}{S_{it}}. \tag{3.18}$$

By an argument similar to the proof of Theorem 3.2.1, it follows that for $0 \le s \le t \le T$

$$\begin{aligned} E_s[\xi_t S_{jt}] &= S_{i0} E_s \left[\frac{z_t S_{jt}}{S_{it}} \right] \\ &= S_{i0} E_s \left[E_t \left[z_\tau \frac{S_{jt}}{S_{it}} \right] \right] \\ &= S_{i0} E_t^{\mathbf{Q}} \left[\frac{S_{jt}}{S_{it}} \right] E_s[z_\tau] \end{aligned} \tag{3.19}$$

for any $j \in \Lambda$. By assumption, S_{jt}/S_{it} is a $\mathbf{Q}$-martingale. Then, (3.19) becomes

$$\begin{aligned} S_{i0} E_s^{\mathbf{Q}} \left[\frac{S_{jt}}{S_{it}} \right] E_s[z_\tau] &= S_{i0} \frac{S_{js}}{S_{is}} \frac{\xi_s S_{is}}{S_{i0}} \\ &= \xi_s S_{js}. \end{aligned} \tag{3.20}$$

Combining (3.19) with (3.20), we see that $E_s[\xi_t S_{jt}] = \xi_s S_{js}$. That is, all $\xi_t S_{jt}, j \in \Lambda$ are **P**-martingales. Thus, $\mathcal{M}$ is arbitrage-free. This completes the proof. □

This theorem shows that if there exists some numéraire asset and a numéraire measure equivalent to **P** such that all relative prices are martingales with respect to the numéraire measure, then the market is arbitrage-free. Usually, **Q** is referred to as an *equivalent martingale measure.*

The difference between Theorem 3.2.1(2) and Theorem 3.2.2 may seem slight, but it is significant in practice. Indeed, in order to define a new measure $\mathbf{P_i}$ in Theorem 3.2.1(2), we need to have the state price deflator. For Theorem 3.2.2, in contrast, we may define ξ artificially by (3.18), and are not concerned with whether ξ is the state price deflator. Succinctly, we need not determine the state price deflator to build an arbitrage-free model. Given this context, Theorem 3.2.2 is more practical than Theorem 3.2.1(2). Moreover, the arbitrage price is defined similarly to that under $\mathbf{P_i}$ as follows.

Arbitrage pricing under Q

Let us consider the arbitrage pricing under **Q**. Recall again the security whose payoff at T is given by X. Set z_t and ξ_t as in (3.17) and (3.18), respectively. Since z_t is a **P**-martingale, the same calculation as (3.12) implies that

$$\begin{aligned} S_{it} E_t^{\mathbf{Q}} \left[\frac{X}{S_{iT}} \right] &= S_{it} E_t \left[\frac{X z_T}{S_{iT}} \right] \frac{1}{E_t[z_T]} \\ &= E_t \left[\frac{X z_T}{S_{iT}} \right] \frac{S_{i0}}{\xi_t}. \end{aligned} \tag{3.21}$$

Similarly to the implication of (3.13), we have

$$E_t \left[\frac{X z_T}{S_{iT}} \right] = \frac{E_t[X \xi_T]}{S_{i0}}. \tag{3.22}$$

Substituting this into (3.21), we have, from (3.5), that

$$S_{it} E_t^{\mathbf{Q}} \left[\frac{X}{S_{iT}} \right] = \frac{E_t[X \xi_S]}{\xi_t} = p_t. \tag{3.23}$$

Hence, the price of this security is given by

$$p_t = S_{it} E_t^{\mathbf{Q}} \left[\frac{X}{S_{iT}} \right]. \tag{3.24}$$

This form is an analogy to the price formula (3.15) derived under $\mathbf{P_i}$, and (3.23) shows that the price is equal to that defined under the real-world measure. In contrast to the real-world measure, $\mathbf{P_i}$ and $\mathbf{Q}$ are referred to as *risk-neutral measures*.

We remark that the price in the form (3.24) is given by a numéraire and the numéraire measure is given without use of the state price deflator. Therefore, the arbitrage pricing within Theorem 3.2.2 can be practically executed. This approach is referred to as a *risk-neutral valuation* or *risk-neutral pricing.*

As a result, for arbitrage pricing, we may choose an arbitrary numéraire according to the properties of the asset. This technique is referred to as *change of numéraire.*

Remark

In this section, we assume no specific properties of an asset price process. In this context, the arbitrage pricing theory has been developed more generally in a mathematical sense. This book does not cover these subjects further. For more advanced study, see Musiela and Rutkowski (2011), or Pliska (1997), among others.

3.3 Market Price of Risk

The previous section presented a general framework of arbitrage pricing without use of a Brownian motion. Next, we introduce another framework for a bond market where bond prices are represented by Ito processes. In this setting, we consider the market price of risk to define the arbitrage-free market.

Let W_t be a d-dimensional $\mathbf{P}$-Brownian motion defined on $(\Omega, \mathcal{F}_{t\in[0,\tau]}, \mathbf{P})$, and let $\{B_{it}\}_{i\in\Lambda}$ be a family of price processes of zero-coupon bonds. We denote by $\mathcal{B} = \{B_{it}\}_{i\in\Lambda}$ the bond market. In this section, we assume that values B_{it} are represented by Ito processes such that

$$\frac{dB_{it}}{B_i} = \mu_{it}dt + v_{it}dW_t, \quad i = 1, \cdots, n, \tag{3.25}$$

where μ_{it} is a one-dimensional adapted process, and v_{it} is a d-dimensional adapted process satisfying

$$\int_0^T |\mu_{it}|ds < \infty, \qquad \int_0^T |v_{it}|^2 ds < \infty, \tag{3.26}$$

respectively. We sometimes denote these as μ_i and v_i, omitting the subscript t. From the Ito formula (2.66), we have

$$B_{it} = B_{i0} \exp\left\{\int_0^t \left(\mu_i - \frac{|v_i|^2}{2}\right) ds + \int_0^t v_i dW_s\right\} \tag{3.27}$$

for each i. Also, ξ_t denotes an adapted process defined by

$$\frac{d\xi_t}{\xi_t} = -r_t dt - \varphi_t dW_t, \tag{3.28}$$

with $\xi_0 = 1$, where r_t is a one-dimensional adapted process, and φ_t is a d-dimensional adapted process such that $\int_0^T |r|ds < \infty$ and $\int_0^T |\varphi|^2 ds < \infty$. We sometimes denote these as r and φ, omitting the subscript t. From (2.66), ξ_t is represented by

$$\xi_t = \exp\left\{\int_0^t \left(-r - \frac{|\varphi|^2}{2}\right) ds - \int_0^t \varphi dW_s\right\}. \tag{3.29}$$

Arbitrage-free bond market

In the bond market $\mathcal{B}$, we have another criterion for the arbitrage-free condition. This is given in the following theorem.

Theorem 3.3.1 *Let $S_{it}, i = 1, \cdots, n$ and ξ be Ito processes defined by (3.25) and (3.28), respectively. Then, the market $\mathcal{M}$ is arbitrage-free if there exist r and φ such that*

$$\mu_i - r = v_i \varphi \tag{3.30}$$

for every i.

Proof From (3.27) and (3.29), we have

$$\begin{aligned} \xi B_{it} &= B_{i0} \exp\left\{\int_0^t \left(\mu_i - r - \frac{|\varphi|^2}{2} - \frac{|v_i|^2}{2}\right) ds + \int_0^t (v_i - \varphi) dW_s\right\} \\ &= B_{i0} \exp\left\{\int_0^t \left(v_i \varphi - \frac{|\varphi|^2}{2} - \frac{|v_i|^2}{2}\right) ds + \int_0^t (v_i - \varphi) dW_s\right\} \\ &= B_{i0} \exp\left\{-\int_0^t \frac{|v_i - \varphi|^2}{2} ds + \int_0^t (v_i - \varphi) dW_s\right\}. \end{aligned} \tag{3.31}$$

The right-hand side is an exponential martingale, as mentioned in Section 2.6, and so ξB_{it} is a martingale under $\mathbf{P}$ for all $i \in \Lambda$. Specifically, ξ is a state price deflator and $\mathcal{B}$ is arbitrage-free. This completes the proof. □

The arbitrage pricing in the market $\mathcal{B}$ is given in the same way as in Sections 3.1 and 3.2. In particular, φ is a *market price of interest rate risk* (hereinafter, *market price of risk*). If we obtain the market price of risk φ, then r is given from (3.30) by $r = \mu_i - v_i\varphi$. The state price deflator ξ_t is obtained by (3.28).

Complete market

If the market price of risk exists and is unique, then the market is called *complete*. Originally, the complete market is defined in the sense of replication of options for option pricing and hedging. However, this book is interested in the uniqueness of the market price of risk, rather than in the replication problem. Therefore, in this book, a "complete market" means that the market price of risk is unique.

Economic interpretation of the market price of risk

To give an economic interpretation of the market price of risk, suppose that W_t is a one-dimensional Brownian motion. Then, the market price of risk is a scalar-valued process. From (3.30), we have

$$\varphi = \frac{\mu_i - r}{v_i}. \tag{3.32}$$

In traditional financial theory, r is regarded as a risk-free interest rate and μ_i is regarded as the expected rate of return for bond i. Then, $\mu_i - r$ indicates the excess return for bond i. Here, v_i is a price volatility of bond i; that is, it is a kind of risk measure of bond i. The market price of risk is traditionally explained as the excess return per unit of risk for investment in bond i. The value r is referred to as the *implied short rate*.

Furthermore, the existence of the market price of risk means that the excess return per unit of risk for each bond is uniform. That is, there is no possibility to find a profitable bond with respect to the risk–return trade-off. This is an intuitive explanation of Theorem 3.3.1.

However the traditional interpretation is limited to a one-dimensional model. In contrast to this, Chapters 6 and 9 will theoretically present a perspective for interpretation of a multi-dimensional model.

CHAPTER 4

HEATH–JARROW–MORTON MODEL

Abstract: For management of interest rate risk, we create an interest rate scenario by using an arbitrage-free model of the bond market, which describes the evolution of the forward rate. With this understanding, this chapter addresses the forward rate model introduced by Heath *et al.* (1992) (hereinafter, HJM). Additionally, we introduce the short rate model introduced by Hull and White (1990), which we treat as a special case in the HJM model.

In interest rate models, the option price is typically valuated under the risk-neutral measure, and so these models have been developed as models specified under the risk-neutral measure.

On the one hand, when we apply a model to risk management, we must use a model specified under the real-world measure. We consider this further by valuating the VaR of a simple example. On the other hand, to construct an interest rate model under the real-world measure, it is necessary to estimate the market price of risk. We briefly summarize some approaches to estimation of that price in the short rate models.

Keywords: Arbitrage-free, Contribution rate, d-factor model, Drift coefficient, Forward rate, HJM model, Hull–White model, Kalman filter, Market price of risk, Mean reversion rate, Principal component analysis (PCA), Real-world measure, Real-world model, Risk-neutral measure, Risk neutral valuation, Savings account, Short rate, Spot measure, State price deflator, Time-homogeneous, Volatility, Volatility component

Takashi Yasuoka

4.1 Heath-Jarrow-Morton Framework

Interest rate model

We introduced a bond market $\mathcal{B}$ in Chapter 3 that did not admit a term structure of interest rates. If, instead, we assume a term structure in the bond market, it becomes possible to relate the bond price to the interest rate. We represent the dynamics of bond price by a stochastic process and use this to specify the corresponding interest rates. Such a system is referred to as a term structure model of interest rates (or put simply, an interest rate model).

A model specified by the dynamics of a short rate is referred to as a short rate model. A model specified by the dynamics of forward rates is referred to as a forward rate model. For management of interest rate risk, it is better to suppose various types of changes in the yield curve, and specifically to suppose changes in the forward rates. Because of this, the forward rate model is more useful in risk management than the short rate model is.

This section briefly introduces the HJM model, which is the most general forward rate model. For additional details, readers are recommended to consult Cairns (2004), Munk (2011), or Shreve (2004), among others. For details on calibration, readers are recommended to consult Wu (2009).

Forward rate process

Let $(\Omega, \mathcal{F}_{t\in[0,\tau]}, \mathbf{P})$ be a filtered probability space, where $\mathcal{F}_{t\in[0,\tau]}$ is the augmented filtration and $\mathbf{P}$ denotes the real-world measure. The instantaneous forward rate with maturity T observed at time t is denoted by $f(t,T)$. When the usage is unambiguous, $f(t,T)$ will be called the forward rate. Typically $f(0,T)$ represents an initial forward rate.

We assume that the dynamics of $f(t,T)$ on $(\Omega, \mathcal{F}_{t\in[0,\tau]}, \mathbf{P})$ is represented by

$$df(t,T) = \alpha(t,T)dt + \sigma(t,T)dW_t, \tag{4.1}$$

where $W_t = (W_t^1, \cdots, W_t^d)^T$ is a d-dimensional $\mathbf{P}$-Brownian motion, and $\alpha(t,T)$ and $\sigma(t,T)$ are predictable processes satisfying some technical conditions. Here, $\sigma(t,T) = (\sigma^1(t,T), \cdots, \sigma^d(t,T))^T$ is a d-dimensional process. The second term, $\sigma(t,T)dW_t$ denotes the inner product of $\sigma(t,T)$ and dW_t in

$\mathbf{R}^d$, specifically

$$\sigma(t,T)dW_t = \sum_{l=1}^{d} \sigma^l(t,T)dW_t^l. \tag{4.2}$$

Adopting this convention for simplicity, ab denotes the inner product of vectors $a = (a_1, \cdots, a_d)^T$ and $b = (b_1, \cdots, b_d)^T$ throughout.

The process $\alpha(t,T)$ is referred to as a *drift coefficient*. Typically, when $\alpha(t,T)$ is positive (resp., negative), the forward rate rises (resp., falls) on average. The process $\sigma(t,T)$ is referred to as a *volatility*; it represents the magnitude of the forward rate diffusion. From these, the equation (4.1) represents a stochastic model in the dynamics of forward rates. In particular, if the model uses a d-dimensional Brownian motion as the above, then it is referred to as a *d-factor model* for discrimination of the dimension size.

Instantaneous short rate and savings account

From equation (4.1), it follows that

$$f(t,T) = f(0,T) + \int_0^t \alpha(s,T)ds + \int_0^t \sigma(s,T)dW_s. \tag{4.3}$$

The instantaneous short rate (hereinafter, short rate) r is given by $r(t) = f(t,t)$. Substituting t into T in equation (4.3), we have

$$r(t) = f(0,t) + \int_0^t \alpha(s,t)ds + \int_0^t \sigma(s,t)dW_s. \tag{4.4}$$

A *savings account* (or *money market account*) B_t is defined by

$$B_t = \exp\left\{\int_0^t r(s)ds\right\}. \tag{4.5}$$

This represents continuous reinvestment at the short rate $r(t)$. In other words, the savings account serves as an indicator of performance by the safest investment. In the HJM model, we take the savings account as a numéraire.

For example, if the short rate is assumed to be constant (i.e., $r(t) = r$), then we have $B_t = \exp\{rt\}$. This is well known as the performance of the investment on the constant short rate r for the period $[0,t]$. This form was used as the example of a risk-free asset in Example 3.1.

Bond price

We denote by $B(t,T)$ the price at time t of a zero-coupon bond with maturity $T, 0 \leq T \leq \tau$. From equation (1.14), it follows that

$$B(t,T) = \exp\left\{-\int_t^T f(t,u)du\right\}. \tag{4.6}$$

A bond market $\mathcal{B}$ is defined as a set of all bonds with maturity $T, 0 \leq T \leq \tau$, where each price of a T-maturity bond is given by equation (4.6).

If $f(t,T)$ is continuous in T, then $B(t,T)$ is differentiable with respect to T. Thus, it follows from equation (4.6) that

$$-\frac{\partial \log B(t,T)}{\partial T} = f(t,T). \tag{4.7}$$

It is shown by Heath *et al.* (1992) that $B(t,T)$ can be represented as

$$\begin{aligned}\log B(t,T) &= \log B(0,T) + \int_0^t \left\{r(s) + b(s,T) - \frac{|v(s,T)|^2}{2}\right\} ds \\ &\quad + \int_0^t v(s,T)dW_s,\end{aligned} \tag{4.8}$$

where $b(s,T)$ and $v(s,T)$ denote processes given by

$$b(s,T) = -\int_s^T \alpha(s,u)du + \frac{|v(s,T)|^2}{2} \tag{4.9}$$

$$v(s,T) = -\int_s^T \sigma(s,u)du, \tag{4.10}$$

respectively.

Relative bond price

Taking the savings account as a numéraire, from equations (4.5) and (4.8), the relative bond price is represented by

$$\begin{aligned}\log \frac{B(t,T)}{B_t} &= \log B(0,T) + \int_0^t \left\{b(s,T) - \frac{|v(s,T)|^2}{2}\right\} ds \\ &\quad + \int_0^t v(s,T)dW_s.\end{aligned} \tag{4.11}$$

We assume the existence of some d-dimensional process φ_t that satisfies

$$b(t,T) = v(t,T)\varphi_t \tag{4.12}$$

for all T. Here, φ_t is called the *market price of risk*. From the above relation, we note that φ_t is independent of T. Substituting $b(t,T)$ into equation (4.11), it follows that

$$\begin{aligned}\frac{B(t,T)}{B_t} &= B(0,T)\exp\left[\int_0^t \left\{v(s,T)\varphi_s - \frac{|v(s,T)|^2}{2}\right\} ds \right.\\ &\quad \left. + \int_0^t v(s,T)dW_s\right].\end{aligned} \tag{4.13}$$

We set a process Z_t as $Z_t = \int_0^t \varphi_s ds + W_t$. From the Girsanov theorem, there exists a measure $\mathbf{Q}$, equivalent to $\mathbf{P}$, such that Z_t is a Brownian motion under $\mathbf{Q}$. Specifically, equation (4.13) becomes

$$\begin{aligned}\frac{B(t,T)}{B_t} &= B(0,T)\exp\left\{-\int_0^t \frac{|v(s,T)|^2}{2}ds + \int_0^t v(s,T)(\varphi_s ds + dW_s)\right\}\\ &= B(0,T)\exp\left\{-\int_0^t \frac{|v(s,T)|^2}{2}ds + \int_0^t v(s,T)dZ_s\right\}.\end{aligned} \tag{4.14}$$

Since the right-hand side is an exponential martingale, the relative bond price $B(t,T)/B_t$ is a martingale for all maturities T. It follows from Theorem 3.2.1(2) that the bond market is arbitrage-free. From these, we have obtained an arbitrage-free interest rate model; this is reflected by the following theorem.

Theorem 4.1.1 *If there exists a market price of risk φ_t satisfying equation (4.12), then the bond market $\mathcal{B}$ is arbitrage-free.*

In the framework of HJM, the savings account is taken as a numéraire, and the measure $\mathbf{Q}$ is the equivalent martingale measure with respect to the savings account. $\mathbf{Q}$ is also referred to as a risk-neutral measure.

Remark

We remark that the sign in the definition of φ_t given in equation (4.12) is opposite that used in Heath *et al.* (1992); however, our usage follows the conventional formulation of the market price of risk, as equation (3.30). This will be verified in the form (4.22).

4.2 Arbitrage Pricing and Market Price of Risk

This section briefly studies some fundamental subjects in the HJM model, specifically, forward rate process, arbitrage pricing, the market price of risk, and state price deflator.

Forward rate process

Here let us represent the forward rate process under the risk-neutral measure $\mathbf{Q}$. Differentiating equation (4.9) with respect to T, we have

$$-\alpha(s,T) - \sigma(s,T)\int_s^T \sigma(s,u)du = \frac{\partial b(s,T)}{\partial T}. \tag{4.15}$$

From equations (4.10) and (4.12), it follows that

$$\begin{aligned} -\alpha(s,T) - \sigma(s,T)\int_s^T \sigma(s,u)du &= \frac{\partial v(s,T)}{\partial T}\varphi_t \\ &= -\sigma(s,T)\varphi_t. \end{aligned} \tag{4.16}$$

Substituting the above into equation (4.1), we obtain

$$df(t,T) = \{-\sigma(t,T)v(t,T) + \sigma(t,T)\varphi(t)\}\,dt + \sigma(t,T)dW_t. \tag{4.17}$$

Recall the $\mathbf{Q}$-Brownian motion $Z_t = \int_0^t \varphi_s ds + W_t$. Substituting this into the above, we have

$$df(t,T) = -\sigma(t,T)v(t,T)dt + \sigma(t,T)dZ_t, \tag{4.18}$$

where the drift under $\mathbf{Q}$ is completely determined by the volatility $\sigma(t,T)$. This form is the well-known forward rate process in the HJM model. For pricing interest rate derivatives, the dynamics of the forward rates are typically simulated by equation (4.18), and the bond pricing is performed by using this form. This method is essentially the same as used with short rate models.

Arbitrage pricing in the HJM model

According to the argument in Section 3.2, let us verify the arbitrage pricing within the HJM framework. Consider a security whose payoff at $T \leq \tau$ is defined by a random variable X. From equation (3.24), the time t price of this security is given by

$$p_t = B_t E_t^{\mathbf{Q}}\left[\frac{X}{B_T}\right]. \tag{4.19}$$

Here, B_t denotes the time t price of the savings account. This formula has two salient points.

- The savings account taken as the numéraire is familiar as a risk-free asset for derivative traders.
- It is not necessary to estimate the market price of risk.

In particular, let us consider a case in which the short rate $r(t)$ is assumed to be a constant process, as $r(t) = r$. In that case, it holds that $B_0 = 1$ and $B_T = \exp^{rT}$. From these, the price formula (4.19) becomes

$$p_0 = \exp\{-rT\}E^{\mathbf{Q}}[X]. \tag{4.20}$$

This expression indicates that the price of this security is the present value of the expectation of the value X at time (T) under the risk-neutral measure $\mathbf{Q}$.

This constant short rate assumption is widely used in the primary model for option pricing. For example, it is assumed for the Black–Scholes model of a stock option and the Black model of a cap (or floor). Because of this, the formulation (4.20) is known as the *risk-neutral valuation.*

Market price of risk

Theorem 4.1.1 assures the existence of an arbitrage-free market under the assumption about the market price of risk φ_t that

$$b(t,T) = v(t,T)\varphi_t. \tag{4.21}$$

This form looks to be different from the original definition given in equation (3.30) as

$$\mu_{it} - r_t = v_{it}\tilde{\varphi}_t. \tag{4.22}$$

However, the two are actually the same, as follows. Here, we denote by $\tilde{\varphi}_t$ the original definition to distinguish it from φ as defined in equation (4.21). Let us examine the property of φ in connection with equation (4.22).

Applying Ito's formula to equation (4.8), we have

$$\frac{dB(t,T)}{B(t,T)} = (r(t) + b(t,T))dt + v(t,T)dW_t. \tag{4.23}$$

From the implications of equation (3.25), the drift $\mu(t,T)$ of the T-maturity bond is represented by $\mu(t,T) = r(t) + b(t,T)$. With this, $b(t,T)$ indicates the excess rate of return for investment in the T-maturity bond relative to the short rate $r(t)$. Combining equation (4.21) with $\mu(t,T)$, we have

$$\mu(t,T) - r(t) = v(t,T)\varphi_t. \tag{4.24}$$

This expression shows the same form as equation (4.22), and so φ_t has the same function as $\tilde{\varphi}_t$ (cf. the remark in Section 4.1).

Negative value of the market price of risk

The market price of risk typically takes a negative value, and we offer a conventional explanation for that. For example, we can find a description in Cairns (2004, p. 62).

Consider a one-dimensional case of equation (4.24); specifically, consider the market price of risk φ_t as being expressed by

$$\varphi_t = \frac{\mu(t,T) - r(t)}{v(t,T)}. \tag{4.25}$$

Since $\mu(t,T)$ represents the expected rate of return for the T-maturity bond, the difference $\mu(t,T) - r(t)$ indicates the excess return rate for the investment in T-maturity bond relative to the short rate $r(t)$. Mostly, it might hold that $\mu(t,T) > r(t)$. Then φ_t will have the same sign as the value $v(t,T)$. Since $v(t,T)$ must be negative from its definition in equation (4.10), we may view the market price of risk as taking a negative value.

However, the truth of this observation is somewhat questionable. Indeed, it is neither trivial to estimate the drift coefficient $\mu(t,T)$ of the bond from a historical price data, nor is it certain that $\mu(t,T) > r(t)$ can be proved. On this topic, we will develop a theoretical study of the value in the market price of risk for the multi-dimensional case in Chapters 6 and 7.

State price deflator

In the previous section, we obtained an arbitrage-free bond market $\mathcal{B}$, where the relative bond prices are $\mathbf{Q}$-martingale. Yet, we have not obtained the state price deflator. Let us derive that from the market price of risk and the short rate.

We suppose that we have already obtained the market price of risk φ_t. We define an Ito process ξ_t by

$$\frac{d\xi_t}{\xi_t} = -r(t)dt - \varphi_t dW_t, \tag{4.26}$$

where $r(t)$ is the short rate process as $r(t) = f(t,t)$. From Ito's formula, ξ_t is represented by

$$\xi_t = \exp\left\{\int_0^t \left(-r(s) - \frac{|\varphi_s|^2}{2}\right) ds - \int_0^t \varphi_s dW_s\right\}. \tag{4.27}$$

Also, the bond price $B(t,T)$ is obtained from equation (4.23) as

$$\begin{aligned} B(t,T) &= B(0,T)\exp\left[\int_0^t \left\{r(s) + b(s,T) - \frac{|v(s,T)|^2}{2}\right\} ds \right. \\ &\quad \left. + \int_0^t v(s,T)dW_s\right]. \end{aligned} \tag{4.28}$$

From these, $\xi_t B(t,T)$ is represented by

$$\begin{aligned} \xi_t B(t,T) &= B(0,T)\exp\left[\int_0^t \left\{-\frac{|\varphi_s|^2}{2} + b(s,T) - \frac{|v(s,T)|^2}{2}\right\} ds \right. \\ &\quad \left. + \int_0^t \{-\varphi_s + v(s,T)\}dW_s\right]. \end{aligned} \tag{4.29}$$

Substituting equation (4.12) into the above, we obtain

$$\begin{aligned} \xi_t B(t,T) &= B(0,T)\exp\left[\int_0^t \left\{-\frac{|\varphi_s|^2}{2} + v(s,T)\varphi_s - \frac{|v(s,T)|^2}{2}\right\} ds \right. \\ &\quad \left. + \int_0^t \{-\varphi_s + v(s,T)\}dW_s\right]. \end{aligned} \tag{4.30}$$

By the same calculation as in the proof of Theorem 3.3.1, we have

$$\begin{aligned} \xi_t B(t,T) &= B(0,T)\exp\left[\int_0^t -\frac{|\varphi_s - v(s,T)|^2}{2} ds \right. \\ &\quad \left. + \int_0^t \{-\varphi_s + v(s,T)\}dW_s\right]. \end{aligned} \tag{4.31}$$

This means that $\xi_t B(t,T)$ is an exponential martingale, and is thus a **P**-martingale for all T. From this, ξ_t is the state price deflator.

As a result, once we obtain the market price of risk φ_t, the state price deflator is given by equation (4.26), where we assign the short rate $r(t)$ as the implied short rate.

Real-world model and risk-neutral model

When an interest rate process and bond price process are represented under **P**, as in equation (4.8), the corresponding market is referred to as a *real-world model.* When they are represented under **Q**, as in equation (4.14), the market is referred to as a *risk-neutral model.*

Note that the risk-neutral model is not unique because the risk-neutral measure is determined according to the choice of numéraire. In contrast, the real-world model is uniquely determined for a complete market.

Null assumption on the market price of risk

When we assume a null market price of risk, $\varphi = 0$, it holds that $Z_t = W_t$ from the relation $Z_t = \int_0^t \varphi_s ds + W_t$. From this, we may see that $\mathbf{Q} = \mathbf{P}$, almost everywhere. Therefore making a null assumption about the market price of risk is equivalent to using a risk-neutral model.

Applying this, we can find many papers that intend to valuate the interest rate risk by using an interest rate model. Many such papers begin with a theoretical setting by using a real-world model. However, at the final step of computing the risk, they assume a null market price of risk. This approach is equivalent to working with the risk-neutral model.

One consequence of this is that many of us may be aware of neither the market price of risk nor the real-world measure in the business of derivatives pricing. Naturally in these circumstances, estimating the market price of risk has not been focused on for several decades.

4.3 Volatility and Principal Components

Approaches to volatility estimation

This section introduces a method for constructing the volatility in the HJM

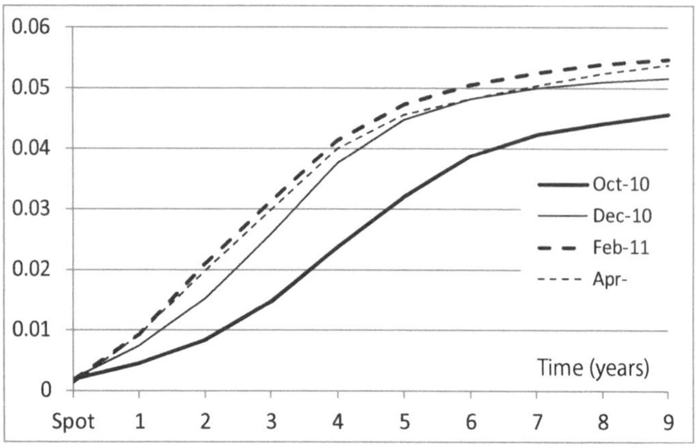

Figure 4.1: Implied forward rate curve in the U.S. Treasury market at October 2010, December 2010, February 2011, and April 2011. Yield data are the same as those for Fig. 1.3.

model. There are two major approaches to do so. One is a market approach; the other is a historical approach.

In the market approach, the volatility is estimated such that the model implies option prices consistent with their market prices. In the historical approach, the volatility is constructed to represent a historical dynamics of an interest rate, for example, the short rate or the forward rate. Experimentally, these two approaches result in quite different volatility structures.

When we calibrate the model for derivatives pricing, the market approach should be employed. In this, it is understood that historical volatility cannot explain market prices because the option prices are determined mostly by traders' forecasts for the future market rather than by historical volatility. Therefore, adopting a historical approach will result in a model that misprices major derivatives. Such a model is not valid for derivatives trading.

However, when we intend to calibrate a model for interest-risk-management, the historical approach is recommended, rather than the market approach. In the historical approach, principal component analysis (PCA) is a standard technique for reducing the dimensionality of the model. PCA will be repeatedly used in this book, and we introduce the construction of volatility by applying PCA. The fundamentals of PCA and the relevant linear algebra are given in Appendix B.

Historical observation

To address the historical approach, let us recall Fig. 1.3 in Section 1.3, which exhibited a historical chart of the implied forward rates in the U.S. Treasury market. Additionally, Fig. 4.1 exhibits some cross sections of those rates. Specifically, it shows the implied forward rate curves observed at October 2010, December 2010, February 2011, and April 2011 for the same U.S. Treasury yields as shown in Fig. 1.3. These graphs suggest that changes in forward rates $f(\cdot, T_i), i = 1, \cdots, n$ are closely correlated with each other. Succinctly, $f(\cdot, T_i)$ moves almost uniformly in $i, i = 1, \cdots, n$.

As an example, consider a case in which the forward rate curve is always moved as a parallel shift, and the dynamics of the forward rate is described by a one-factor model as

$$df(t, T_i) = \cdots dt + \sigma dW_t \;\; ; \quad i = 1, \cdots, n \tag{4.32}$$

where σ is a scalar constant and W_t is a one-dimensional Brownian motion. Here, we focus our argument on the volatility structure, which means that we may not exactly specify the second term. From Fig. 4.1, we may adopt the view that the one-factor model can simply approximate the change in the forward rates.

Covariance matrix

Let $x_i, i = 1, \cdots, n$ with $x_i < x_{i+1}$ be a sequence of time length. At time t, the variable $T_i = x_i + t$ represents a maturity date of a bond i. Let Δt be a time interval to observe the forward rates. In the HJM model, the change in the forward rate $f(t, T_i)$ is specified as $\Delta f(t, T_i) = f(t + \Delta t, T_i) - f(t, T_i)$ with fixed maturity T_i. Using the time length x_i, this is represented as

$$\Delta f(t, t + x_i) = f(t + \Delta t, t + x_i - \Delta t) - f(t, t + x_i). \tag{4.33}$$

We typically observe the change in the forward rate in this form with a fixed time length x_i. Applying this form, the covariance matrix $V = \{V_{ij}\}$ is given by the observation of $\Delta f(\ , x_i)$ as

$$V_{ij} = \frac{1}{\Delta t} Cov(\Delta f(\ , x_i), \Delta f(\ , x_j)). \tag{4.34}$$

Principal volatility component

PCA is a statistical technique for reducing the dimensionality of the model. For the covariance matrix V, we have from equation (B.11) in Appendix B that

$$V_{ij} = (e^1, \cdots, e^n) \begin{pmatrix} (\rho_1)^2 & 0 & 0 \\ 0 & \ddots & 0 \\ 0 & 0 & (\rho_n)^2 \end{pmatrix} (e^1, \cdots, e^n)^T, \tag{4.35}$$

where $e^l = (e_1^l, \cdots, e_n^l)^T$ is the lth principal component and $(\rho_l)^2$ is the lth eigenvalue. In this, we assume that the eigenvalues are chosen such that $\rho_1 > \rho_2 > \cdots > \rho_n > 0$, and $|e^l|^2 = 1$ for all l. The first principal component explains the largest portion of the covariance V, and the second one explains the largest portion of the remaining covariance, and so on. The set of principal components is orthonormal from equation (B.4); in other words, the components are uncorrelated with each other (cf. Appendix B.1).

Let $\sigma^l = (\sigma_1^l, \cdots, \sigma_n^l)^T$ denote the *lth principal volatility component* (briefly, the *lth volatility component*) defined by $\sigma_i^l = \rho_l e_i^l$. It follows from the orthonormality condition that

$$\begin{aligned} |\sigma^l|^2 &= \sum_{i=1}^n (\rho_l e_i^l)^2 = (\rho_l)^2 \sum_{i=1}^n (e_i^l)^2 \\ &= (\rho_l)^2. \end{aligned} \tag{4.36}$$

This means that the lth eigenvalue $(\rho_l)^2$ indicates the magnitude of the lth volatility component.

Principal component in the forward rates

Here we summarize the basic property of the principal components in connection with the changes of the forward rates. Using this, Litterman and Scheinkman (1991) applied PCA to U.S. Treasury yields. They showed that the first factor essentially represents a parallel change in yields; this is called a level factor. The second factor is called steepness (or slope), and the third factor is called curvature (or hump-shapedness). Empirically, these three factors explain most of the changes in the yields. This feature is generally observed in the bond market and widely applied for interest-rate-risk management.

Additionally, a property similar to the above is observed in the forward rate dynamics. Specifically, the first principal component represents a parallel change in the forward rate curve change, the second component indicates a steepening or flattening, and the third component represents a curvature change.

Fig. 4.2 illustrates a representative example of the first three components in the forward rate dynamics. In this figure, the bold line e^1 shows the first principal component, which typically takes a strictly positive value. This component represents parallel change in the forward rate curve. The thin line e^2 shows the second component, which takes positive values in short forward rates and negative values in long forward rates. This indicates the steepness of change. The dashed line e^3 indicates the third component, which takes positive values in short and long forward rates and takes negatives value in middle forward rates. This represents curvature change.

From these observations, the principal components are used to construct a scenario of the forward rate changes for use in risk management. A numerical example of the principal components will be shown in Chapter 10.

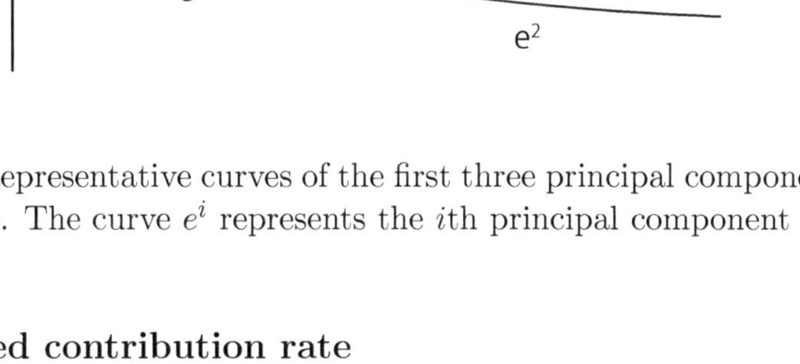

Figure 4.2: Representative curves of the first three principal components of forward rate dynamics. The curve e^i represents the ith principal component for $i = 1, 2, 3$.

Accumulated contribution rate

When a d-factor model is constructed by using the first d principal components, we call it the *first d-factor model.* Throughout this book, we always work with the first d-factor model, which we abbreviate to *d-factor model.*

A *contribution rate* of the lth principal component is defined by

$$\frac{(\rho_l)^2}{(\rho_1)^2 + \cdots + (\rho_n)^2}. \tag{4.37}$$

This indicates the portion of the lth principal component in the covariance. An *accumulated contribution rate* C_d for the first d principal components is defined by

$$C_d = \frac{(\rho_1)^2 + \cdots + (\rho_d)^2}{(\rho_1)^2 + \cdots + (\rho_n)^2}. \tag{4.38}$$

Dimensionality reduction

When we work with an n-factor model, the volatility structure is represented by an $n \times n$ matrix chosen such that

$$\begin{pmatrix} df(t,T_1) \\ \vdots \\ df(t,T_n) \end{pmatrix} = \begin{pmatrix} \cdots \\ \vdots \\ \cdots \end{pmatrix} dt + \begin{pmatrix} \sigma_1^1 & \cdots & \sigma_1^n \\ \vdots & \vdots & \vdots \\ \sigma_n^1 & \cdots & \sigma_n^n \end{pmatrix} \begin{pmatrix} dW_t^1 \\ \vdots \\ dW_t^n \end{pmatrix}, \tag{4.39}$$

where $\sigma_i^l = \rho_l e_i^l$ for $i, l = 1, \cdots, n$. The accumulated contribution rate is a traditional criterion used when reducing the dimensionality of the forward rate model. When C_d is almost equal to 1 for an integer $d > 0$, then the above equation is successfully approximated by the d-factor model.

It is empirically known that the first three-factor model adequately approximates the n-factor model of equation (4.39). When an observation such as this is known to hold, we may work with a three-factor model. The equation (4.39) is remarkably reduced to a three-factor model as

$$\begin{pmatrix} df(t,T_1) \\ \vdots \\ df(t,T_n) \end{pmatrix} = \begin{pmatrix} \cdots \\ \vdots \\ \cdots \end{pmatrix} dt + \begin{pmatrix} \sigma_1^1 & \sigma_1^2 & \sigma_1^3 \\ \vdots & \vdots & \vdots \\ \sigma_n^1 & \sigma_n^2 & \sigma_n^3 \end{pmatrix} \begin{pmatrix} dW_t^1 \\ dW_t^2 \\ dW_t^3 \end{pmatrix}. \tag{4.40}$$

Thus, it remains to determine the drift term; this will be studied in Chapter 6.

4.4 The Hull–White Model

In the early days, many stochastic models were introduced to describe the dynamics of the short rate. As examples, see Cox *et al.* (1985; hereinafter,

CIR), Ho and Lee (1986), Hull and White (1990), and Vasicek (1977), among others. A strong point of these models is their parsimoniousness. Additionally, these models are described by affine term structures. For details of affine models, readers are recommended to consult Duffie and Kan (1996), Björk (2004), or Munk (2011).

It is known that the Ho–Lee model and the Hull–White model are special cases of the Gaussian HJM model. The Hull–White model, in particular, is one of the most popular models in many financial institutions. Following along these lines, this section introduces the Hull–White model as a special case of the HJM model.

Short rate process

Let us consider a one-dimensional process of the short rate $r(t)$ represented by

$$dr(t) = \kappa\left\{\theta(t) - r(t) + \frac{\sigma}{\kappa}\varphi_t\right\}dt + \sigma dW_t, \tag{4.41}$$

where W_t is a one-dimensional Brownian motion under the real-world measure $\mathbf{P}$; κ and σ are positive constants; $\theta(t)$ is a positive process; and φ_t denotes the market price of risk.

It is empirically observed that the volatility of long-term interest rates is less than that of short term rates, reflecting a general phenomenon referred to as mean reversion. To model this feature, the rate at which $r(t)$ reverts to $\theta(t)$ is the speed κ, called the *mean reversion rate*.

The savings account $B_t = \exp\{\int_0^t r(s)ds\}$ is taken as a numéraire. We set $Z_t = \int_0^t \varphi_s ds + W_t$. By the Girsanov theorem, there exists a risk-neutral measure $\mathbf{Q}$ equivalent to $\mathbf{P}$ such that Z_t is a Brownian motion under $\mathbf{Q}$. From these, the short rate $r(t)$ is represented under $\mathbf{Q}$ as

$$dr(t) = \kappa(\theta(t) - r(t))dt + \sigma dZ_t. \tag{4.42}$$

It is known that the price of a zero-coupon bond with maturity T is given by

$$B(t,T) = \exp\{-a(t,T) - b(T-t)r(t)\}, \tag{4.43}$$

where $a(t,T)$ and $b(s)$ are defined by

$$
\begin{aligned}
a(t,T) &= \kappa \int_t^T \theta(s) b(T-s) ds + \frac{\sigma^2}{4\kappa} b(T-t)^2 \\
&\quad + \frac{\sigma^2}{2\kappa^2}\{b(T-t) - (T-t)\}. \qquad (4.44) \\
b(s) &= \frac{1}{\kappa}[1 - \exp\{-\kappa(s)\}] \qquad (4.45)
\end{aligned}
$$

For an arbitrary initial forward rate $f(0,T)$, we define $\theta(t)$ by

$$\theta(t) = f(0,t) + \frac{1}{\kappa}\frac{\partial f(0,t)}{\partial t} + \frac{\sigma^2}{2\kappa^2}(1 - e^{-2\kappa t}). \qquad (4.46)$$

With this, it is known that $B(0,T)$ coincides with the zero-coupon bond price implied from the initial rate $f(0,T)$.

Substituting equation (4.46) into equation (4.42), $r(t)$ is described as

$$dr(t) = \kappa \left\{ f(0,t) + \frac{1}{\kappa}\frac{\partial f(0,t)}{\partial t} + \frac{\sigma^2}{2\kappa^2}(1 - e^{-2\kappa t}) - r(t) \right\} dt + \sigma dZ_t. \qquad (4.47)$$

This is the formulation of the short rate process $r(t)$ used in the Hull–White model.

In this model, when $\theta(t)$ is determined by equation (4.46), $B(0,T)$ is equal to the initial bond price implied from arbitrarily given the forward rate $f(0,T)$. In this context, the Hull–White model is referred to as an arbitrage-free model. Among examples in Gaussian short rate models, the Ho–Lee model is known as an arbitrage-free model but the Vasicek model is not. For more about this, refer to the works of Ho and Lee (1986) and Hull and White (1990), or see Munk (2011) or Wu (2009), among others.

Hull–White model as an HJM model

The previous argument is derived from the short rate process (4.41). Next, we obtain the Hull–White model as a special case of HJM's forward rate process. Consider a one-factor volatility in the HJM model given by

$$\sigma(t,T) = \sigma \exp\{-\kappa(T-t)\}, \qquad (4.48)$$

where σ and κ are positive constants. This volatility admits an exponentially decaying structure with respect to the time length $T-t$ from the time t to the maturity T. From equation (4.18), the drift term is represented under $\mathbf{Q}$ by

$$\begin{aligned}\sigma(t,T)\upsilon(t,T) &= -\sigma e^{-\kappa(T-t)}\int_t^T \sigma e^{-\kappa(T-s)}ds \\ &= -\frac{\sigma^2}{\kappa}e^{-\kappa(T-t)}[1-e^{-\kappa(T-t)}]. \end{aligned} \tag{4.49}$$

Substituting this into equation (4.18), $f(t,T)$ is described as

$$\begin{aligned}f(t,T) &= f(0,T)+\int_0^t \frac{\sigma^2}{\kappa}e^{-\kappa(T-s)}[1-e^{-\kappa(T-s)}]ds \\ &\quad +\sigma\int_0^t e^{-\kappa(T-s)}dZ_s. \end{aligned} \tag{4.50}$$

Since $r(t)=f(t,t)$, putting $T=t$ in the above results in expressing the short rate process as

$$\begin{aligned}r(t) &= f(0,t)+\int_0^t \frac{\sigma^2}{\kappa}e^{-\kappa(t-s)}[1-e^{-\kappa(t-s)}]ds \\ &\quad +\int_0^t \sigma e^{-\kappa(t-s)}dZ_s \\ &= f(0,t)+\frac{\sigma^2}{2\kappa^2}(1-e^{-\kappa t})^2+\sigma e^{-\kappa t}\int_0^t e^{\kappa s}dZ_s. \end{aligned} \tag{4.51}$$

Next, we define a process X_t by $X_t=\int_0^t e^{\kappa s}dZ_s$, and a process $g(t,X_t)$ by

$$g(t,X_t)=f(0,t)+\frac{\sigma^2}{2\kappa^2}(1-e^{-\kappa t})^2+\sigma e^{-\kappa t}X_t. \tag{4.52}$$

From equation (4.51), we see that $g(t,X_t)=r(t)$. In order to obtain $dr=dg(t,X_t)$ by Ito's formula, we calculate the following:

$$\frac{\partial g}{\partial t} = \frac{\partial f(0,t)}{\partial t}+\frac{\sigma^2}{\kappa}(1-e^{-\kappa t})e^{-\kappa t}-\kappa\sigma e^{-\kappa t}X_t \tag{4.53a}$$

$$\frac{\partial g}{\partial X} = \sigma e^{-\kappa t} \tag{4.53b}$$

$$\frac{\partial^2 g}{\partial X^2} = 0. \tag{4.53c}$$

From Ito's formula, it follows that

$$\begin{aligned} dr(t) &= dg(t, X_t) \\ &= \left\{ \frac{\partial f(0,t)}{\partial t} + \frac{\sigma^2}{\kappa}(1 - e^{-\kappa t})e^{-\kappa t} - \kappa\sigma e^{-\kappa t} X_t \right\} dt + e^{\kappa t}\sigma e^{-\kappa t} dZ_s \\ &= \left\{ \frac{\partial f(0,t)}{\partial t} + \frac{\sigma^2}{\kappa}(1 - e^{-\kappa t})e^{-\kappa t} - \kappa\sigma e^{-\kappa t} \int_0^t e^{\kappa s} dZ_s \right\} dt \\ &\quad + \sigma dZ_s. \end{aligned} \tag{4.54}$$

Substituting equation (4.51) into the above, we have

$$\begin{aligned} dr(t) &= \left\{ \frac{\partial f(0,t)}{\partial t} + \frac{\sigma^2}{\kappa}(1 - e^{-\kappa t})e^{-\kappa t} \right\} dt \\ &\quad + \kappa \left\{ f(0,t) + \frac{\sigma^2}{2\kappa^2}(1 - e^{-\kappa t})^2 - r(t) \right\} dt + \sigma dZ_s \\ &= \left\{ \kappa f(0,t) + \frac{\partial f(0,t)}{\partial t} + \frac{\sigma^2}{2\kappa}(1 - e^{-2\kappa t}) - \kappa r(t) \right\} dt \\ &\quad + \sigma dZ_s. \end{aligned} \tag{4.55}$$

Setting $\theta(t)$ as

$$\theta(t) = f(0,t) + \frac{1}{\kappa}\frac{\partial f(0,t)}{\partial t} + \frac{\sigma^2}{2\kappa^2}(1 - e^{-2\kappa t}), \tag{4.56}$$

we have

$$dr(t) = \kappa(\theta(t) - r(t))dt + \sigma dZ_s. \tag{4.57}$$

This coincides precisely with equation (4.46). From these, the Hull–White model with mean reversion rate κ and volatility σ is exactly an HJM model with volatility $\sigma(t,T) = \sigma \exp\{-\kappa(T - t)\}$.

Distribution of short rate

From equation (4.51), the short rate $r(t)$ is normally distributed with mean

$$E^{\mathbf{Q}}[r(t)] = f(0,t) + \frac{\sigma^2}{2\kappa^2}(1 - e^{-\kappa t})^2 \tag{4.58}$$

under $\mathbf{Q}$. The variance of the distribution is obtained from equation (2.33) as

$$\begin{aligned} Var[r(t)] &= E\left[(\sigma e^{-\kappa t}\int_0^t e^{\kappa s}dZ_s)^2\right] \\ &= \sigma^2\int_0^t e^{2\kappa(t-s)}ds \\ &= \frac{\sigma^2}{2\kappa}(1-e^{-2\kappa t}). \end{aligned} \tag{4.59}$$

We note, in particular, that the variance is independent on the measure.

We will address the calibration of this model for risk management in Chapter 8.

4.5 VaR Computed in the Real-world

This section studies the reason that the VaR should be computed using a real-world model. For this purpose, the valuation of the VaR depends on the choice of measure. We use the following simple example to illustrate this. For simplicity, we assume a null discount rate in the following argument (i.e. the forward price is equal to the present price).

Suppose a binary bond with expiry at time T and with payoff X at T is given as follows.

$$\begin{cases} \text{If} \quad L > 5\% \quad \text{at } T, \quad \text{then} \quad X = 0 \\ \text{If} \quad L \le 5\% \quad \text{at } T, \quad \text{then} \quad X = 1.01, \end{cases} \tag{4.60}$$

where L indicates the 6-month LIBOR at T. Succinctly, the payoff is determined by the level of the 6-month LIBOR at the expiry date.

The price of this security is computed by using some interest rate model under some risk-neutral measure $\mathbf{Q}$. For the model, we assume the probability distribution of L as

$$\begin{cases} \mathbf{Q}(L > 5\%) = 0.09\% \\ \mathbf{Q}(L \le 5\%) = 99.01\%. \end{cases} \tag{4.61}$$

With this distribution, the arbitrage price of this bond at $t = 0$ is calculated by

$$(1.01 \times 0.9901 + 0 \times 0.0009) \times 1 = 1.00 \tag{4.62}$$

because of the assumption of a null discount rate.

We buy this bond at price 1.00. Let us valuate the 99% VaR of this bond for holding period T. We can sell this for the price 1.01 at time T at a probability of more than 99%. The 99% VaR is valuated as the profit of -0.01(=1.00-1.01) under **Q**.

Next, we assume that historical observation estimates for the 6-month LIBOR are

$$\begin{cases} \mathbf{P}(L > 5\%) = 2\% \\ \mathbf{P}(L \leq 5\%) = 98\%, \end{cases} \tag{4.63}$$

where **P** denotes the real-world probability. From this, the 99% VaR is the loss of 1.00 $(= 1.00 - 0)$. So the valuation of the VaR is absolutely affected by the measure. Even assuming a non-zero interest rate as the discount rate might affect little in this example.

Table 4.1 summarizes these figures. Here, the second column exhibits the payoff of this security, and the third column exhibits the profit and loss. The last row exhibits the 99% VaR under the measures **P** and **Q**, respectively.

Moreover, let us depart from the assumption of a null discount rate, and suppose an alternative numéraire measure. This might imply yet another 99% VaR depending on the measure. These observations means that the VaR depends on the choice of the measure, in contrast to the arbitrage price, which does not vary with the choice of measure. Naturally, we have no probability more reliable than the real-world probability.

Because of this, when we valuate the VaR by using some existing system at our institution, we must confirm whether the VaR has been calculated under the real-world measure and examine what method was employed to estimate the market price of risk.

Taken all together, when we intend to construct a real-world model, it is possible to determine the volatility σ from the market data. It remains to estimate the market price of risk. This subject will be theoretically investigated in Chapters 6 and 8.

Table 4.1: 99% VaR of the binary bond for holding period T. The initially invested amount is 1.00.

			Probability	
6-month LIBOR	Payoff	P/L	Real-world	Risk-neutral
$L > 0.05$	0	-1.00	0.02	0.0009
$L \leq 0.05$	1.01	0.01	0.98	0.9901
VaR			1.00	-0.01 (profit)

4.6 Estimation of the Market Price of Risk

In empirical analysis concerning the term structure of interest rates, we are observing historical data under the real-world measure. To give an example, when we use the Hull–White model, the dynamics of the short rate is described from equation (4.41) as

$$dr(t) = \kappa \left\{ \theta(t) - r(t) + \frac{\sigma}{\kappa}\varphi_t \right\} dt + \sigma dW_t. \tag{4.64}$$

To calibrate this model such that this equation explains the historical dynamics of the short rate, we must estimate the parameters σ and κ and the market price of risk φ_t. In this way, we inevitably estimate φ_t as part of fitting any interest rate model with the historical dynamics of the interest rates.

Along these lines, there are many studies on estimating the market price of risk in the field of economics. Some papers in this vein are Ahn and Gao (1999), Cheridito *et al.* (2007), Cochrane and Piazzesi (2010), De Jong (2000), and Duffee (2002). However, there are few papers that explicitly describe the method used in estimating the market price of risk in short rate models. It is even more difficult to find such papers that work with forward rate models.

In this section, we briefly describe three approaches to estimating the market price of risk in short rate models. For a more advanced treatment of this subject, we study theoretical methods for estimating the market price of risk in the forward rate model from Chapter 6.

Time-homogeneous short rate model

To define the term "time-homogeneous" in relation to short rate models, let us consider the Vasicek model, which represents the short rate dynamics as

$$dr_t = \kappa(\theta - r_t)dt + \sigma dZ_t. \tag{4.65}$$

Here, κ, θ, and σ are constants[1], and Z_t is a one-dimensional Brownian motion under a risk-neutral measure. When κ, θ, and σ are assumed to be constant, as here, the model is called *time-homogeneous* For example, the CIR model and the so-called CKLS model (Chan *et al.*, 1992) are other time-homogeneous models.

Stanton (1997) introduced a numerical technique for studying the term structure of interest rates in time-homogeneous short rate models. Parameters, such as those above, are estimated empirically, and an approximation formula for the market price of risk is obtained.

This approach is restricted to time-homogeneous models. As an example, the short rate dynamics in the Hull–White model was described by equation (4.64), above. Since the parameter $\theta(t)$ is not a constant in that model, the model is not time-homogeneous. However, time-homogeneous models are not arbitrage-free in the sense that it is impossible to fit a term structure with arbitrary initial forward rates in the manner described in Section 4.4. Specifically, this approach is difficult to apply to risk management.

Multi-factor time-homogeneous model

In the multi-dimensional case, Dempster *et al.* (2010) studied methods to estimate the market price of risk in a Gaussian three-factor model under the additional assumption that the model is a time-homogeneous Markov model. The three factors are defined as a long rate X_1, the slope of the yield curve X_2, and the short rate X_3. Their model is formulated as

$$dX_{it} = (\mu_i - \lambda_i X_{it} + \varphi_i \sigma_i)dt + \sigma_i dW_{it}, \quad ; \quad i = 1, 2 \tag{4.66a}$$

$$dX_{3t} = (\kappa(X_{1t} + X_{2t} - X_{3t}) + \varphi_3 \sigma_3)dt + \sigma_3 dW_{3t}, \tag{4.66b}$$

where φ_i denotes the market price of X_i-risk for $i = 1, 2, 3$.

[1]The difference between the Vasicek model and the Hull–White model is that θ is assumed to be constant in the former.

By the Euler approximation, the above equations are discretized as

$$X_{i(t+\Delta t)} = X_{it} + (\mu_i - \lambda_i X_{it} + \varphi_i \sigma_i)\Delta t + \sigma_i \sqrt{\Delta t} W_{i1} \quad ; \quad i = 1, 2 \quad (4.67a)$$

$$X_{3(t+\Delta t)} = X_{3t} + (\kappa(X_{1t} + X_{2t} - X_{3t}) + \varphi_3 \sigma_3)\Delta t + \sigma_3 \sqrt{\Delta t} W_{31}, \quad (4.67b)$$

where each of W_{i1} $(i = 1, 2, 3)$ is regarded as the standard normal distribution[2]. The market price of X_i-risk φ_i is estimated by applying regression analysis to historical data. Dempster *et al.*'s approach is basically similar to the method introduced in Chapter 6 of this book.

Broadly speaking, the regression formulation can be used to immediately and comprehensively estimate the market price of risk. However, the last equation in the above set contains the state variables X_{1t} and X_{2t}, and so it is not trivial to estimate φ_3 in the manner described in Appendix C. To overcome this, the computationally intensive Kalman filter technique is applied for solving the regression model, and so this approach requires software to perform the calculation.

Although this model is not arbitrage-free in the sense described above, a naive method of approximately fitting arbitrary initial forward rates is offered by three-factor models.

Drift difference

In an another approach from the above studies, Cheridito *et al.* (2007) estimates the market price of risk in affine models, with some implications consistent with the results of Chapters 6 and 9 of this book. We sketch their approach by using the Hull–White model as follows.

The short rate $r(t)$ is represented by

$$dr(t) = a_{\sigma\kappa}(t, r)dt + \sigma dZ_t, \quad (4.68)$$

where $a_{\sigma\kappa}(t, r)$ indicates the drift term in equation (4.47), and Z_t is a Brownian motion under a risk-neutral measure $\mathbf{Q}$. For this argument, the term $a_{\sigma\kappa}(t, r)$ is referred to as a *risk-neutral drift*.

[2] W_t denotes a Brownian motion with respect to time t. W_1 has the standard normal distribution for $t = 1$. For convenience, we regard W_1 as the standard normal distribution throughout this book. Then, Monte Carlo simulation is executed by substituting numbers generated according to a standard normal distribution into W_1.

Under the real-world measure $\mathbf{P}$, we may represent $r(t)$ by

$$dr(t) = b(t)dt + \sigma dW_t, \tag{4.69}$$

where W_t is the Brownian motion under $\mathbf{P}$, and $b(t)$ is the drift estimated by the observation under $\mathbf{P}$, which is referred to as *historical drift* here (in contrast to the risk-neutral drift).

We assert that $Z_t = \int_0^t \phi_s ds + W_t$, where ϕ_t denotes the market price of risk. From this, we have that $b(t) = a_{\sigma\kappa}(t,r) + \sigma\phi_t$. Then, ϕ_t is obtained by

$$\phi_t = \frac{b(t) - a_{\sigma\kappa}(t,r)}{\sigma}, \tag{4.70}$$

where $b(t) - a_{\sigma\kappa}(t,r)$ represents the difference between the historical drift and the risk-neutral drift. Equation (4.70) means that ϕ_t is characterized by the ratio given by the difference between historical drift and risk-neutral drift over short rate volatility. Specifically, if the historical drift is larger (resp., smaller) than the risk-neutral drift, then the market price of risk takes a positive (resp., negative) value. From this, the formulation as equation (4.70) has features in common with the results in Chapters 6 and 9, where we will give a theoretical interpretation of implications of the market price of risk.

CHAPTER 5

LIBOR MARKET MODEL

Abstract: This chapter introduces the LIBOR market model, which is the standard model for derivatives pricing. Because the topic of this book is risk management, we do not deal with the details of pricing. Instead, this chapter introduces the model, focusing on the implications of the real-world model.

First, we give a definition of the LIBOR market model, following Jamshidian (1997). Next, we define the LIBOR market model under the real-world measure (hereinafter, LMRW), and show, following the method of Yasuoka (2013b), that the model exists. Additionally we find the models under the spot LIBOR measure and under a forward measure that are implied by the LMRW.

Finally, we verify the numerical differences of the LIBOR process according to choice of measure. The study on the real-world model will be developed in Chapter 9.

Keywords: Arbitrage-free, Arbitrage pricing, BGM model, Change of numéraire, Deterministic volatility, Forward LIBOR, Forward measure, HJM model, LIBOR market model, LIBOR volatility, LMRW, Lognormal distribution, Market price of risk, Martingale approach, Positive interest rate, Real-world measure, Risk-neutral model, Spot LIBOR measure, State price deflator, Terminal measure

Takashi Yasuoka

5.1 LIBOR market Model

LIBOR market models

The LIBOR market model was introduced by Miltersen *et al.* (1997), Brace *et al.* (1997; hereinafter, BGM), Musiela and Rutkowski (1997), and Jamshidian (1997). The notable points of this model are listed here:

- The model has positive LIBOR.
- The model admits an arbitrary deterministic volatility structure.
- The price formulae of a caplet and a floorlet are derived so as to be consistent with the corresponding Black's price.
- An approximated price formula for a swaption is derived.

From these, the LIBOR market model has a usability advantage in calibration, and so it is widely applied as a standard model for derivatives pricing. As a particular example, the BGM model is the most well-known type of LIBOR market model, and is built in the HJM framework. The BGM approach requires a kind of differentiability for LIBOR volatility. It is impossible to satisfy this smoothness in practice because the volatility cannot be constructed except as a piecewise continuous, but not necessarily smooth, function. Because of this, the BGM model is not strictly supported in the HJM framework. For more advanced study of this problem, see Yasuoka (2001, 2013b).

At one end of the spectrum of models, the approaches by Musiela and Rutkowski (1997) and Jamshidian (1997) stand on a martingale pricing theory, with no theoretical imperfections. However, their models are constructed under a risk-neutral measure without referring to the real-world measure.

In this section and the next, we introduce the LIBOR market model as described by Jamshidian (1997). Because the topic of this book is risk management, pricing of derivatives is not addressed here at length. For a more advanced treatment of pricing, readers are recommended to consult Brigo and Mercurio (2007) or Gatarek *et al.* (2007).

Similarly to the argument for the HJM model, when the LIBOR and bond prices are represented under a risk-neutral measure, we call the resulting system a *risk-neutral model*. When, instead, they are represented under $\mathbf{P}$, the resulting system is referred to as a *real-world model.* Strict definitions of these terms will be given later.

Definition of the LIBOR market model

Let $\tau > 0$ be a time horizon, and let $(\Omega, \mathcal{F}_{t\in[0,\tau]}, \mathbf{P})$ be a probability space, where $\mathcal{F}_{t\in[0,\tau]}$ is the augmented filtration and $\mathbf{P}$ is the real-world measure. In this, W_t denotes a d-dimensional $\mathbf{P}$-Brownian motion defined on $(\Omega, \mathcal{F}_{t\in[0,\tau]}, \mathbf{P})$.

Let $0 = T_0 < T_1 < \cdots < T_n = \tau$ be a sequence of times. Let $B_i(t)$ denote a price process of a zero-coupon bond with maturity T_i such that $B_i(T_i) = 1$ for $i = 1, \cdots, n$, and let $\mathcal{B} = \{B_i(t)\}_{i=1,\cdots,n}$ denote the bond market. We remark that the market $\mathcal{B}$ is not assumed to be complete in this setup, again following Jamshidian (1997).

We set δ_i as

$$\delta_i = T_{i+1} - T_i \quad ; \quad i = 0, \cdots, n-1, \tag{5.1}$$

and denote by $L_i(t)$ the forward LIBOR observed at t over the period $[T_i, T_{i+1}]$, which is given by

$$1 + \delta_i L_i(t) = \frac{B_i(t)}{B_{i+1}(t)} \quad ; \quad i = 0, \cdots, n-1. \tag{5.2}$$

We first construct a positive LIBOR process under some measure $\mathbf{Q}$ equivalent to $\mathbf{P}$. We assume that L_i is represented by an Ito process such that

$$\frac{dL_i(t)}{L_i(t)} = \cdots dt + \lambda_i(t) dZ_t, \tag{5.3}$$

where Z_t is a d-dimensional Brownian motion under $\mathbf{Q}$, and $\lambda_i(t)$ is an $\mathbf{R}^d$-valued volatility of $L_i(t)$. The mathematical definition of the LIBOR market model ("the LIBOR model") is given as follows.

Definition 5.1 (Jamshidian model) $\mathcal{B}$ is called the *LIBOR market model* if the LIBOR process $L_i(t)$ is specified by a deterministic volatility $\lambda_i(t), i = 1, \cdots, n$, such that $L_i(t) > 0$, $B_i(t) > 0$ for $i = 1, \cdots, n$, and $\mathcal{B}$ is arbitrage-free.

In this definition, the bond price process $B_i(t)$ does not have to be an Ito process. Then, this model does not deal with the market price of risk and is constructed within the martingale framework introduced in Chapter 3.

5.2 Existence of LIBOR Market Model

The existence of the LIBOR model is shown in the following theorem.

Theorem 5.2.1 *For arbitrary deterministic volatility $\lambda_i(t), i = 1, \cdots, n-1$, the LIBOR market model exists.*

The LIBOR model can be constructed under any of several risk-neutral measures. Applying this, we will show the existence of the LIBOR model under the real-world measure in the next section, and show how the models are implied under other measures in Sections 5.4 and 5.5 of this chapter. It is thought that this approach is the simplest method of constructing the LIBOR market model for practical use. Therefore, we here only sketch Jamshidian's LIBOR market model under a forward measure, omitting the proof.

Let each of $\lambda_i(t)$ be an arbitrary deterministic function in t for $i = 1, \cdots, n-1$. Consider the following equation:

$$\frac{dL_i(t)}{L_i(t)} = \sum_{j=i+1}^{n-1} \frac{\delta_j L_j(t)\lambda_i(t)\lambda_j(t)}{1+\delta_j L_j} dt + \lambda_i(t) dZ_t. \tag{5.4}$$

Here, Z_t is a d-dimensional Brownian motion with respect to a measure $\mathbf{Q}(\sim \mathbf{P})$. With this setup, the following proposition is given in Jamshidian (1997, Corollary 2.1).

Proposition 5.2.2 *The equation (5.4) admits a unique positive solution for an arbitrary initial condition $L_i(0) > 0$ for all i. Further, $Y_i(t) = (1 + \delta_i L_i(t)) \cdots (1 + \delta_i L_{n-1}(t))$ is a $\mathbf{Q}$-martingale.*

Let $B_n(t)$ be an arbitrary bond price process such that $B_n(T_n) = 1$ and

$$B_n(T_i) = \frac{1}{\prod_{j=i}^{n-1}(1+\delta_j L_j(T_j))} \tag{5.5}$$

at each T_i. Accordingly, we define $B_i(t)$ for $i < n$ by

$$\frac{B_i(t)}{B_n(t)} = \prod_{j=i}^{n-1}(1 + \delta_j L_j(t)). \tag{5.6}$$

From these, we see that $B_i(T_i) = 1$ and the relation (5.2) is satisfied for all i. By Proposition 5.2.2, $\prod_{j=i}^{n-1}(1 + \delta_j L_j(t))$ is a $\mathbf{Q}$-martingale for every i. Hence $B_i(t)/B_n(t)$ is a $\mathbf{Q}$-martingale for all i.

Along these lines, $\mathbf{Q}$ is a B_n numéraire measure and is referred to as a *forward measure*. As a result, the bond market $\mathcal{B}$ is arbitrage-free from Theorem 3.2.2.

In this way, when the market $\mathcal{B}$ is represented under the forward measure $\mathbf{Q}$, the market $\mathcal{B}$ is referred to as a *forward measure model* for simplicity. By changing the numéraire to a different bond B_i, we can derive the B_i numéraire measure in the manner described in Section 3.2. With this measure, we can obtain another forward measure model with respect to the B_i numéraire measure.

Non-uniqueness of the LIBOR model

In the above sketch, the bond price process is allowed to have arbitrary value during the interval between each pair of successive maturity dates ending at T_i, because $B_n(t)$ must satisfy the relation (5.5) only at each T_i. Thus, there exist infinitely many bond markets consistent with the LIBOR process (5.4).

For some such markets, the bond price processes may be represented by Ito processes; for others, they may not. From this, the class of LIBOR market models is more relaxed than the class of HJM models.

Comparison with HJM models

In order to study the LMRW, it is worthwhile to verify the differences between LIBOR models and HJM models from the viewpoint of arbitrage theory.

In an HJM model, the price processes of bonds are assumed to be Ito processes, and so the market price of risk is a critical factor in ensuring an arbitrage-free market. Additionally, the HJM framework for models is first constructed under the real-world measure $\mathbf{P}$. Such a model is then reduced

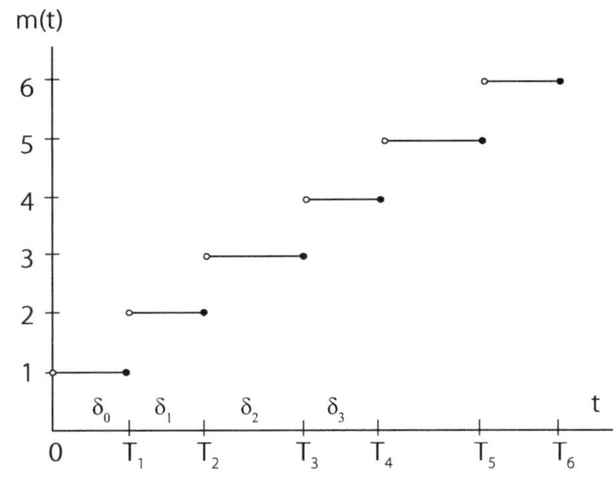

Figure 5.1: Graph of $m(t)$

to a model under a risk-neutral measure $\mathbf{Q}$ by applying the Girsanov theorem with the market price of risk. Therefore, the relation between $\mathbf{P}$ and $\mathbf{Q}$ is theoretically clear except for the estimation of the market price of risk.

In contrast, the LIBOR market model is constructed under a risk-neutral measure in the martingale framework, as described above. Indeed, the price processes of bonds are not assumed to be Ito processes, and the market price of risk does not appear in the formulation. Instead, the model is initially constructed under the forward measure $\mathbf{Q}$, where the relation between $\mathbf{Q}$ and $\mathbf{P}$ remains to be elucidated. We will address this relation in Section 5.5.

5.3 LIBOR Market Model under a Real-world Measure

Within the same setting as in Sections 5.1 and 5.2, we give a definition of the LMRW and show the existence of the model, following Yasuoka (2013a).

Definition 5.3 The bond market $\mathcal{B}$ is called the *LMRW* when the following conditions are satisfied.

1. The LIBOR processes $L_i, i = 1, \cdots, n$, with $L_i(t) > 0$, are represented under the real-world measure $\mathbf{P}$ such that each volatility $\lambda_i(t)$ and the market price of risk φ_t are deterministic in t.

2. The bond market $\mathcal{B}$ is arbitrage-free; here this means that $B_i(t) \in \mathcal{B}, i = 1, \cdots, n$ and the state price deflator ξ_t are positive Ito processes represented under $\mathbf{P}$.

For this, we define a left-continuous function $m(t)$ by $m(t) = j$, while $t \in (T_{j-1}, T_j]$. Succinctly, $m(t)$ represents the index of the next maturity date[1]. Examination of Fig. 5.1 may help to see the features of $m(t)$.

To show the existence of the LMRW, it is sufficient to give the simplest example for arbitrarily given volatility λ and market price of risk φ. For this, we define a process $\bar{\mu}(t)$ by $\bar{\mu}(t) = \bar{\mu}(T_{m(t)})$ such that

$$\bar{\mu}(T_i) = \frac{1}{\delta_{i-1}} \log\{1 + \delta_{i-1} L_{i-1}(T_{i-1})\} \tag{5.7}$$

at each time T_i. Specifically, $\bar{\mu}(t)$ represents the yield for the shortest maturity bond, with the next maturity $T_{m(t)}$. As a consequence, $\bar{\mu}(t)$ is constant on each period $(T_{i-1}, T_i]$, $i = 1, \cdots, n$.

Let φ_t be an arbitrarily given market price of risk such that φ_l is an $\mathbf{R}^d$-valued deterministic function with

$$\int_0^T |\varphi_t|^2 ds < \infty. \tag{5.8}$$

Let $\lambda_i(t), i = 1, \cdots, n$ be deterministic volatilities. We set $\chi_i(t)$ as

$$\chi_i(t) = \frac{\lambda_i(t)\delta_i L_i(t)}{1 + \delta_i L_i(t)} \quad ; \quad i = 1, \cdots, n. \tag{5.9}$$

Consider the following equation with the initial LIBOR $L_i(0) > 0$,

$$\frac{dL_i(t)}{L_i(t)} = \left\{ \lambda_i(t) \sum_{j=m(t)}^{i} \chi_j(t) + \lambda_i(t)\varphi_t \right\} dt + \lambda_i(t) dW_t, \tag{5.10}$$

for $i = 1, \cdots, n$. It is known that the solution $L_i(t)$ exists uniquely and $L_i(t) > 0$. We assume that bond price processes $B_i(t), i = 1, \cdots, n$ are Ito processes with initial values $B_0(0) = 1$ and

$$B_i(0) = \prod_{j=0}^{i-1} (1 + \delta_j L_j(0))^{-1} \tag{5.11}$$

[1]The same function is used in BGM (1997, p. 130) and in Jamshidian (1997, p. 315).

such that

$$\frac{dB_i(t)}{B_i(t)} = \left\{ \bar{\mu}(t) - \sum_{j=m(t)}^{i-1} \chi_j(t)\varphi_t \right\} dt - \sum_{j=m(t)}^{i-1} \chi_j(t) dW_t. \tag{5.12}$$

Under this setup, we give the following theorem, which shows the existence of the LMRW.

Theorem 5.3.1 *For arbitrary deterministic volatilities $\lambda_i(t), i = 1, \cdots, n$ and the deterministic market price of risk φ_t satisfying the condition (5.8), we define $B_i(t), i = 1, \cdots, n$ by equations (5.11) and (5.12). Then, the market $\mathcal{B} = \{B_i(t)\}_{i=1,\cdots,n}$ is the LMRW.*

Proof Since $L_i(t) > 0$, $\bar{\mu}(t)$ is positive. Hence, $\bar{\mu}(t)$ is well defined. The proof is divided into the proofs of the following four claims.

Claim 1: For all i,

$$1 + \delta_i L_i(t) = \frac{B_i(t)}{B_{i+1}(t)} \qquad a.s. \tag{5.13}$$

Proof of Claim 1 We may set $B_0(0) = 1$. From equation (5.11), we see that

$$1 + \delta_i L_i(0) = \frac{B_i(0)}{B_{i+1}(0)} \quad ; \quad i = 0, \cdots, n-1. \tag{5.14}$$

Equation (5.12) admits a unique positive solution, as

$$\begin{aligned} B_i(t) &= B_i(0) \exp\left\{ \int_0^t \left(\bar{\mu} - \sum_{j=m(s)}^{i-1} \chi_j \varphi_s - \frac{1}{2} \left| \sum_{j=m(s)}^{i-1} \chi_j \right|^2 \right) ds \right. \\ &\quad \left. - \int_0^t \sum_{j=m(s)}^{i-1} \chi_j dW_s \right\}. \end{aligned} \tag{5.15}$$

It follows that

$$\begin{aligned}\frac{B_i(t)}{B_{i+1}(t)} &= \frac{B_i(0)}{B_{i+1}(0)} \exp\left\{\int_0^t \left(\chi_i\varphi_s + \frac{1}{2}\left|\sum_{j=m(s)}^{i} \chi_j\right|^2 \right.\right.\\ &\quad \left.\left. -\frac{1}{2}\left|\sum_{j=m(s)}^{i-1} \chi_j\right|^2\right) ds + \int_0^t \chi_i dW_t\right\}\\ &= \frac{B_i(0)}{B_{i+1}(0)} \exp\left\{\int_0^t \left(\chi_i\varphi_s + \chi_i \sum_{j=m(s)}^{i} \chi_j - \frac{|\chi_i|^2}{2}\right) ds\right.\\ &\quad \left. + \int_0^t \chi_i dW_s\right\}. \qquad (5.16)\end{aligned}$$

Multiplying both sides of equation (5.10) by $\delta_i L_i(t)/(1+\delta_i L_i(t))$, we have

$$\frac{d\delta_i L_i}{1+\delta_i L_i} = \frac{\delta_i L_i}{1+\delta_i L_i}\left\{\left(\lambda_i \sum_{j=m(t)}^{i} \chi_j + \lambda_i\varphi_t\right) dt + \lambda_i dW_t\right\}. \qquad (5.17)$$

Substituting equation (5.9) into the right-hand side of the above, we obtain

$$\frac{d\delta_i L_i}{1+\delta_i L_i} = \left(\chi_i \sum_{j=m(t)}^{i} \chi_j + \chi_i\varphi_t\right) dt + \chi_i dW_t. \qquad (5.18)$$

The solution of this equation is uniquely given by

$$\begin{aligned}1+\delta_i L_i(t) &= (1+\delta_i L_i(0)) \exp\left\{\int_0^t \left(\chi_i\varphi_s + \chi_i \sum_{j=m(s)}^{i} \chi_j\right.\right.\\ &\quad \left.\left. -\frac{|\chi_i|^2}{2}\right) ds + \int_0^t \chi_i dW_s\right\}. \qquad (5.19)\end{aligned}$$

From equation (5.14), the initial conditions are the same for each of the equations (5.16) and (5.19). Then, the right-hand sides of equations (5.16) and (5.19) are equal. Hence, we have equation (5.13) for $t \geq 0$. This completes the proof of the first claim.

Claim 2: The price of each bond becomes 1 at its maturity date.

Proof of Claim 2 Since $B_0(0) = 1$, equation (5.14) implies

$$B_1(0) = \frac{1}{(1 + \delta_0 L_0(0))}. \tag{5.20}$$

Substituting $i = 1$ into equation (5.15), we have $B_1(T_1) = B_1(0)\exp\{\int_0^{T_1} \bar{\mu}(s)ds\}$.

From (5.7), it follows that

$$\begin{aligned} B_1(T_1) &= \frac{1}{1 + \delta_0 L_0(0)} \exp\left\{\int_0^{T_1} \frac{\log\{1 + \delta_0 L_0(T_0)\}}{\delta_0} ds\right\} \\ &= \frac{1}{1 + \delta_0 L_0(0)} \exp\left\{\log\{1 + \delta_0 L_0(T_0)\}\frac{T_1}{\delta_0}\right\}. \end{aligned} \tag{5.21}$$

We see that $\delta_0 = T_1$ from equation (5.1). From this, we have

$$\begin{aligned} B_1(T_1) &= \frac{1}{1 + \delta_0 L_0(0)} \exp\left\{\log\{1 + \delta_0 L_0(0)\}\frac{\delta_0}{\delta_0}\right\} \\ &= 1. \end{aligned} \tag{5.22}$$

Inductively, we obtain $B_i(T_i) = 1$ for all i. This proves the second claim.

Claim 3: $\mathcal{B}$ is arbitrage-free.

Proof of Claim 3 Let ξ_t be an Ito process defined by

$$\frac{d\xi_t}{\xi_t} = -\bar{\mu}(t)dt - \varphi_t dW_t, \tag{5.23}$$

with $\xi_0 = 1$. There exists a unique positive solution, given by

$$\xi_t = \exp\left\{-\int_0^t \left(\bar{\mu}(s) + \frac{|\varphi_s|^2}{2}\right) ds - \int_0^t \varphi_s dW_s\right\}. \tag{5.24}$$

Combining equation (5.15) with equation (5.24), we obtain

$$\begin{aligned}
\xi_t B_i(t) &= B_i(0)\exp\left\{\int_0^t \left(-\frac{|\varphi_s|^2}{2} - \sum_{j=m(s)}^{i-1} \chi_j\varphi_s \right.\right.\\
&\quad \left.\left. -\frac{|\sum_{j=m(s)}^{i-1}\chi_j|^2}{2}\right) ds - \int_0^t \left(\varphi_s + \sum_{j=m(s)}^{i-1}\chi_j\right) dW_s\right\}\\
&= B_i(0)\exp\left\{-\int_0^t \frac{1}{2}\left(\varphi_s + \sum_{j=m(s)}^{i-1}\chi_j\right)^2 ds\right.\\
&\quad \left. -\int_0^t \left(\varphi_s + \sum_{j=m(s)}^{i-1}\chi_j\right) dW_s\right\}. \qquad (5.25)
\end{aligned}$$

Hence, $\xi_t B_i(t)$ is a **P**-martingale for all i, and ξ_t is the state price deflator. From these, $\mathcal{B}$ is arbitrage-free.

Claim 4: φ_t is well defined as the market price of risk.
Proof of Claim 4 Since ξ_t is the state price deflator, $\bar{\mu}(t)$ may be regarded as the implied short rate from equation (5.23). Indeed, equation (5.7) defines $\bar{\mu}(t)$ as the return rate of the bond with the least time to maturity.

We define processes $\mu_i(t)$ and $\upsilon_i(t)$ by

$$\mu_i(t) = \bar{\mu}(t) - \sum_{j=m(t)}^{i-1}\chi_j(t)\varphi_t, \qquad (5.26)$$

$$\upsilon_i(t) = -\sum_{j=m(t)}^{i-1}\chi_j(t), \qquad (5.27)$$

respectively. Substituting these into equation (5.12), we obtain

$$\frac{dB_i(t)}{B_i(t)} = \mu_i(t)dt + \upsilon_i(t)dW_t. \qquad (5.28)$$

Then, $\mu_i(t)$ and $\upsilon_i(t)$ indicate the drift coefficient and the volatility, respectively, of the ith bond. From equations (5.26) and (5.27), it follows that $\mu_i(t) = \bar{\mu}(t) + \upsilon_i(t)\varphi_t$; here, φ_t is independent of the bond i. This coincides

LIBOR market model (Jamshidian,1997)

$\lambda \to L_i$: under Q $\to B_n \to B_i \to B_i/B_n$: Q-MG

LMRW

$\lambda, \phi \to L_i, B_i$: under P $\to \xi \to \xi B_i$: P-MG

Figure 5.2: Structures to construct the LIBOR market models

with the definition of the market price of risk φ_t in Theorem 3.3.1. This completes the proof of the claim and the theorem. □

Comparison with Jamshidian's LIBOR model

Let us verify the difference between the LMRW and the Jamshidian model from the viewpoint of arbitrage theory. In Section 5.2, the LIBOR market model is initially constructed as a LIBOR process with given volatility under a measure $\mathbf{Q} \sim \mathbf{P}$. Taking the bond n as a numéraire, the bond family $\mathcal{B}$ is constructed from the LIBOR process. Along these lines, each relative bond price B_i/B_n is a $\mathbf{Q}$-martingale. This approach is illustrated in the upper part of Fig. 5.2. Because of this, there is no information from which to practically derive the state price deflator in this setting, which means that it is not trivial to change the model to a real-world model.

In contrast, the LMRW begins with constructing LIBOR and bond price processes such that they are Ito processes represented under the $\mathbf{P}$ associated with volatility λ and the market price of risk φ. From this, we show that the bond price is consistent with the LIBOR. Next, we define the state price deflator ξ_t, and so each $\xi_t B_i(t)$ is a $\mathbf{P}$-martingale. This approach is illustrated in the lower part of Fig. 5.2. By changing the numéraire, we can derive a risk-neutral model from the LMRW. This will be introduced in Sections 5.4 and 5.5 of this chapter.

Arbitrage pricing in the LMRW

In the LMRW, we can calculate the state price deflator ξ_t from equation (5.24).

After this, arbitrage pricing can be executed in the LMRW.

For example, consider a security with expiry T_i with payoff at T_i given by a random variable X. The price c_t of this security at time t is given by $c_t = \frac{1}{\xi_t} E_t[\xi_{T_i} X]$. When the expiry T of the security does not coincide with any of $T_i, i = 1, \cdots, n$, the pricing is assumed to be constructed by some technical argument.

Resemblance to the BGM model

Here, we remark on the resemblance between the LMRW and the BGM model. From equation (5.12), it holds for each i that

$$\frac{dB_i(t)}{B_i(t)} = \bar{\mu}(t)dt \quad ; \quad t \in (T_{i-1}, T_i]. \tag{5.29}$$

This indicates that each B_i has null volatility in $(T_{i-1}, T_i]$, the period just prior to its maturity.

This assumption is held in common with the setting in the BGM model. Specifically, the BGM model (BGM, 1997, p. 129) assumes the bond price process is given by

$$\frac{dB(t,T)}{B(t,T)} = r(t)dt - \tilde{\sigma}(t, T-t)dZ_t, \tag{5.30}$$

where $\tilde{\sigma}(t, T-t)$ denotes the bond price volatility, the second variable $T-t$ of $\tilde{\sigma}$ represents the time length to the maturity T, and Z_t denotes a Brownian motion under the spot measure in the HJM framework. Additionally, the BGM model assumes that $\tilde{\sigma}(t, T-t) = 0$ for t with $0 \leq T-t < \delta$. With this, $B(t,T)$ is represented by

$$\frac{dB(t,T)}{B(t,T)} = r(t)dt \quad ; \quad t \in (T-\delta, T]. \tag{5.31}$$

This shows the same structure as equation (5.29). Thus, the null volatility of the shortest maturity bond in the LMRW is essentially the same as the assumption on BGM's volatility $\tilde{\sigma}(t, T-t)$. For details, see BGM (1997).

5.4 Spot LIBOR Model

This section shows how the LIBOR model under the spot LIBOR measure is implied by the LMRW.

Numéraire

From Theorem 5.3.1, we may assume that the LIBOR process $L_i(t)$ and the bond price process $B_i(t)$ of the LMRW already exist. Here, we define a process $B^*(t)$ for $t \in [0, \tau]$ by

$$B^*(t) = \frac{B_{m(t)}(t)}{B_1(0)} \prod_{j=1}^{m(t)-1} (1 + \delta_j L_j(T_j)). \tag{5.32}$$

Note that the process $B^*(t)$ did not appear during the construction of the LMRW in Section 5.3. It holds from equation (5.29) that

$$\frac{dB^*(t)}{B^*(t)} = \frac{dB_{m(t)}(t)}{B_{m(t)}(t)} = \bar{\mu}(t)dt. \tag{5.33}$$

Specifically, $B^*(t)$ is expressed by

$$B^*(t) = \exp\left\{\int_0^t \bar{\mu}(s)ds\right\}. \tag{5.34}$$

From this, $B^*(t)$ represents a continuous reinvestment in the shortest maturity bonds. Thus, we may adopt the view that $B^*(t)$ is a tradable asset. Obviously, it holds that $B^*(0) = 1$ and $B^*(t) > 0$. Given this, we may take $B^*(t)$ as a numéraire.

From equation (5.32), it follows that

$$B^*(T_i) = B^*(T_{i-1})\{1 + \delta_{i-1} L_{i-1}(T_{i-1})\} \tag{5.35}$$

at each T_i. Since $L_{i-1}(T_{i-1})$ indicates the spot LIBOR at $t = T_{i-1}$, $B^*(t)$ can be understood as continuous reinvestment at the spot LIBOR.

Spot LIBOR measure

Combining equations (5.24) and (5.34), we obtain

$$\xi_t B^*(t) = \exp\left\{-\int_0^t \frac{|\varphi_s|^2}{2} ds - \int_0^t \varphi_s dW_s\right\}. \tag{5.36}$$

From this, $\xi_t B^*(t)$ is a $\mathbf{P}$-martingale. We define the B^* *numéraire measure* $\mathbf{P}^*$ by

$$\frac{d\mathbf{P}^*}{d\mathbf{P}} = \xi(\tau)B^*(\tau). \tag{5.37}$$

Since $B^*(t)$ indicates continuous investment at the spot LIBOR, $\mathbf{P}^*$ is referred to as the *spot LIBOR measure.*

Setting $Z_t = \int_0^t \varphi_s ds + W_t$, Z_t is a $\mathbf{P}^*$-Brownian motion, by the Girsanov theorem. Substituting Z_t into equations (5.10) and (5.12), we obtain

$$\frac{dL_i(t)}{L_i(t)} = \lambda_i(t) \sum_{j=m(t)}^{i} \chi_j(t)dt + \lambda_i(t)dZ_t, \tag{5.38}$$

$$\frac{dB_i(t)}{B_i(t)} = \bar{\mu}_{m(t)}(t)dt - \sum_{j=m(t)}^{i-1} \chi_j(t)dZ_t, \tag{5.39}$$

for all i. From these, the bond price process $B_i(t)$ and the LIBOR process $L_i(t)$ are specified under the spot LIBOR measure. We call this system a *spot LIBOR model* to distinguish it from the LMRW.

Additionally, we want to verify that the relative bond price is a martingale. Since $\xi_t B_i(t)$ are $\mathbf{P}$-martingales, each $\xi_t B_i(t)/E_t[d\mathbf{P}^*/d\mathbf{P}]$ is a $\mathbf{P}^*$-martingale, from Proposition 2.4.2. It follows from equation (5.37) that

$$\begin{aligned} \frac{\xi_t B_i(t)}{E_t[d\mathbf{P}^*/d\mathbf{P}]} &= \frac{\xi_t B_i(t)}{\xi_t B^*(t)} \\ &= \frac{B_i(t)}{B^*(t)} \quad ; \quad i = 1, \cdots, n, \qquad a.s. \end{aligned} \tag{5.40}$$

This means that $B_i(t)/B^*(t), i = 1, \cdots, n$ are $\mathbf{P}^*$-martingales.

Null market price of risk

Here, we examine the case of null market price of risk. When we set $\varphi_t = 0$, it then holds that $Z_t = W_t$. From equations (5.24) and (5.34), it holds that

$$\xi_t = \exp\{-\int_0^t \bar{\mu}(s)ds\} = \frac{1}{B^*(t)}. \tag{5.41}$$

By equation (5.37), we have $d\mathbf{P}^*/d\mathbf{P} = \xi(\tau)B^*(\tau) = 1$. Specifically, it holds that $\mathbf{P}^* = \mathbf{P}$ almost everywhere. From this, when we assume the null market price of risk on the LMRW, the model is equivalent to the spot LIBOR model. This argument has the same structure as that applied to the HJM model in Section 4.2.

5.5 $\mathbf{P}_k$ Measure Model

Let k be a fixed integer with $0 < k \leq n$. This section shows how the LIBOR model under a B_k numéraire measure is implied from the LMRW.

From equation (5.12), the bond price process $B_k(t)$ is given by

$$\frac{dB_k(t)}{B_k(t)} = \left(\bar{\mu}(t) - \sum_{j=m(t)}^{k-1} \chi_j \varphi \right) dt - \sum_{j=m(t)}^{k-1} \chi_j dW_t. \tag{5.42}$$

The B_k numéraire measure $\mathbf{P}_k$ is defined from equation (3.8) as

$$\frac{d\mathbf{P}_k}{d\mathbf{P}} = \xi_\tau \frac{B_k(\tau)}{B_k(0)}. \tag{5.43}$$

The measure $\mathbf{P}_k$ is also referred to as a *forward measure*, in contrast to the spot LIBOR measure. Of particular note, $\mathbf{P}_n$ is referred to as a *terminal measure.*

From equation (5.25), it follows that

$$\begin{aligned} \frac{\xi_t B_k(t)}{B_k(0)} &= \exp\left\{ -\int_0^t \frac{|\varphi_s + \sum_{j=m(s)}^{k-1} \chi_j(s)|^2}{2} ds \right. \\ &\left. - \int_0^t \left(\varphi_s + \sum_{j=m(s)}^{k-1} \chi_j(s) \right) dW_s \right\}. \end{aligned} \tag{5.44}$$

We define a process $Z_{k,t}$ by[2]

$$Z_{k,t} = \int_0^t \left(\varphi_s + \sum_{j=m(s)}^{k-1} \chi_j(s) \right) ds + W_t. \tag{5.45}$$

The process $Z_{k,t}$ is a $\mathbf{P}_k$-Brownian motion, from the Girsanov theorem. Substituting $Z_{k,t}$ into equation (5.10), the LIBOR process $L_i(t)$ is represented by

$$\frac{dL_i(t)}{L_i(t)} = -\lambda_i(t) \sum_{j=i+1}^{k-1} \chi_j(t) dt + \lambda_i(t) dZ_{k,t} \ ; \ \ i < k. \tag{5.46}$$

From equation (5.12), the bond price $B_i(t)$ is represented under $\mathbf{P}_k$ by

$$\frac{dB_i(t)}{B_i(t)} = \left\{ \bar{\mu}(t) + \sum_{j=m(t)}^{i-1} \chi_j(t) \sum_{k=m(t)}^{k-1} \chi_k(t) \right\} dt - \sum_{j=m(t)}^{i-1} \chi_j(t) dZ_{k,t}. \tag{5.47}$$

[2]We denote the Brownian motion under $\mathbf{P}_k$ by $Z_{k,t}$ using a subscript k to distinguish it from the lth component of a multi-dimensional Brownian motion Z_t^l with superscript l.

With these, the LIBOR model under $\mathbf{P}_k$ is implied from the LMRW. We call the resulting system a $\mathbf{P}_k$ *measure model* (or forward measure model) to distinguish it from the spot measure model.

Next, we show that the relative bond prices $B_i(t)/B_k(t), i = 1, \cdots, n$ are each a $\mathbf{P}_k$-martingale. Since $\xi_t B_k(t)$ is a P-martingale, we see that

$$\xi_t B_k(t) = E_t\left[\frac{d\mathbf{P}_k}{d\mathbf{P}}\right]. \tag{5.48}$$

Proposition 2.4.2 implies that $\xi_t B_i(t)/E_t[d\mathbf{P}_k/d\mathbf{P}]$ is a $\mathbf{P}_k$-martingale. It follows from equation (5.48) that

$$\begin{aligned}\frac{\xi_t B_i(t)}{E_t[d\mathbf{P}_k/d\mathbf{P}]} &= \frac{\xi_t B_i(t)}{\xi_t B_k(t)} \\ &= \frac{B_i(t)}{B_k(t)} \quad ; \quad i = 1, \cdots, n \qquad a.s.\end{aligned} \tag{5.49}$$

This means that each of $B_i(t)/B_k(t), i = 1, \cdots, n$ is a $\mathbf{P}_k$-martingale.

Lognormal distribution

Substituting $i = k - 1$ into equation (5.46), we have

$$\frac{dL_{k-1}(t)}{L_{k-1}(t)} = \lambda_{k-1}(t)dZ_{k,t}. \tag{5.50}$$

From this equation, $L_{k-1}(t)$ can be written as

$$L_{k-1}(t) = L_{k-1}(0)\exp\left\{-\int_0^t \frac{|\lambda_{k-1}(s)|^2}{2}ds + \int_0^t \lambda_{k-1}(s)dZ_{k,s}\right\}. \tag{5.51}$$

Since $\lambda_{k-1}(t)$ is deterministic in t, the forward LIBOR $L_{k-1}(t)$ is lognormally distributed under $\mathbf{P}_k$. This is the most important result for option pricing in the LIBOR market model.

Remark

In derivatives pricing, the forward measure is chosen according to the properties of each derivative. When we use some computer system for derivatives pricing in the LIBOR market model, we typically do not concern ourselves with which measure is used. In practice, such programs typically choose the measure in an automatic way according to the properties of each product. For this reason, when we use that model in risk valuation, we have to pay attention to the measure used by the pricing software.

Comparison with other measure models

As mentioned in Section 4.5, the valuation of the VaR depends on the measure. In this respect, let us compare the value of the LIBOR $L_i(t)$ in connection with the choice of measure.

In the spot LIBOR model, $L_i(t)$ was given in equation (5.38) as

$$\frac{dL_i(t)}{L_i(t)} = \lambda_i(t) \sum_{j=m(t)}^{i} \chi_j(t)dt + \lambda_i(t)dZ_t, \tag{5.52}$$

where $Z_t = \int_0^t \varphi_s ds + W_t$. In the $\mathbf{P}_k$ measure model, $L_i(t)$ was represented in equation (5.46) as

$$\frac{dL_i(t)}{L_i(t)} = -\lambda_i(t) \sum_{j=i+1}^{k-1} \chi_j(t)dt + \lambda_i(t)dZ_t^l, \tag{5.53}$$

where $Z_{k,t}$ is defined by equation (5.45) as

$$Z_{k,t} = \int_0^t \left\{ \varphi_s + \sum_{j=m(s)}^{k-1} \chi_j(s) \right\} ds + W_t. \tag{5.54}$$

Specifically, the difference of two Brownian motions is expressed by

$$Z_{k,t} - Z_t = \int_0^t \sum_{j=m(s)}^{k-1} \chi_j(s)ds. \tag{5.55}$$

With this, the numerical difference in $L_i(t)$ between the two models is equal to

$$\lambda_i(t) \int_0^t \sum_{j=m(s)}^{k-1} \chi_j(s)ds. \tag{5.56}$$

Since $\chi_j(t) > 0$, this difference widens as k or t becomes large.

This means that the $\mathbf{P}_k$ measure model exhibits a more positive bias in the distribution of $L_i(t)$ than the spot LIBOR model does.

Example 5.5

In practice, a terminal measure $\mathbf{P}_n$ is successfully chosen as the risk-neutral measure. To verify the numerical difference between $L_i(t)$ as calculated with respect to the measure, let us calculate equation (5.56) in a simple example.

We set $\delta = 0.5$ (year) and $T_i = \delta i$ for $i = 1, \cdots, 40$. We consider the forward LIBOR $L_i(t)$ for $i = 1, \cdots, 39$. In this case, the terminal measure $\mathbf{P}_{40}$ indicates the B_{40} numéraire measure. Assume a flat term structure, such that the initial LIBOR and the volatility are flat at $L_i(0) = 0.03$ and $\lambda_i(t) = 0.2$ for all i. We have

$$\begin{aligned} \chi_i(0) &= \frac{\lambda_i(0)\delta L_i(0)}{1+\delta L_i(0)} \\ &= \frac{0.2 \times 0.5 \times 0.03}{1+0.5 \times 0.03} \\ &= \frac{0.003}{1.015} \\ &= 0.002956 \;\; ; \;\; i = 1, \cdots, 39. \end{aligned} \tag{5.57}$$

By putting $i = 39$ and $l = 40$, the Euler integral of (5.56) gives the difference for $L_{40}(0.5)$ as

$$\begin{aligned} \lambda_{39}(0) \sum_{i=1}^{40-1} \chi_i(0) \times 0.5 &= 0.2 \times 0.002956 \times 39 \times 0.5 \\ &= 0.01153. \end{aligned} \tag{5.58}$$

From this, the $\mathbf{P}_{40}$ measure model simulates a LIBOR that is 115 basis points higher at $L_{39}(0.5)$ (on average) than the spot measure model. This difference strongly affects the computation of VaR. This illustrates that no risk-neutral model is reliable for risk valuation.

CHAPTER 6

REAL-WORLD MODEL IN THE GAUSSIAN HJM MODEL

Abstract: This chapter theoretically investigates a real-world model within the Gaussian HJM model. In order to construct the real-world model, it is vital to estimate the market price of risk. For this purpose, we assume that the market price of risk is constant during each observation period. Representing the forward rate process in a principal component space, we introduce a formula for the market price of risk as the maximum likelihood estimate.

Next, we investigate the numerical properties of the market price of risk, after which we give an interpretation of that price with respect to the historical trend of the forward rates. Furthermore, we show that the interest rate simulation admits historical drift and volatility. Finally, we present a numerical procedure for real-world modeling. These results are essentially those from Yasuoka (2015). Of particular note, however, is that applying maximum likelihood estimation to finding the market price of risk is newly written for this book, in Section 6.2. Additionally, a numerical procedure is introduced in Section 6.9 for implementing the real-world model.

Keywords: Butterfly trading strategy, Dimension reduction, Flattening strategy, Forward rate curve, Full-factor model, Gaussian HJM model, Market price of risk, Monte Carlo simulation, Maximum likelihood estimation, Musiela's parametrization, Numerical procedure, Observable trend, PCA, Principal volatility component, Real-world simulation, Rolled trend, Rolled trend score, Roll-down, Roll-up, State price deflator, State space, Steepening strategy

Takashi Yasuoka

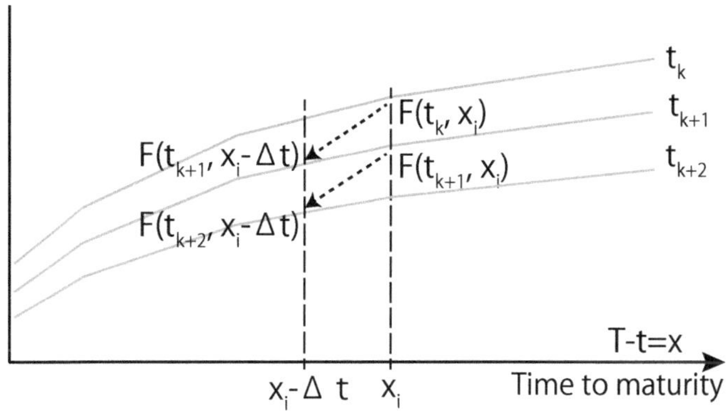

Figure 6.1: Forward rate curves and observation of the forward rates

6.1 Discretization of Forward Rate Process

We recall the forward rate process in the HJM model as

$$\begin{aligned} f(t,T) &= f(0,T) + \int_0^t \{-\sigma(s,T)v(s,T) + \sigma(s,T)\varphi_s\}ds \\ &\quad + \int_0^t \sigma(s,T)dW_s, \end{aligned} \tag{6.1}$$

where W_t is a d-dimensional $\mathbf{P}$-Brownian motion. The HJM model is called *Gaussian* if $\sigma(t,T)$ is a deterministic function of t and T. In this book, we always assume that volatility $\sigma(t,T)$ is deterministic and continuous with respect to t and T. Then, $v(t,T)$ is also deterministic and continuous. In the following, the market price of risk is assumed to be constant. The validity of the constancy assumption will be examined in the context of risk management in Chapter 7.

Data observation

Denoting the market price of risk as a constant φ, the above forward rate process is expressed by

$$\begin{aligned} f(t,T) &= f(0,T) + \int_0^t \{-\sigma(s,T)v(s,T) + \sigma(s,T)\varphi\}ds \\ &\quad + \int_0^t \sigma(s,T)dW_s. \end{aligned} \tag{6.2}$$

Next, we specify a historical dataset as follows. Let a time interval $\Delta t > 0$ be fixed, and $\{t_k\}_{k=1,\cdots,J+1}$ be a sequence of observation dates such that $t_1 = 0$ and $t_{k+1} - t_k = \Delta t$, where $J+1$ is the number of observation times. We denote the time length to a maturity T from t by $x = T - t$. For an integer $n \geq d$, $x_1, \cdots, x_n$ denotes a sequence of time lengths to maturity.

Typically, we observe the instantaneous forward rate $F(t_k, x_i)$ with respect to fixed x_i. Fig. 6.1 illustrates an example of forward rate curves observed at t_k,t_{k+1}, and t_{k+2}, showing $F(t_k, x_i), F(t_{k+1}, x_i - \Delta t)$, and so on. We assume that the dynamics of these observations follow equation (6.2).

We substitute $F(t_k, x_i)$ and $F(t_{k+1}, x_i - \Delta t)$ into $f(0, x_i)$ and $f(\Delta t, x_i)$, respectively, in equation (6.2) for every t_k, $k = 1, \cdots, J$. Then, it follows that

$$\begin{aligned} F(t_{k+1}, x_i - \Delta t) &= F(t_k, x_i) + \int_0^{\Delta t} \{-\sigma(s, x_i) v(s, x_i) \\ &\quad + \sigma(s, x_i)\varphi\} ds + \int_0^{\Delta t} \sigma(s, x_i) dW_s \end{aligned} \tag{6.3}$$

for $i = 1, \cdots, n$ and $k = 1, \cdots, J$, where x_i is identified with a maturity date at $t = 0$.

Since σ is assumed to be continuous, the Euler integral implies

$$\begin{aligned} F(t_{k+1}, x_i - \Delta t) &= F(t_k, x_i) + \{-\sigma(0, x_i) v(0, x_i) + \sigma(0, x_i)\varphi\}\Delta t \\ &\quad + \sqrt{\Delta t}\, \sigma_{0i} W_1 \end{aligned} \tag{6.4}$$

for all i and k, where $W_1 = (W_1^1, \cdots, W_1^d)^T$ corresponds to a d-dimensional standard normal distribution. To simplify the notation, we write $\sigma(0, x_i)$ and $v(0, x_i)$ as σ_{0i} and v_{0i}, respectively, where $\sigma_{0i} = (\sigma_{0i}^1, \cdots, \sigma_{0i}^d)^T$ and $v_{0i} = (v_{0i}^1, \cdots, v_{0i}^d)^T$. This yields a kind of regression form, as

$$F(t_{k+1}, x_i - \Delta t) = F(t_k, x_i) + \{-\sigma_{0i} v_{0i} + \sigma_{0i}\varphi\}\Delta t + \sqrt{\Delta t}\, \sigma_{0i} W_1, \tag{6.5}$$

for all i and k.

Remark

When we put $t = k + 1$ into the above, we obtain the next observation, which occurs at time t_{k+1}, as

$$F(t_{k+2}, x_i - \Delta t) = F(t_{k+1}, x_i) + \{-\sigma_{0i} v_{0i} + \sigma_{0i}\varphi\}\Delta t + \sqrt{\Delta t}\, \sigma_{0i} W_1. \tag{6.6}$$

The left-hand side of equation (6.5) does not appear in the right-hand side of the above equation because $F(t_{k+1}, x_i - \Delta t) \neq F(t_{k+1}, x_i)$. Thus, the formulation (6.5) is slightly different from the usual regression model that appears in Appendix C.

6.2 Estimation of Market Price of Risk

We recall the volatility structure associated with PCA in Section 4.3. A sample covariance matrix V is defined by

$$\begin{aligned} V_{ij} &= \frac{1}{\Delta t}\mathrm{Cov}(F(t_k + \Delta t, x_i - \Delta t) - F(t_k, x_i), \\ &\quad F(t_k + \Delta t, x_j - \Delta t) - F(t_k, x_j)) \;\; ; \;\; i, j = 1, \cdots, n. \end{aligned} \tag{6.7}$$

We assume that V has rank $d \leq n$. By the argument in Appendix B, the covariance matrix is decomposed into $V_{ij} = \sum_{l=1}^{d} e_i^l \rho_l^2 e_j^l$ for $i, j \leq n$, where ρ_l^2 is the lth eigenvalue, and $e^l = (e_1^l, \cdots, e_n^l)^T$ is the lth principal component of the covariance for $l = 1, \cdots, d$.

We always assume that

$$e_1^l > 0, \qquad \rho_l > 0 \;\; ; \;\; l = 1, \cdots, d. \tag{6.8}$$

This assumption is significant in the interpretation of the meaning of the market price of risk in Sections 6.4 and 6.5. Recall the equation (B.4), that is, that the principal components $e^1, \cdots, e^d$ form an orthonormal set. Thus,

$$\sum_{i=1}^{n} e_i^l e_i^h = \delta_{lh} \;\; ; \;\; l, h = 1, \cdots, d. \tag{6.9}$$

Representation in principal component space

Next we represent the dynamics of the forward rates in the principal component space. We suppose that the volatility is given by the principal component as

$$\sigma_{0i}^l = \rho_l e_i^l \;\; ; \;\; l = 1, \cdots, d, \; i = 1, \cdots, n. \tag{6.10}$$

Here, σ^l is the lth volatility component. From equation (4.36), we see that $|\sigma^l|^2 = (\rho_l)^2$, and so ρ_l represents the magnitude of the lth volatility component σ^l.

With respect to the sequence $\{x_i\}_{i=1,\cdots,n}$, we assume that the rank of the $n \times d$-matrix

$$(\sigma^1, \cdots, \sigma^d) = \begin{pmatrix} \sigma_{01}^1 & \cdots & \sigma_{01}^d \\ \vdots & \vdots & \vdots \\ \sigma_{0n}^1 & \cdots & \sigma_{0n}^d \end{pmatrix} \tag{6.11}$$

is equal to d. Next, we set $\Delta F_i(t_k)$ by letting

$$\Delta F_i(t_k) = F(t_{k+1}, x_i - \Delta t) - F(t_k, x_i). \tag{6.12}$$

With this, equation (6.5) becomes

$$\begin{aligned} \Delta F_i(t_k) &= \{-\sigma_{0i}v_{0i} + \sigma_{0i}\varphi\}\Delta t + \sqrt{\Delta t}\,\sigma_{0i}W_1 \\ &= -\sigma_{0i}v_{0i}\Delta t + \sum_{l=1}^{d}\sigma_{0i}^l\varphi_l\Delta t + \sqrt{\Delta t}\sum_{l=1}^{d}\sigma_{0i}^l W_1^l, \end{aligned} \tag{6.13}$$

where the left-hand side represents an observation and the right-hand side represents a random variable.

Let us consider a d-dimensional principal component space with a basis $e^1, \cdots, e^d$. Regarding

$$\left(\frac{\Delta F_1(t_k)}{\Delta t}, \cdots, \frac{\Delta F_n(t_k)}{\Delta t}\right)^T \tag{6.14}$$

as an n-dimensional vector in $\mathbf{R}^n$, we denote by $\alpha_l(t_k)$ the inner product[1] of the above with e^l as

$$\alpha_l(t_k) = \sum_{i=1}^{n}\frac{\Delta F_i(t_k)}{\Delta t}e_i^l. \tag{6.15}$$

In other words, $\alpha_l(t_k)$ represents the lth projection of the vector (6.14).

Additionally, we define a constant β_l by

$$\begin{aligned} \beta_l &= \sum_{i=1}^{n}\sigma_{0i}v_{0i}\,e_i^l \\ &= \sum_{i=1}^{n}\left(\sum_{l=1}^{d}\sigma_{0i}^l v_{0i}^l\right)e_i^l \;\; ; \;\; l = 1, \cdots, d. \end{aligned} \tag{6.16}$$

[1]The α in the following is not related to the α of Chapter 4.

From equation (6.9), the lth projection of equation (6.13) is represented as

$$\begin{aligned}\alpha_l(t_k)\Delta t &= \sum_{i=1}^{n} \Delta F_i(t_k) e_i^l \\ &= -\sum_{i=1}^{n} \sigma_{0i} v_{0i} \Delta t e_i^l + \sum_{i=1}^{n}\sum_{m=1}^{d} \sigma_{0i}^m \varphi_m \Delta t e_i^l \\ &\quad +\sqrt{\Delta t}\sum_{i=1}^{n}\sum_{m=1}^{d} \sigma_{0i}^m W_1^m e_i^l \\ &= -\beta_l \Delta t + \sum_{m=1}^{d} \rho_m \varphi_m \sum_{i=1}^{n} e_i^m e_i^l \Delta t \\ &\quad +\sqrt{\Delta t}\sum_{m=1}^{d} \rho_m W_1^m \sum_{i=1}^{n} e_i^m e_i^l \\ &= (-\beta_l + \rho_l \varphi_l)\Delta t + \sqrt{\Delta t}\rho_l W_1^l \end{aligned} \tag{6.17}$$

at all observation times $t_k, k = 1, \cdots, J$. This is an expression of equation (6.13) in the space spanned by the principal components $e^1, \cdots, e^d$. We remark again that the left-hand side is an observation at time t_k, and the right-hand side is represented by a random variable.

Maximum likelihood estimation of the market price of risk

The last term in the right-hand side of equation (6.17) is normally distributed. From Proposition C.0.1, the maximum likelihood estimate of φ_l is given by the solution to the least squares problem with minimization of the following:

$$\sum_{k=1}^{J} |\alpha_l(t_k)\Delta t + (\beta_l - \rho_l\varphi_l)\Delta t|^2. \tag{6.18}$$

Alternatively, we may reduce the above to the problem of minimizing $\theta_l(\varphi_l)$ with

$$\theta_l(\varphi_l) = \sum_{k=1}^{J} |\alpha_l(t_k) + (\beta_l - \rho_l\varphi_l)|^2. \tag{6.19}$$

This follows because Δt is a non-zero constant. Since each $\theta_l(\varphi_l)$ is a one-variable function of φ_l, it is sufficient to solve d minimization problems independently, one for each of $\theta_l(\varphi_l), l = 1, \cdots, d$.

Then, the PCA setup simplifies maximum likelihood estimation. Although the PCA formulation is indirect, this setup provides us with a perspective on estimation of the market price of risk. As a result, the next theorem gives an exact formulation of the market price of risk, framing it as the solution to the minimization problem.

Theorem 6.2.1 *For a Gaussian HJM model, if the volatility $\sigma(t,T)$ is continuous on t and T, and σ^l is given as the lth volatility component for each l, then the maximum likelihood estimate of the market price of risk φ_l is uniquely given by*

$$\varphi_l = \frac{1}{\rho_l}\left\{E^H\left[\alpha_l\right] + \beta_l\right\} \quad ; \quad l = 1, \cdots, n, \tag{6.20}$$

where $\alpha_l(t_k) = \frac{1}{\Delta t}\sum_{i=1}^{n} \Delta F_i(t_k)e_i^l$, $\beta_l = \sum_{i=1}^{n} \sigma_{0i}v_{0i}e_i^l$, and $E^H[\ ]$ denotes a sample mean of the historical data for $t_1, \cdots, t_J$.

Proof Direct calculation implies

$$\frac{\partial\theta(\varphi_l)}{\partial\varphi_l} = -2\sum_{k=1}^{J}\{\alpha_l(t_k) + (\beta_l - \rho_l\varphi_l)\}\rho_l \tag{6.21}$$

and

$$\frac{\partial^2\theta}{\partial\varphi_l^2} = 2(\rho_l)^2 J. \tag{6.22}$$

From this, $\theta_l(\varphi_l)$ is strictly convex with respect to φ_l for all l because of the assumption $\rho^l > 0$.

Therefore, the least squares solution exists uniquely as the root of the equation such that $\partial\theta(\varphi_l)/\partial\varphi_l = 0$. From equation (6.21) and $\rho_l \neq 0$, we may solve the following equation:

$$\sum_{k=1}^{J}\{\alpha_l(t_k) + (\beta_l - \rho_l\varphi_l)\} = 0. \tag{6.23}$$

Denoting by $E^H[\ ]$ the sample mean for the observation $t_1, \cdots, t_J$, we have $E^H[\alpha_l] = \frac{1}{J}\sum_{k=1}^{J}\alpha_l(t_k)$. Substituting this into equation (6.23), it follows that

$$\begin{aligned}\rho_l\varphi_l &= \frac{1}{J}\sum_{k=1}^{J}\alpha_l(t_k) + \beta_l \\ &= E^H[\alpha_l] + \beta_l.\end{aligned} \tag{6.24}$$

Consequently, φ_l is solved as $\varphi_l = \frac{1}{\rho_l}\left\{E^H\left[\alpha_l\right] + \beta_l\right\}$. This completes the proof. □

The exact formulation (6.20) for the market price of risk enables two significant applications. First, it becomes possible to systematically study the properties of the market price of risk. Second, the properties of the interest rate simulation can be theoretically examined, which will be described in Sections 6.5, 6.6, and 6.7. However, in this approach, we have not dealt with the t-value for the statistics in the market price of risk estimation; this is a further subject.

Remark

There is another approach to represent the dynamics of the forward rates $g(t,x)$, applying the so-called Musiela's parametrization as

$$dg(t,x) = \left(\frac{\partial}{\partial x}g(t,x) + a(t,x)\right) + \tilde{\sigma}(t,x)dW_t, \tag{6.25}$$

where $x = T - t$ is the time length from time t to maturity T. For details, see Brace and Musiela (1994). Usually, we observe the interest rate with respect to the variable x, and so the above equation might be more suitable for specifying historical data on the forward rates than the HJM model is.

However, because we are considering the real-world model as our primary focus, the difference between these two approaches seems less important in the beginning. Therefore, we employ the simple representation in the HJM model.

6.3 Market Price of Risk: State Space Setup

This section introduces another method to estimate the market price of risk: working in a state space.

Denoting the market price of risk by $\varphi' = (\varphi'_1, \cdots, \varphi'_d)^T$, we return to the discretization as equation (6.13), which we reproduce below:

$$\Delta F_i(t_k) = -\sigma_{0i}v_{0i}\Delta t + \sigma_{0i}\varphi'\Delta t + \sqrt{\Delta t}\,\sigma_{0i}W_1 \ ; \ i = 1, \cdots, n, \ k = 1, \cdots, J. \tag{6.26}$$

We remark that the volatility is assumed to be determined by a principal component. Our objective here is to directly obtain φ' from the above equations.

We denote by $\epsilon(\varphi')$ the sum of the squared difference between each side of equation (6.26) in the time series and cross sections, neglecting the random part, such that

$$\epsilon(\varphi') = \frac{1}{J}\sum_{k=1}^{J}\sum_{i=1}^{n}\{\Delta F_i(t_k) + (\sigma_{0i}v_{0i} - \sigma_{0i}\varphi')\Delta t\}^2 . \tag{6.27}$$

Let φ' be the solution that minimizes $\epsilon(\varphi')$. We call this setting a *state space setup*, and call that used in the previous section a *PCA setup* to distinguish between the two approaches. We note the implications of both definitions below.

- φ is the solution that minimizes $\theta_l(\varphi_l)$ in equation (6.19) in the principal component space, and also is the maximum likelihood estimate.
- φ' is the solution that minimizes $\epsilon(\varphi')$ of equation (6.27) in the state space.

Note that the definition of $\epsilon(\varphi')$ does not deal with the PCA. Then, the derivation of $\epsilon(\varphi')$ is immediate and more comprehensive than that of $\theta(\varphi)$. Accordingly, the definition of φ' is simpler than that of φ. However, the minimization problem (6.27) is too complicated to allow deriving φ' by maximum likelihood estimation.

Apart from this, let us solve this least squares problem. We have the following result.

Proposition 6.3.1 *For a d-dimensional discretization of equation (6.26) with $d \le n$, let $\epsilon(\varphi')$ be a function of d variables in $\varphi'_1, \cdots, \varphi'_d$ and defined by equation (6.27). Then, the solution φ' that minimizes $\epsilon(\varphi')$ is uniquely given as the solution of the system of linear equations, as*

$$\sum_{m=1}^{d}\left(\sum_{i=1}^{n}\sigma_{0i}^{m}\sigma_{0i}^{l}\right)\varphi'_m = \sum_{i=1}^{n}\gamma_i\sigma_{0i}^{l} \quad ; \quad l = 1, \cdots, d, \tag{6.28}$$

where

$$\gamma_i = E^H\left[\frac{\Delta F_i}{\Delta t}\right] + \sigma_{0i}v_{0i} \quad ; \quad i = 1, \cdots, n. \tag{6.29}$$

Proof We may assume that the matrix

$$(\sigma^1, \cdots, \sigma^d) = \begin{pmatrix} \sigma_{01}^1 & \cdots & \sigma_{01}^d \\ \vdots & \vdots & \vdots \\ \sigma_{0n}^1 & \cdots & \sigma_{0n}^d \end{pmatrix} \tag{6.30}$$

has rank d. From $\sigma_{0i}\varphi' = \sum_{l=1}^{d} \sigma_{0i}^l \varphi_l'$, it follows that

$$\frac{\partial \sigma_{0i}\varphi'}{\partial \varphi_l'} = \sigma_{0i}^l. \tag{6.31}$$

Then, the partial derivative of $\epsilon(\varphi')$ in φ_l' is

$$\begin{aligned} \frac{\partial \epsilon(\varphi')}{\partial \varphi_l'} &= \frac{-2}{J} \sum_{k=1}^{J} \sum_{i=1}^{n} \{\Delta F_i(t_k) + (\sigma_{0i}v_{0i} - \sigma_{0i}\varphi')\Delta t\}\, \sigma_{0i}^l \Delta t \\ &= -2 \sum_{i=1}^{n} \left\{E^H[\Delta F_i] + (\sigma_{0i}v_{0i} - \sigma_{0i}\varphi')\, \Delta t\right\} \sigma_{0i}^l \Delta t \end{aligned} \tag{6.32}$$

for $l = 1, \cdots, d$. From equations (6.31) and (6.32), we have

$$\frac{\partial^2 \epsilon(\varphi')}{\partial \varphi_l' \partial \varphi_m'} = 2 \sum_{i=1}^{n} \sigma_{0i}^l \sigma_{0i}^m \Delta t^2. \tag{6.33}$$

From this, the Hessian matrix of $\epsilon(\varphi')$ is represented by

$$\nabla^2 \epsilon(\varphi') = 2\Delta t^2 \{\sigma^1, \cdots, \sigma^d\}^T \{\sigma^1, \cdots, \sigma^d\}. \tag{6.34}$$

It holds that for an arbitrary vector $y(\neq 0) \in \mathbf{R}^d$,

$$y^T \{\sigma^1, \cdots, \sigma^d\}^T \{\sigma^1, \cdots, \sigma^d\} y = |\{\sigma^1, \cdots, \sigma^d\} y|^2 > 0, \tag{6.35}$$

because the rank of $\{\sigma_{01}, \cdots, \sigma_{0n}\}$ is d. That is, $\nabla^2 \epsilon(\varphi')$ is positive definite. Hence, the solution φ' to the minimization problem exists uniquely and is obtained by solving the equation $\nabla \epsilon(\varphi') = 0$.

For a simple expression, we define a constant vector $\gamma = (\gamma_1, \cdots, \gamma_n)^T$ by setting

$$\gamma_i = E^H \left[\frac{\Delta F_i}{\Delta t}\right] + \sigma_{0i} v_{0i}. \tag{6.36}$$

Note that γ is completely determined by the historical data, and specifically by the forward rates and the volatility. Upon substituting equation (6.36) into (6.32), it should hold that

$$\frac{\partial \epsilon(\varphi')}{\partial \varphi'_l} = -2\sum_{i=1}^{n}(\gamma_i - \sigma_{0i}\varphi')\sigma_{0i}^l \Delta t^2 = 0. \tag{6.37}$$

This can be reduced to

$$\sum_{i=1}^{n}(\gamma_i - \sigma_{0i}\varphi')\sigma_{0i}^l = 0 \;\; ; \;\; l = 1, \cdots, d. \tag{6.38}$$

By direct calculation,

$$\begin{aligned}\sum_{i=1}^{n}\sigma_{0i}\varphi'\sigma_{0i}^l &= \sum_{i=1}^{n}\left\{\sum_{m=1}^{d}\sigma_{0i}^m\varphi'_m\right\}\sigma_{0i}^l \\ &= \sum_{m=1}^{d}\left\{\sum_{i=1}^{n}\sigma_{0i}^m\sigma_{0i}^l\right\}\varphi'_m. \end{aligned}\tag{6.39}$$

Substituting this into equation (6.38), we obtain the system of linear equations on φ',

$$\sum_{m=1}^{d}\left\{\sum_{i=1}^{n}\sigma_{0i}^m\sigma_{0i}^l\right\}\varphi'_m = \sum_{i=1}^{n}\gamma_i\sigma_{0i}^l \;\; ; \;\; l = 1, \cdots, d. \tag{6.40}$$

Since the $d \times d$ matrix $\left\{\sum_{i=1}^{n}\sigma_{0i}^m\sigma_{0i}^l\right\}_{ml}$ is positive definite and has rank d, φ' is obtained as a unique solution to equation (6.40). This completes the proof. □

Proposition 6.3.1 does not assume orthogonality within the volatility structure. This means that the result is available for an artificially given volatility; for example, it can be applied with a Nelson–Siegel type volatility, Hull–White type volatility, and so forth. Furthermore, this proposition is applicable to a kind of a Markovian model studied by Ritchken and Sankarasubramanian (1995), being available whenever the volatility is deterministic and continuous.

Principal volatility component

We remark that Proposition 6.3.1 does not involve the maximum likelihood estimate for the market price of risk. To change that, we additionally suppose that the volatility is given by the principal volatility components as

$$\sigma_{0i}^l = \rho_l e_i^l \ ; \ \ l = 1, \cdots, d, I = 1, \cdots, n, \tag{6.41}$$

where $\rho_l^2 (> 0)$ is the lth eigenvalue, and $e^l = (e_1^l, \cdots, e_n^l)$ is the lth principal component of the covariance.

We reproduce the least squares problem (6.27) in the state space as

$$\epsilon(\varphi') = \frac{1}{J} \sum_{k=1}^{J} \sum_{i=1}^{n} \{\Delta F_i(t_k) + (\sigma_{0i} v_{0i} - \sigma_{0i} \varphi') \Delta t\}^2 . \tag{6.42}$$

We have the following theorem.

Theorem 6.3.2 *For a Gaussian HJM model, we assume that the volatility $\sigma(t, T)$ is continuous on t and T, and the values of σ_{0i} are given as the principal components by equation (6.41). Then, φ_l' is uniquely given by*

$$\varphi_l' = \frac{1}{\rho_l} \sum_{i=1}^{n} \{E^H \left[\frac{\Delta F_i}{\Delta t}\right] + \sigma_{0i} v_{0i}\} e_i^l \ ; \ \ l = 1, \cdots, d. \tag{6.43}$$

Proof From Proposition 6.3.1, we have

$$\sum_{m=1}^{d} \left\{ \sum_{i=1}^{n} \sigma_{0i}^m \sigma_{0i}^l \right\} \varphi_m' = \sum_{i=1}^{n} \gamma_i \sigma_{0i}^l . \tag{6.44}$$

From equation (6.41), the left-hand side of the above becomes

$$\sum_{m=1}^{d} \left\{ \sum_{i=1}^{n} \sigma_{0i}^m \sigma_{0i}^l \right\} \varphi_m' = \sum_{m=1}^{d} \left\{ \rho_m \rho_l \sum_{i=1}^{n} e_i^m e_i^l \right\} \varphi_m' . \tag{6.45}$$

By the orthonormality of the principal components, the above equation can be reduced to

$$\begin{aligned} \sum_{m=1}^{d} \left\{ \sum_{i=1}^{n} \sigma_{0i}^m \sigma_{0i}^l \right\} \varphi_m' &= \sum_{m=1}^{d} \rho_m \rho_l \varphi_m' \delta_{ml} \\ &= (\rho_l)^2 \varphi_l' . \end{aligned} \tag{6.46}$$

Similarly, the right-hand side of equation (6.44) can be written as

$$\sum_{i=1}^{n} \gamma_i \sigma_{0i}^l = \rho_l \sum_{i=1}^{n} \gamma_i e_i^l . \tag{6.47}$$

Since equations (6.46) and (6.47) are the same, it follows that

$$\varphi'_l = \frac{1}{\rho_l} \sum_{i=1}^{n} \gamma_i e_i^l, \tag{6.48}$$

where γ_i was given by equation (6.29) as $\gamma_i = E^H[\Delta F_i/\Delta t] + \sigma_{0i} v_{0i}$. Substituting this into equation (6.48), φ'_l is represented by equation (6.43). This completes the proof. □

Accordingly, we have the following corollary, which shows that the market price of risk derived in the state space setup is implied as the maximum likelihood estimate.

Corollary 6.3.3 *Under the same conditions as in Theorem 6.3.2, it holds that*

$$\varphi'_l = \varphi_l \quad ; \quad l = 1, \cdots, d. \tag{6.49}$$

Proof From equation (6.20) of Theorem 6.2.1, φ_l is given by

$$\varphi_l = \frac{1}{\rho_l} \left\{ E^H[\alpha_l] + \beta_l \right\}, \tag{6.50}$$

where $\alpha_l(t_k) = \frac{1}{\Delta t} \sum_{i=1}^{n} \Delta F_i(t_k) e_i^l$ and $\beta_l = \sum_{i=1}^{n} \sigma_{0i} v_{0i} e_i^l$. Substituting these into equation (6.50), we obtain

$$\varphi_l = \frac{1}{\rho_l} \sum_{i=1}^{n} \left\{ E^H\left[\frac{\Delta F_i(t_k)}{\Delta t}\right] + \sigma_{0i} v_{0i} \right\} e_i^l = \varphi'_l. \tag{6.51}$$

This completes the proof. □

6.4 Historical Trend of Forward Rate

By using Theorem 6.2.1, we investigate the numerical implications of the market price of risk with respect to the historical change in the forward rates. For this purpose, we provide some definitions to use in describing this change. Note that approximations and deductions here have been inferred from empirical observation.

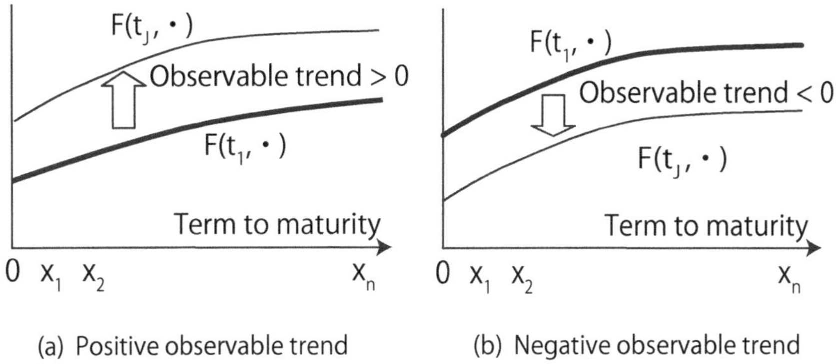

Figure 6.2: Change in the forward rates and the observable trend

Observable trend

Let $t_k, k = 1, \cdots, J+1$ be a sequence of observation dates of the forward rates $F(t_k, x_i)$ such that $t_{k+1} - t_k = \Delta t > 0$. The *observable trend* of the historical forward rate $F(\cdot, x_i)$ is defined by

$$E^H\left[\frac{F(t_{k+1}, x_i) - F(t_k, x_i)}{\Delta t}\right], \tag{6.52}$$

where $E^H[\,]$ denotes the sample mean. We see that

$$\begin{aligned} E^H\left[\frac{F(t_{k+1}, x_i) - F(t_k, x_i)}{\Delta t}\right] &= \frac{1}{\Delta t J}[\{F(t_2, x_i) - F(t_1, x_i)\} \\ &\quad + \cdots + \{F(t_{J+1}, x_i) - F(t_J, x_i)\}] \\ &= \frac{1}{\Delta t J}\{F(t_{J+1}, x_i) - F(t_1, x_i)\}. \end{aligned} \tag{6.53}$$

From this, the observable trend for x_i is positive when $F(t_{J+1}, x_i) - F(t_1, x_i) > 0$. Fig. 6.2(a) illustrates a case in which the observable trends are positive for all x_i. Conversely, this trend is negative when $F(t_{J+1}, x_i) - F(t_1, x_i) < 0$, as shown in Fig. 6.2(b), which illustrates a case in which observable trends are negative for all x_i.

Thus, the observable trend represents the average change in the forward rate $F(\cdot, x_i)$ for a fixed x_j during the sample period $[t_1, t_{J+1}]$. More precisely, this trend represents the average speed of change in the forward rate.

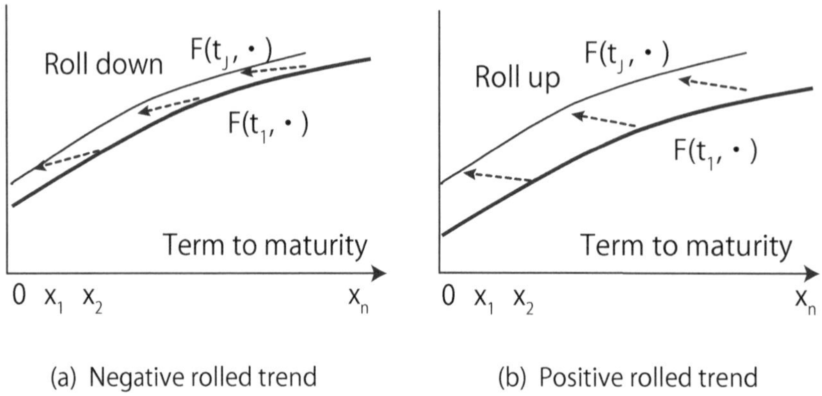

Figure 6.3: Rolled trend and roll-up/down of the forward rates

Rolled trend

The observable trend is visually comprehensive, as shown in Fig. 6.2. Although the term "observable trend" is newly coined for our investigation, this measure is common in the analysis of market interest rates. So, knowing this trend is not sufficient for exactly investigating the implications of the market price of risk. To supplement this trend, we introduce the rolled trend, as follows.

The *rolled trend* of the historical forward rate $F(\cdot, x_i)$ is defined for fixed x_i as

$$E^H\left[\frac{\Delta F_i}{\Delta t}\right], \tag{6.54}$$

where $\Delta F_i(t_k) = F(t_{k+1}, x_i - \Delta t) - F(t_k, x_i)$. It follows that

$$\begin{aligned} E^H\left[\frac{\Delta F_i(t_k)}{\Delta t}\right] &= E^H\left[\frac{F(t_{k+1}, x_i) - F(t_k, x_i)}{\Delta t}\right] \\ &\quad -E^H\left[\frac{F(t_{k+1}, x_i) - F(t_{k+1}, x_i - \Delta t)}{\Delta t}\right]. \end{aligned} \tag{6.55}$$

The first term is equal to the observable trend of $F(\ , x_i)$, and the second term corresponds to the historical mean of the slope of the forward rate at $x = x_i$.

Roll down and roll up

For example, let us consider a case in which the forward rate curve has positive

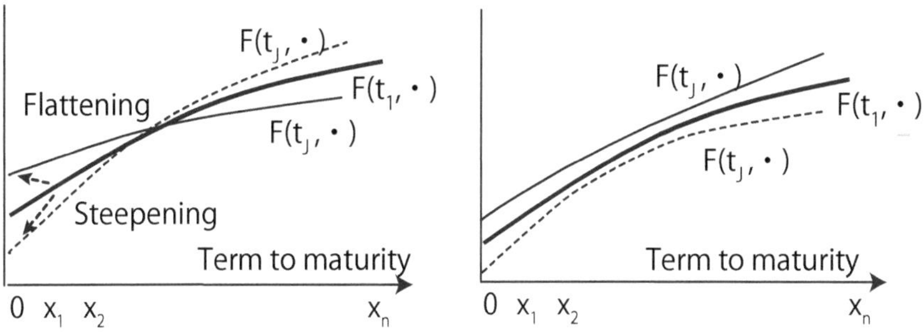

(a) Second score (b) Third score

Figure 6.4: Second and third score of rolled trend

slope and rises slowly, as in Fig. 6.3(a). In this case, the first term of equation (6.55) is nearly equal to 0, and the second term is negative because

$$E^H\left[\frac{F(t_{k+1}, x_i) - F(t_{k+1}, x_i - \Delta t)}{\Delta t}\right] > 0. \tag{6.56}$$

This case implies that the rolled trend is negative, as $E^H\left[\Delta F_i/\Delta t\right] < 0$, which is known as the *roll-down* of the forward rate curve in practice.

When the upward-sloping forward rate curve rises quickly across its entirety, the curve rolls up, as shown in Fig. 6.3(b). Although the second term might be positive, the first term is both positive and larger than the second term. As a result, the rolled trend might be positive in this case.

Thus, the rolled trend corresponds to the roll-down or roll-up of the forward rate curve, with which we are familiar from financial experience.

lth trend score

Next, we represent both trends in the principal component space.

Definition 6.4 For $l = 1, \cdots, d$, the *lth observable trend score* O_l is defined by

$$O_l = \sum_{i=1}^{n} E^H\left[\frac{F(t_{k+1}, x_i) - F(t_k, x_i)}{\Delta t}\right] e_i^l. \tag{6.57}$$

The *lth rolled trend score* R_l is defined by

$$R_l = \sum_{i=1}^{n} E^H \left[\frac{\Delta F_i}{\Delta t} \right] e_i^l. \tag{6.58}$$

The following lemma is directly obtained from equations (6.15) and (6.58).

Lemma 6.4.1

$$R_l = E^H[\alpha_l] \;\; ; \;\; l = 1, \cdots, d \tag{6.59}$$

Meaning of R_1

As mentioned in Section 4.3, the first principal component represents a parallel shift, with an example shown in Fig. 6.2. If the entire forward rate curve with positive-slope rises slowly, like that shown in Fig. 6.3(a), then the first rolled trend score is negative, that is, $R_1 < 0$. In contrast, if the entire forward rate curve rises fast, as shown in Fig. 6.3(b), then it follows that $R_1 > 0$.

Table 6.1 roughly shows the value of R_1 with respect to the shape of the forward rate curve and the observable trend. For example, the value of the latter case above is exhibited in the cell in the "Upward sloping" row and "Rising fast" column, where R_1 is positive.

Table 6.1: Qualitative estimation of the first rolled trend R_1

Shape of forward rate curve	Observable trend		
	Falling fast	Stable	Rising fast
Upward-sloping	Negative	Negative	Positive
Flat	Negative	Near zero	Positive
Downward-sloping	Negative	Positive	Positive

Meaning of R_2 and R_3

Next, we examine the meaning of the second rolled trend. We assumed that $e_1^l > 0$ in equation (6.8) for all l, which affects the sign of the score. We suppose that the forward rate curve is upward sloping and steepening during the sample period, as illustrated by the dashed line in Fig. 6.4(a). This change is opposite to the second component of the forward rates at Fig. 6.2 in Section

4.3. Then, the first rolled trend score might be negative, and the second rolled score is negative; that is, $R_1 < 0$ and $R_2 < 0$.

Conversely, if the forward rate curve is flattening, illustrated by the narrow line in Fig. 6.4(a), then the first rolled trend score might be negative, and the second one positive; we then see that $R_1 < 0$ and $R_2 > 0$.

Accordingly, Table 6.2 qualitatively estimates the values R_1 and R_2 with respect to the observable trend scores O_1 and O_2. The former example in the above is shown in the row marked "Steep." The latter example is shown in the row marked "Flat." The explanation for the third rolled trend score is similar to the explanations above.

Summarizing the above argument, O_1, O_2, and O_3 represent the level, slope, and curvature factors of the observed trend. Similarly, R_1, R_2, and R_3 represent the same factors of the rolled trend.

Remark

In Table 6.2, "bull" means that the forward rate curve is falling, and "bear" means it is rising. Additionally, "steepening" means the slope of the forward rate curve is become larger, with "flattening" meaning the slope is becoming smaller. "Bull steepening" is a combination of the bull and steepening changes in the forward rate curve, and other combinations are analogously defined.

Table 6.2: Qualitative estimation of R_1 and R_2 with respect to the observable trends. Forward rate curves are assumed to be upward sloping during the sample period.

Observable trend	R_1	R_2
Bull steep	Negative	Negative
Steep	Negative	Negative
Bear steep	Near zero	Negative
Bull flat	Negative	Positive
Flat	Negative	Positive
Bear flat	Near zero	Positive

6.5 Market Price of Risk and the Trends

This section briefly examines the numerical meaning of the market price of risk in connection with the rolled trend. For this, Theorem 6.2.1 makes it possible to derive a qualitative estimate of the value of the market price of risk.

Approximation of the market price of risk

The next proposition shows that the lth market price of risk is approximately explained as the ratio of the lth rolled trend score to the magnitude of the lth volatility component. The argument here is developed in the principal component space.

Proposition 6.5.1 *For a d-dimensional Gaussian HJM model, we assume that the volatility $\sigma(t,T)$ is continuous on t and T, and σ_{0i} is given as the principal component by equation (6.10). If the inequality*

$$|\sigma_{0i}v_{0i}| \ll E^H\left[\frac{\Delta F_i}{\Delta t}\right] \tag{6.60}$$

holds for all i, then the lth market price of risk is approximated by

$$\varphi_l \approx \frac{R_l}{\rho_l} \quad ; \quad l = 1, \cdots, d, \tag{6.61}$$

where R_l is the lth rolled trend score, and ρ_l is the magnitude of the lth volatility component.

Proof From equation (6.60), we have

$$|\sum_{i=1}^{n} \sigma_{0i}v_{0i}e_i^l| \ll \sum_{i=1}^{n} E^H\left[\frac{\Delta F_i}{\Delta t}\right] e_i^l \tag{6.62}$$

for all l. Substituting equations (6.15) and (6.16) into the above, it follows that

$$\begin{aligned} |\beta_i| &\ll \sum_{i=1}^{n} E^H\left[\frac{\Delta F_i}{\Delta t}\right] e_i^l \\ &= E^H\left[\alpha_l\right]. \end{aligned} \tag{6.63}$$

By Theorem 6.2.1, we have

$$
\begin{aligned}
\varphi_l &= \frac{1}{\rho_l}\left\{E^H\left[\alpha_l\right] + \beta_l\right\} \\
&\approx \frac{1}{\rho_l}E^H\left[\alpha_l\right].
\end{aligned}
\tag{6.64}
$$

From equation (6.59) in Lemma 6.4.1, it holds for all l that $R_l = E^H[\alpha_l]$. Substituting this into equation (6.64), we obtain equation (6.61). This completes the proof. □

A remark on inequality (6.60)

We want to note here that the condition (6.60) is empirically feasible. From the definition of v in equation (4.10), we have, roughly,

$$
\begin{aligned}
v_{0i}\ (= v(0,T_i)) &= -\int_0^{T_i}\sigma(0,u)du \\
&\approx \sigma(0,T_i)T_i \\
&= \sigma_{0i}T_i.
\end{aligned}
\tag{6.65}
$$

Accordingly, it holds that $|\sigma_{0i}^l v_{0i}^l| \approx |\sigma_{0i}^l|^2 T_i$ for each l. Then, if the volatility σ is uniformly low in i, the left-hand side value of equation (6.60) may be assumed to be sufficiently small.

Additionally when we work with a period where the interest rate rises (or falls) a consider amount, we may expect that the following will hold: $E^H\left[\Delta F_i/\Delta t\right] \gg 0$. Therefore, when the volatility is sufficiently low, the condition $|\sigma_{0i}v_{0i}| \ll E^H\left[\Delta F_i/\Delta t\right]$ can be satisfied. The approximation (6.61) is practically useful for investigating the implications of the market price of risk. Of course, we are not asserting that the above inequality always holds.

Qualitative estimation for φ_1

Proposition 6.5.1 states that the market price of risk is largely determined by the rolled trend in the principal component space. Recall that R_1, R_2, and R_3 represent the level, slope, and curvature factors of the rolled trend, respectively. Since ρ_l represents the magnitude of the lth volatility component, we may take the view that ρ_l indicates the "lth volatility risk." Hence, we may say that lth market price of risk is approximately equal to the magnitude of the lth rolled trend per unit risk of the lth volatility component; that is,

$$\{l^{th} \text{ market price of risk}\} \approx \frac{\{\text{Magnitude of } l^{th} \text{ rolled trend}\}}{\{l^{th} \text{ volatility risk}\}}. \tag{6.66}$$

Accordingly, this interpretation can be roughly rephrased in terms of the observable trend. In particular, for $l = 1$, from equation (6.55) we may accept that

$$R_1 \approx O_1 - \{\text{Slope of forward rate curve}\} \tag{6.67}$$

holds approximately. Combining equations (6.61) with (6.67), Table 6.3 presents a rough estimate of φ_1 in terms of the observable trend, where each result corresponds to the relevant entry in Table 6.1.

As an example, suppose that the forward rate curve is upward-sloping and stably unchanged, as shown in Fig. 6.5(a). Then, O_1 is almost equal to zero and R_1 is negative; that is, this is the roll-down. Hence, φ_1 might be negative. Moreover, if the forward rate curve rises fast as shown in Fig. 6.5(b), such that O_1 is positive and larger than the second term in equation (6.67), then R_1 is positive. Hence, φ_1 might be positive. These two cases are shown in the first row of Table 6.3.

Following this line of reasoning, φ_1 is roughly estimated for other shapes of the forward rate curve. If the curve is almost flat during the sample period, then the second term in equation (6.67) is nearly equal to zero. We may assume that $O_1 \approx R_1$. Therefore, φ_1 is almost estimated by the observable trend, which is shown in the second row of Table 6.3. In Section 7.2, we will work with this particular case for studying the negative price tendency of φ_1. An example with actual data will be presented in Section 10.4.

At last, we examine the case in which the forward rate curve is downward-sloping. This means that the second term in equation (6.67) is negative, and so it roughly holds that $R_1 > O_1$. With this, φ_1 is estimated to be a bit larger than in the case of a flat curve, which is shown in the bottom row of Table 6.3.

Qualitative estimation for φ_2

Next, we examine the properties of the first and second market price of risk φ_1 and φ_2 in connection with R_1 and R_2, respectively.

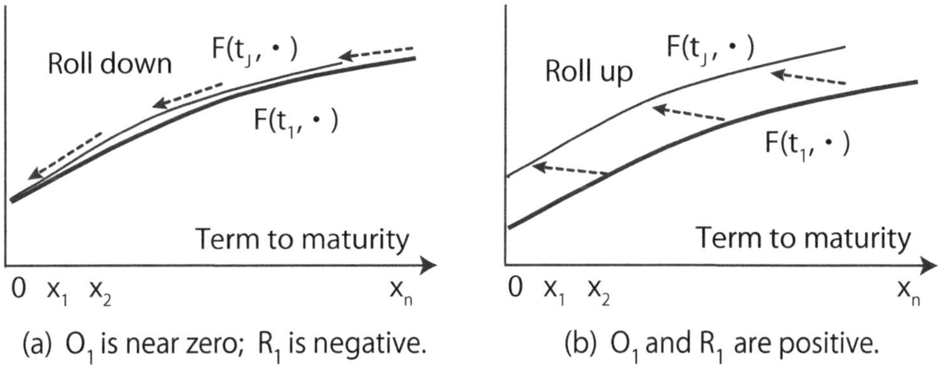

Figure 6.5: First observable trend score and rolled trend

Table 6.3: First market price of risk φ_1 with respect to the observable trend and average shape of the forward rate curve.

Shape of forward rate curve	Observable trend		
	Fast fall	Stable	Fast rise
Upward-sloping	Negative	Negative	Positive
Flat	Negative	Near zero	Positive
Downward-sloping	Negative	Positive	Positive

We assume that the forward rate curve is almost upward-sloping through the observation period. We have roughly estimated the rolled trend score R_1 and R_2 for each observable trend in Table 6.2. From those estimations, the market prices of risk φ_1 and φ_2 are roughly inferred by Proposition 6.5.1, with the results summarized in Table 6.4.

For example, the steepening of the forward rates implies that $O_1 \approx 0$ (or $\leq$ 0) and $O_2 < 0$, as shown in Fig. 6.6, Then, O_1 is near zero and R_1 might be a little negative because of the roll-down effect. Hence, φ_1 might be a little negative. Since O_2 is negative, R_2 might be negative, and so φ_2 takes a negative value. This case is shown in the second row of Table 6.4.

Table 6.4: First and second market prices of risk with respect to the observable trend. The forward rate curve is assumed to be upward-sloping through a sample period.

Observable trend	φ_1	φ_2
Bull steep	Negative	Negative
Steep	Negative	Negative
Bear steep	Near zero	Negative
Bull flat	Negative	Positive
Flat	Negative	Positive
Bear flat	Near zero	Positive

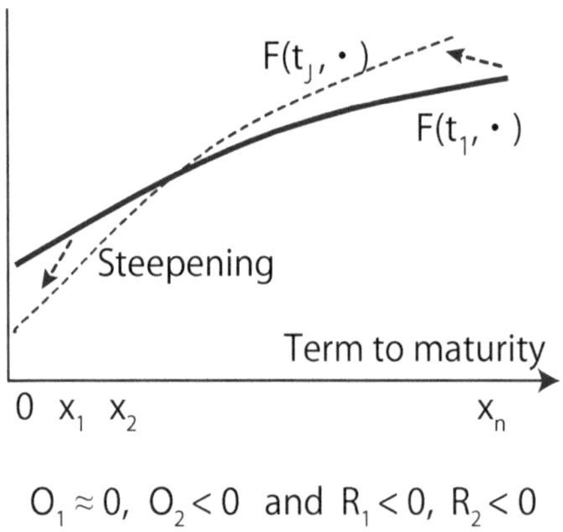

Figure 6.6: Observable trend and rolled trend. The forward rate curve is steepening through a sample period.

Furthermore, when the forward rate curve is flat or has negative slope, we can estimate the market price of risk by a method similar to the above.

6.6 Interpretation of Market Price of Risk

Recall the conventional argument on the negative market price of risk, discussed in Section 4.2. From equation (4.22), the market price of risk satisfies $\mu_i(t) - r(t) = v(t)\varphi_t$ for all T_i. This means that φ_t is independent from the

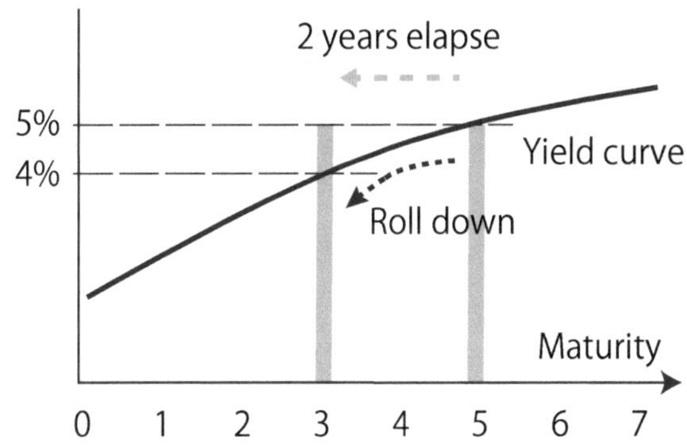

Figure 6.7: Yield curve and roll-down

maturity T_i. In the one-dimensional case, the above equation is reduced to

$$\varphi_t = \frac{\mu_i(t) - r(t)}{v(t)}. \tag{6.68}$$

From this form, the market price of risk is traditionally explained as the excess return per unit risk for investment in the ith bond; that is, it is the same risk–return no matter which bond we invest in within an arbitrage-free market. The traditional interpretation is familiar within the usual investment theory, but it is difficult to develop along these lines for the higher-order market price of risk.

In this respect, this section presents another interpretation of the market price of risk, employing Proposition 6.5.1 to do so. We begin with addressing the roll-down return from bond investment.

Roll-down return

In order to explain the roll-down effect in the context of bond investment, we work with the yield rates instead of the forward rates for a while. We assume that the yield curve has positive slope, as shown in Fig. 6.7. Recall the five-year bond with coupon rate 5% in Example 1.4.1. From calculation with equation (1.29), we can buy that bond at the face value 1.00. Two years later, we will own a three-year bond with coupon rate 5%.

If the yield curve has not changed, then the yield of the three-year bond rolls down to 4%, as shown in Fig. 6.7. This rate is taken as the discount rate, as follows. Specifically, the price of this bond is equal to the present value of the three-year bond with 5% coupon by applying the discount rate of 4%. From the calculation of equation (1.34), the price rises to 1.02775; that is, we gain 0.02775 (= 1.02775 – 1.00) by the roll-down. Therefore, the roll-down on the yield provides excess return for a bond holder.

Conversely, if the three-year yield rises to 6% after two years, that will be a roll-up of the yield. Then, the price of the bond will fall to 0.9733 from the calculation of equation (1.36). We then lose 0.0267 (= 0.9733 – 1.00) due to the roll-up.

Therefore, when the yield curve is steep, the bond holder can expect an excess return from the roll-down. The roll-down and roll-up correspond to excess return and loss, respectively, for the investor. These observations approximately follow the analogous observations for the roll-down and roll-up in the forward rates. Now we return to the argument on forward rates.

The first market price of risk for investor

Now we explain the first market price of risk in connection with the roll-down return by referring to Fig. 6.8. The bar graph in the lower part of Fig. 6.8(a) shows a uniform portfolio consisting of one-year to six-year bonds. The investor expects the roll-down of the entire forward rate curve for the excess return. Specifically,

$$R_1 < 0 \tag{6.69}$$

is expected. The risk for the investor is the roll-up of the entire forward rates, in other words, the level change of the rates. The magnitude of this risk is evaluated as ρ_1, which is the norm of the first volatility component. By Proposition 6.5.1, we have the approximation

$$\varphi_1 \approx \frac{R_1}{\rho_1} \tag{6.70}$$

under a low-volatility condition. This means that *the first market price of risk φ_1 is a risk-adjusted measure for the roll-down return of the entire forward rate curve.*

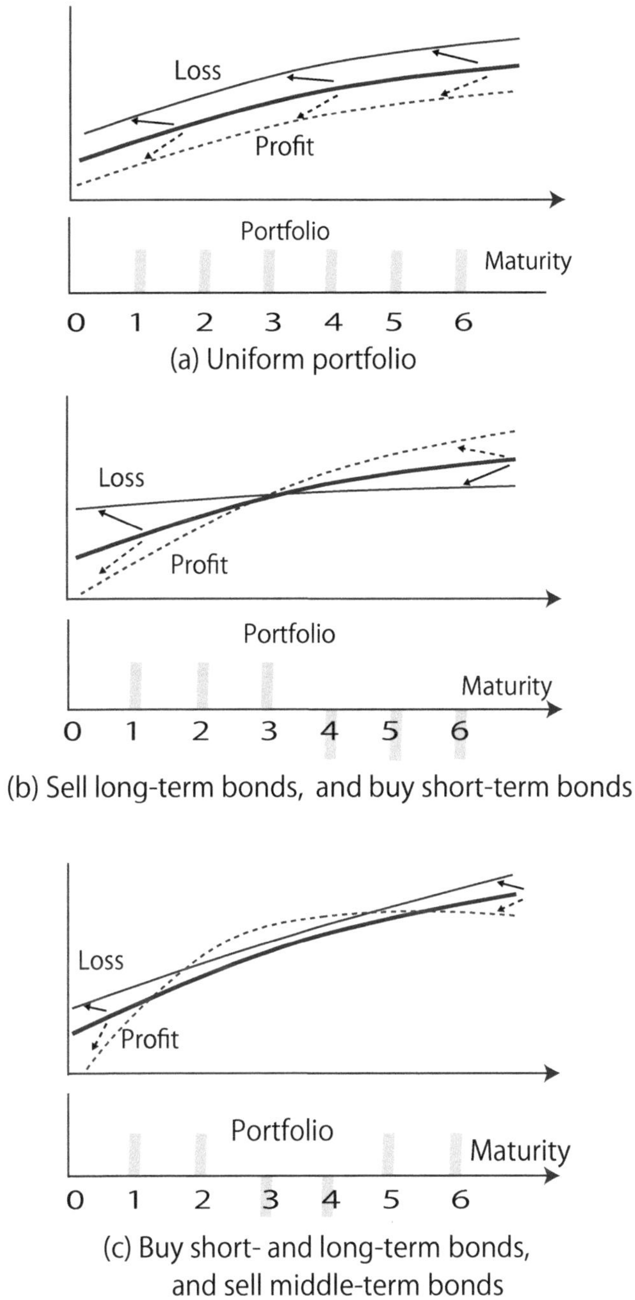

Figure 6.8: Risk–return in three investment strategies

Thus, we have quantitatively obtained another interpretation of φ_1. The most important advantage of this observation is that the following systematic interpretation can be given for $\varphi_i, i = 1, 2, 3, \cdots$.

The second market price of risk for investor

We next examine the meaning of the second market price of risk in the principal component space by applying the above method. The bar graph in Fig. 6.8(b) represents a so-called steepening position, where the investor buys short-term bonds and sells long-term bonds. We may regard it as given that this portfolio's value is not affected by the parallel shift of the entire forward rates (i.e., the first principal component of the covariance). Thus, the portfolio risk is hedged against the first volatility component.

If the forward rate curve becomes steeper—for example, if the one-, two-, and three-year forward rates fall, and the four-, five-, and six-year forward rates rise, as shown by the dashed line in Fig. 6.8(b)—then the price of short-term bonds will rise, but the price of the long-term bonds might fall[2]. Then, the investor gains from both the buying and selling of bonds and expects the steepening trend implied by

$$R_2 < 0. \tag{6.71}$$

This investment style is known as the *steepening strategy.*

The only risk in this strategy is from the flattening of the forward rate curve because the parallel shift risk is already hedged against. The magnitude of the slope change in this context is measured by the magnitude of the second volatility component ρ_2. Letting $l = 2$ in Corollary 6.5.1 gives

$$\varphi_2 = R_2/\rho_2, \tag{6.72}$$

which is interpreted as the risk–return ratio of the steepening position. From this, *the second market price of risk* φ_2 *is a risk-adjusted measure for the steepening strategy.*

[2]More precisely, for the argument on the second market price of risk, the prices of the four-year and five-year bonds might not fall when the forward rates become steeper. This is because the discount factors to four and five years are also affected by the falls of the short-term forward rates. In practice, a steepening position is numerically designed to hedge against a risk of parallel shift.

The converse portfolio strategy, in which short-term bonds are sold and long-term bonds are purchased, is called the flattening strategy. The risk–return ratio for this strategy is represented by φ_2.

The third market price of risk and investment

The bar graphs in Fig. 6.8(c) shows the so-called *butterfly trading strategy* or *butterfly position*, where the investor buys short- and long-term bonds and sells the middle-term bonds. The value of the butterfly position is affected by neither level changes nor slope changes for the same reason that the steepening position has these properties[3]. In other words, the risk caused by the first and second volatility components is eliminated in this portfolio. The risk of the butterfly position is only that the curvature will change in the forward rate curve.

If the curvature becomes large, for example, short- and long-term forward rates will fall, and middle-term forward rates will rise, as shown by the dashed line in Fig. 6.8(c). In that case, the prices of short- and long-term bonds rises, but the middle-term bonds fall in price. The investor gains from each bond and expects that the curvature becomes larger as $R_3 < 0$. The narrow line shows the converse case.

The magnitude of this risk is measured by the norm of the third volatility component ρ_3. Proposition 6.5.1 shows that, for the case $l = 3$, $\varphi_3 = R_3/\rho_3$; that is, *the third market price of risk* φ_3 *is a risk-adjusted measure for the butterfly trading strategy*

Accordingly, the higher-order market prices of risk can be interpreted in a similar manner.

The market price of risk has been econometrically studied in relation to state variables such as the instantaneous spot rate r. For example, a functional form of $\varphi(r) = a\sqrt{b^2 + c^2 r}$ is assumed in De Jong and Santa-Clara (1999), where a, b, and c are constants. Stanton (1997) empirically estimates the market price of risk in the form of $\varphi(r)$. In contrast, we provide a theoretical interpretation of the market price of risk in relation to the average changes in the historical forward rate curve, rather than to the state of the interest rate.

[3]The remarks in the above footnote apply to the butterfly position.

6.7 Property of Real-world Simulation

In the previous sections, we have systematically and qualitatively examined the numerical properties of the market price of risk. Next, we study the properties of the real-world model for simulation. In the following, interest rate simulation under the real-world measure is referred to as *real-world simulation.*

Approach

Before investigating the simulation properties, let us consider how to approach examining them. Monte Carlo simulation will yield too many numerical results, obscuring the features of the model. However, in cases where we use only a few random numbers for simulation, the results will depend on the specific numbers. Moreover, the results will depend on not only the volatility structure but also the initial forward rates. In light of this, such an experiment seems no better than ad hoc testing. Instead, it might be better to employ a theoretical approach for our objective.

For this, we again work in the principal component space by using the exact formula (6.20) of the market price of risk.

Real-world simulation

We recall the relation $T = x - t$, which was given in Section 6.1. We set $T_i = x_i$ for $t = 0$ and $i = 1, \cdots, n$. For a short time interval $\Delta s > 0$ and the initial forward rates $f(0, T_i)$, $f(\Delta s, x_i)$ is represented under $\mathbf{P}$ by equation (6.2), as

$$\begin{aligned} f(\Delta s, T_i) &= f(0, T_i) + \int_0^{\Delta s} \{-\sigma(s, T_i)v(s, T_i) + \sigma(s, T_i)\varphi\} ds \\ &\quad + \int_0^{\Delta s} \sigma(s, T_i) dW_s, \end{aligned} \tag{6.73}$$

where W_s denotes a d-dimensional Brownian motion. We then have

$$f(\Delta s, T_i) = f(0, T_i) + \{-\sigma_{0i}v_{0i} + \sigma_{0i}\varphi\}\Delta s + \sqrt{\Delta s}\sigma_{0i}W_1. \tag{6.74}$$

Here, we adopt the notation $\sigma_{0i} = \sigma(0, T_i)$ and $v_{0i} = v(0, T_i)$ for convenience. This equation presents a simulation model, substituting a d-dimensional number generated according to a standard normal distribution in W_1.

We define the volatility structure σ_{0i}^l from the principal components, where the market price of risk is estimated by Theorem 6.2.1. Then, the single-period simulation is executed according to the above form.

Real-world model in principal component space

In particular, when $d = n$ and $(\sigma_{01}, \cdots, \sigma_{0n})$ is rank n, the above interest rate model is referred to as a *full-factor model.* In this section, we work with this model. The lth projection of equation (6.74) can be described as

$$\begin{aligned}\sum_{i=1}^{n} f(\Delta s, T_i)e_i^l &= \sum_{i=1}^{n} f(0, T_i)e_i^l + \sum_{i=1}^{n}\{-\sigma_{0i}v_{0i}e_i^l + \sigma_{0i}\varphi e_i^l\}\Delta s \\ &\quad + \sum_{i=1}^{n}\sqrt{\Delta s}\sigma_{0i}e_i^l W_1. \end{aligned} \tag{6.75}$$

This is a representation of the real-world model in a principal component space. We set $\beta_l = \sum_{i=1}^{n} \sigma_{0i}v_{0i}e_i^l$, with $l = 1, \cdots, d$. By the orthonormality of the set of principal components, it holds that

$$\begin{aligned}\sum_{i=1}^{n} \sigma_{0i}\varphi e_i^l &= \sum_{i=1}^{n}\sum_{m=1}^{n} \rho_m e_i^m \varphi_m e_i^l \\ &= \rho_l\varphi_l \end{aligned} \tag{6.76}$$

and

$$\begin{aligned}\sum_{i=1}^{n} \sigma_{0i}e_i^l W_1 &= \sum_{i=1}^{n}\sum_{m=1}^{n} \rho_m e_i^m W_1^m e_i^l \\ &= \rho_l W_1^l. \end{aligned} \tag{6.77}$$

From these, we have

$$\sum_{i=1}^{n} f(\Delta s, T_i)e_i^l = \sum_{i=1}^{n} f(0, T_i)e_i^l + \{-\beta_l + \rho_l\varphi_l\}\Delta s + \sqrt{\Delta s}\rho_l W_1^l. \tag{6.78}$$

From Theorem 6.2.1, we already know that $\varphi_l\rho_l = E^H[\alpha_l] + \beta_l$. Substituting this into the above, we obtain

$$\begin{aligned}\sum_{i=1}^{n} f(\Delta s, T_i)e_i^l &= \sum_{i=1}^{n} f(0, T_i)e_i^l + \left(-\beta_l + \left\{E^H[\alpha_l] + \beta_l\right\}\right)\Delta s \\ &\quad +\sqrt{\Delta s}\rho_l W_1^l \\ &= \sum_{i=1}^{n} f(0, T_i)e_i^l + E^H[\alpha_l]\Delta s + \sqrt{\Delta s}\rho_l W_1^l. \end{aligned} \tag{6.79}$$

This represents a simulation model in the principal component space.

Properties of simulation model

Lemma 6.4.1 gives $E^H[\alpha_l] = R_l$. Then, equation (6.79) becomes

$$\sum_{i=1}^{n} f(\Delta s, T_i)e_i^l = \sum_{i=1}^{n} f(0, T_i)e_i^l + R_l\Delta s + \sqrt{\Delta s}\rho_l W_1^l \tag{6.80}$$

for $l = 1, \cdots, n$.

In practice, this structure is comprehensive. Indeed, the first term is the lth principal component score of the initial rates. The drift term is equal to the lth rolled trend, and the diffusion coefficient is equal to the size of the lth volatility component. In other words, we may say that *a real-world simulation model consists of a historical drift and a historical volatility in PCA representation.* It is worth noting that this feature follows from the exact formulation of the market price of risk in Theorem 6.2.1.

6.8 Simulation Model in State Space

This section converts the real-world model in the principal component space to the real-world model in the state space. From the simulation having the form of equation (6.80) with $l = 1, \cdots, n$, we have

$$\begin{pmatrix} \sum_{i=1}^{n} f(\Delta s, T_i)e_i^1 \\ \vdots \\ \sum_{i=1}^{n} f(\Delta s, T_i)e_i^n \end{pmatrix} = \begin{pmatrix} \sum_{i=1}^{n} f(0, T_i)e_i^1 + R_1\Delta s + \sqrt{\Delta s}\rho_1 W_1^1 \\ \vdots \\ \sum_{i=1}^{n} f(0, T_i)e_i^n + R_n\Delta s + \sqrt{\Delta s}\rho_n W_1^n \end{pmatrix}. \tag{6.81}$$

Following the method in Appendix B, we multiply both sides of equation (6.81) by $(e^1, \cdots, e^n)$ to represent the model in the state space. Then, the left-hand side becomes

$$
\begin{aligned}
(e^1, \cdots, e^n) \begin{pmatrix} \sum_{i=1}^n f(\Delta s, T_i) e_i^1 \\ \vdots \\ \sum_{i=1}^n f(\Delta s, T_i) e_i^n \end{pmatrix}
&= (e^1, \cdots, e^n)(e^1, \cdots, e^n)^T \begin{pmatrix} f(\Delta s, T_1) \\ \vdots \\ f(\Delta s, T_n) \end{pmatrix} \\
&= \begin{pmatrix} f(\Delta s, T_1) \\ \vdots \\ f(\Delta s, T_n) \end{pmatrix}. \qquad (6.82)
\end{aligned}
$$

We calculate each term in the right-hand side of equation (6.81) as follows. The leftmost term becomes

$$
(e^1, \cdots \ , \ e^n) \begin{pmatrix} \sum_{i=1}^n f(0, T_i) e_i^1 \\ \vdots \\ \sum_{i=1}^n f(0, T_i) e_i^n \end{pmatrix} = \begin{pmatrix} f(0, T_1) \\ \vdots \\ f(0, T_n) \end{pmatrix}. \qquad (6.83)
$$

From equation (6.58), the next term is reduced to

$$
\begin{aligned}
(e^1, \cdots, e^n) \begin{pmatrix} R_1 \Delta s \\ \vdots \\ R_n \Delta s \end{pmatrix} &= (e^1, \cdots, e^n) \begin{pmatrix} \sum_{i=1}^n E^H[\Delta F_i / \Delta t] e_i^1 \Delta s \\ \vdots \\ \sum_{i=1}^n E^H[\Delta F_i / \Delta t] e_i^n \Delta s \end{pmatrix} \\
&= \begin{pmatrix} E^H[\Delta F_1 / \Delta t] \Delta s \\ \vdots \\ E^H[\Delta F_n / \Delta t] \Delta s \end{pmatrix}. \qquad (6.84)
\end{aligned}
$$

Since $\sigma_{0i}^l = \rho_l e_i^l$, the third term becomes

$$
\begin{aligned}
(e^1, \cdots, e^n) \begin{pmatrix} \rho_1 W_1^1 \\ \vdots \\ \rho_n W_1^n \end{pmatrix} &= \begin{pmatrix} \sum_{l=1}^n e_1^l \rho_l W_1^l \\ \vdots \\ \sum_{l=1}^n e_n^l \rho_l W_1^l \end{pmatrix} \\
&= \begin{pmatrix} \sum_{l=1}^n \sigma_{01}^l W_1^l \\ \vdots \\ \sum_{l=1}^n \sigma_{0n}^l W_1^l \end{pmatrix}. \qquad (6.85)
\end{aligned}
$$

Summarizing these, we have the simulation model represented in state space as

$$f(\Delta s, T_i) = f(0, T_i) + E^H \left[\frac{\Delta F_i}{\Delta t} \right] \Delta s + \sqrt{\Delta s} \sigma_{0i} W_1. \tag{6.86}$$

From this, we have obtained the following theorem.

Theorem 6.8.1 *For a full-factor Gaussian HJM model, let σ_{0i} be given by the principal components of the sample covariance as $\sigma_{0i}^l = \rho_l e_i^l$. Let φ be the market price of risk as obtained by Theorem 6.2.1. Then, for an arbitrary initial forward rate $f(0, T_i)$ and a short time step Δs with $0 < \Delta s < T_1$, $f(\Delta s, T_i)$ is simulated by*

$$f(\Delta s, T_i) = f(0, T_i) + E^H \left[\frac{\Delta F_i}{\Delta t} \right] \Delta s + \sqrt{\Delta s} \sigma_{0i} W_1 \ ; \ i = 1, \cdots, n. \tag{6.87}$$

From this theorem, the full-factor simulation is achieved, eliminating the market price of risk. Furthermore, the drift term is made equal to the rolled trend, and the volatility is made equal to the historical volatility. In this context, we may say that *the real-world model represents a historical model admitting an arbitrage-free pricing system.*

Arbitrage pricing in the real-world model

Let us trace the examination from Theorem 6.2.1 up to Theorem 6.8.1. First, we derived the formula for the market price of risk in Theorem 6.2.1. Next, we substituted this formula into the discretized forward rate process. Working with the full factor model, we eliminated the market price of risk in the real-world model, formulating it in the principal component space as equation (6.80). As a result, we have represented a simulation model in the state space in the above theorem, and this result is a historical term structure model.

Some readers might question whether any historical term structure model is arbitrage-free. On this issue, let us recall the definition of an arbitrage-free market from Section 3.1, and that the arbitrage-free condition is ensured by the existence of a state price deflator. Then, the difference between the real-world model and the historical term structure model is that the former includes the market price of risk and the state price deflator, but the latter does not.

Indeed, once we obtain the market price of risk φ, the state price deflator is implied by equation (4.26), such that

$$d\xi_t/\xi_t = -r(t)dt - \varphi_t dW_t. \tag{6.88}$$

This is solved as

$$\xi_t = \exp\left\{\int_0^t \left(-r(t) - \frac{|\varphi|^2}{2}\right) ds - \int_0^t \varphi dW_s\right\}. \tag{6.89}$$

Using the Euler approximation, we obtain $\xi_{\Delta s}$ by

$$\xi_{\Delta s} = \exp\left\{\left(-f(0,0) - \frac{|\varphi|^2}{2}\right) \Delta s - \sqrt{s}\varphi W_1\right\}. \tag{6.90}$$

Consider a security with a payoff at T given by a random variable X. Then, the time t price p_t of this security is given by equation (3.5) as $p_t = \frac{1}{\xi_t} E_t[\xi_T X]$. Thus, the arbitrage price is numerically computable in the real-world model.

Key points for Theorem 6.8.1

There are two key items in deriving Theorem 6.8.1. The first is discretization by the Euler integral, which simplifies the discrete-time representation of the forward rate evolution in equation (6.5). Indeed, if we attempt analytic estimation of $v(r, T)$, we find that the approximation (6.5) is nontrivial in a continuous-time framework.

The second is that the HJM framework admits an arbitrary volatility structure in a multi-dimensional model. Most studies on term structure modeling begin with a one-factor model and extend that model to a multi-factor model. In contrast, the previous section starts the investigation from a full-factor model, where PCA allows converting the model from the principal component space to the state space.

Dimension reduction

The full-factor model is not feasible for numerical simulation because of the large volatility matrix. Here, we investigate a method to reduce the dimensionality of the simulation model.

For convenience, we recommend using equation (6.87) rather than equation (6.74) because the drift term $-\sigma_{0i}v_{0i} + \sigma_{0i}\varphi$ in equation (6.74) should be computed for full factors. In contrast, the drift term $E^H\left[\Delta F_i/\Delta t\right]\Delta s$ in equation

(6.87) is independent to the dimensionality. From this starting point, we need only to approximate the diffusion term $\sqrt{\Delta s}\sigma_{0i}W_1 = \sum_{l=1}^{n} \sigma_{0i}^{l} W_1^l$ by a d-factor model with $d < n$ and use the form given in equation (6.87). Thus, we may determine the dimension d such that the accumulated contribution rate C_d is sufficiently close to 1. As a result, a d-dimensional model for real-world simulation is described as

$$f(\Delta s, T_i) = f(0, T_i) + E^H \left[\frac{\Delta F_i}{\Delta t} \right] \Delta s + \sqrt{\Delta s} \sum_{l=1}^{d} \sigma_{0i}^{l} W_1^l. \tag{6.91}$$

Remark

In a strict sense, equation (6.91) is not supported in the arbitrage-pricing framework because the state price deflator ξ_t in equation (6.89) is valid for only the full-factor model. Of course, in practice, we may approximate this state price deflator ξ_t.

6.9 Numerical Procedure

To complete this chapter, we summarize a numerical procedure to build the real-world model in the Gaussian HJM framework.

Let $x_i, i = 1, \cdots, n$ be a sequence of time lengths, and set $\delta_i = x_{i+1} - x_i$. For a positive constant $\Delta t > 0$, we set the sequence of observation dates as $t_k = \Delta t k$ for $k = 1, \cdots, J + 1$.

Numerical calculation of $\Delta F_i(t_k)$

We practically observe the forward rates in the form $F(t_k, x_i)$ at t_k for a fixed time length x_i. Recall the definition of ΔF_i in equation (6.12):

$$\Delta F_i(t_k) = F(t_{k+1}, x_i - \Delta t) - F(t_k, x_i). \tag{6.92}$$

Usually, we set $\delta_i = 0.5$ or 1 (years), and the time step Δt should be taken to be shorter than δ_1. Then, we may assume that $\Delta t < \min_i \delta_i$. For this, the time length $x_i - \Delta t$ is not contained in the set of $\{x_i\}_{i=1,\cdots,n}$. Thus, $F(t_{k+1}, x_i - \Delta t)$ is not directly observed in the market.

The most convenient way to obtain $F(t_{k+1}, x_i - \Delta t)$ is to use $F(t_{k+1}, x_i)$ as a proxy. However, the rolled trend exactly determines the drift of the simulation and the market price of risk, as mentioned in Section 6.5. This means that we should avoid using $F(t_{k+1}, x_i)$ in place of $F(t_{k+1}, x_i - \Delta t)$. For the sake of expedience, $F(t_{k+1}, x_i - \Delta t)$ is approximately calculated by linear interpolation:

$$F(t_{k+1}, x_i - \Delta t) = \left(1 - \frac{\Delta t}{\delta_{i-1}}\right) F(t_{k+1}, x_i) + \frac{\Delta t}{\delta_{i-1}} F(t_{k+1}, x_{i-1}). \qquad (6.93)$$

Thus, we approximately obtain $\Delta F_i(t_k)$. The importance of this interpolation will be verified in a numerical example, Case B4 in Section 10.2.3, which is given in the LMRW.

Calculation of the market price of risk

Below, we list the procedure to estimate the market price of risk from Theorem 6.3.2. For this, the rank of the covariance matrix is assumed to be n.

1. $F(t_{k+1}, x_i - \Delta t)$ is obtained by the interpolation (6.93), and then $\Delta F_i(t_k)$ is calculated by equation (6.92) for $i = 1, \cdots, n,\ k = 1, \cdots, J$.

2. By PCA of $Cov(\Delta F_i,\ \Delta F_j)/\Delta t$, the eigenvalue $(\rho_l)^2$, the principal component e^l, and the volatility σ^l are obtained for $l = 1, \cdots, n$.

3. The number of factors d is chosen such that the accumulated contribution rate C_d is sufficiently close to 1.

4. The lth volatility component σ^l is determined by

$$\sigma^l_{0i} = \rho_l e^l_i \ ; \ i = 1, \cdots, n, \ l = 1, \cdots, d. \qquad (6.94)$$

5. The rolled trend is calculated as

$$E^H\left[\frac{\Delta F_i}{\Delta t}\right] \ ; \ i = 1, \cdots, n. \qquad (6.95)$$

6. From equation (4.9), v_{0i} is obtained by solving the integral

$$v_{0i} = -\int_0^{x_i} \sigma(0, u)du \ ; \ i = 1, \cdots, n. \qquad (6.96)$$

7. Next, $\sigma_{0i}v_{0i}$ is computed from

$$\sigma_{0i}v_{0i} = \sum_{l=1}^{d} \sigma_{0i}^{l} v_{0i}^{l} \quad ; \quad i = 1, \cdots, n. \tag{6.97}$$

   More precisely, the right-hand side is an approximation of $\sigma_{0i}v_{0i}$ when $d < n$ and is in agreement when $d = n$.

8. From Theorem 6.3.2, we calculate the lth market price of risk by solving

$$\varphi_l = \frac{1}{\rho_l} \sum_{i=1}^{n} \left\{ E^H \left[\frac{\Delta F_i}{\Delta t} \right] + \sigma_{0i}v_{0i} \right\} e_i^l \quad ; \quad l = 1, \cdots, d. \tag{6.98}$$

Real-world simulation

Lastly, we summarize the procedure for single-period simulation of forward rates by using equation (6.91). Here, the volatility is inferred by PCA and the market price of risk is eliminated.

1. The procedure from 1) to 7) is the same as that given above.

2. We set the initial instantaneous forward rate $f(0, x_i)$ and generate a d-dimensional sequence of standard normal random numbers.

3. Identifying the time period x_i with the maturity date, we set $T_i = x_i$. Let Δs $(< T_1)$ be the time period for simulation. From equation (6.91), $f(\Delta s, T_i)$ is simulated by

$$f(\Delta s, T_i) = f(0, T_i) + E^H \left[\frac{\Delta F_i}{\Delta t} \right] \Delta s + \sqrt{\Delta s} \sum_{l=1}^{d} \sigma_{0i}^{l} W_1^l. \tag{6.99}$$

Some numerical examples will be presented in Section 10.1.

CHAPTER 7

REMARKS ON REAL-WORLD MODELS

Abstract: This chapter presents some remarks about real-world modeling. First, we examine the numerical differences between real-world simulations and risk-neutral simulations, comparing the drift terms in each type of model.

Next, we investigate the reason that the market price of risk is negative by using a simplified model, which we refer to as a flat yield model. This subject is motivated by the following research question: *Why does long-period observation tend to imply a negative value for the market price of risk?* We obtain an answer to this question by introducing simplified models (specifically, the flat yield model and the positive slope model).

Through this book, we have estimated the market price of risk under the assumption that it is constant in the sample period. Addressing this, we examine the validity of the constancy assumption for risk management by using a simplified model. It is worth nothing here that Section 7.1 is basically the contents of Yasuoka (2015), and Sections 7.2 and 7.3 are newly written for this book.

Keywords: Constant market price of risk, Drift, Flat yield model, Interest rate shock, Interest rate risk management, Long-period observation, Negative price tendency, Null market price of risk, Positive slope model, Real-world model, Risk management, Risk-neutral model, Time-varying market price of risk

Takashi Yasuoka

7.1 Differences between Real-world and Risk-neutral Models

In this section, we investigate the differences in interest rate simulation between real-world models and risk-neutral models. Although there are multiple risk-neutral models, characterized by the choice of a numéraire, for this analysis, we employ the spot measure model as a benchmark for risk-neutral models.

To highlight the differences, we compare the expectations from forward rate simulation under both measures, doing so for the reasons explained at the beginning of Section 6.7. We have the following theorem, which evaluates the expectations for each measure.

Theorem 7.1.1 *Under the assumptions of Theorem 6.8.1, $f(\Delta s, T_i)$ is normally distributed under both* **P** *and* **Q**, *and the expectations of $f(\Delta s, T_i)$ under each measures are given by*

$$E[f(\Delta s, T_i)] = f(0, T_i) + E^H\left[\frac{\Delta F_i}{\Delta t}\right]\Delta s, \tag{7.1}$$

$$E^{\mathbf{Q}}[f(\Delta s, T_i)] = f(0, T_i) - \sigma_{0i} v_{0i} \Delta s, \tag{7.2}$$

respectively. The variance of $f(\Delta s, T_i)$ in both simulations is

$$\Delta s \sum_{l=1}^{n} (\sigma_{0i}^l)^2. \tag{7.3}$$

Proof Note that we are working with the full-factor model under the conditions of Theorem 6.8.1. From equation (6.87), $f(\Delta s, T_i)$ is represented by

$$f(\Delta s, T_i) = f(0, T_i) + E^H\left[\frac{\Delta F_i}{\Delta t}\right]\Delta s + \sqrt{\Delta s}\sigma_{0i} W_1. \tag{7.4}$$

Thus, $f(\Delta s, T_i)$ is normally distributed under **P** with mean $f(0, T_i) + E^H[\Delta F_i/\Delta t]\Delta s$ and variance $\Delta s \sum_{l=1}^{n} (\sigma_{0i}^l)^2$.

By the argument as in Section 4.2, when we assume the null market price of risk, the model is equivalent to the spot measure model. Then, substituting $\varphi = 0$ into equation (6.74) in Section 6.7, we have the discretization under **Q** as

$$f(\Delta s, T_i) = f(0, T_i) - \sigma_{0i} v_{0i} \Delta s + \sqrt{\Delta s}\, \sigma_{0i} Z_1, \tag{7.5}$$

where Z_1 is an n-dimensional standard normal distribution under $\mathbf{Q}$. Thus, $f(\Delta s, T_i)$ is normally distributed under $\mathbf{Q}$ with mean $f(0, T_i) - \sigma_{0i} v_{0i} \Delta s$ and variance $\Delta s \sum_{l=1}^{n} (\sigma_{0i}^{l})^2$. This completes the proof. □

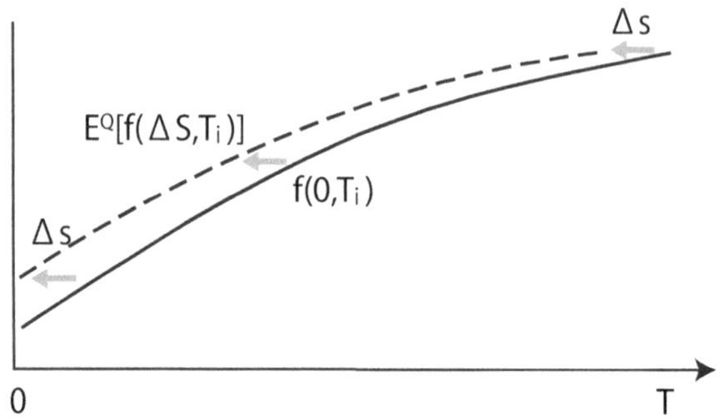

Figure 7.1: Initial forward rate and the expectation of the simulation in the risk-neutral model. $E^{\mathbf{Q}}[f(\Delta s, T_i)]$ is approximately equal to the parallel shift of $f(0, T_i)$ to the left for Δs when the volatility is low.

Property of drift

As described in the remark after Proposition 6.5.1, it sometimes happens that $|\sigma_{0i} v_{0i}| \Delta s$ takes a negligibly small value. In such cases, the equation (7.2) can be approximated by $E^{\mathbf{Q}}[f(\Delta s, T_i)] \approx f(0, T_i)$. Fig. 7.1 illustrates this relation, where the bold line represents the initial forward rates $f(0, T_i)$, and the dashed line represents $E^{\mathbf{Q}}[f(\Delta s, T_i)]$. Specifically, the expectation $E^{\mathbf{Q}}[f(\Delta s, T_i)]$ is almost equal to the parallel shift in the initial curve to the left for Δs. We usually observe this property when working with a term structure model for derivatives pricing.

In contrast, equation (7.1) indicates that the drift of the real-world model is equal to the rolled trend. The following corollary roughly explains the difference between them.

Corollary 7.1.2 *Under the assumptions of Theorem 7.1.1, if it holds that*

$$|\sigma_{0i} v_{0i}| \ll E^{H} \left[\frac{\Delta F_i}{\Delta t} \right], \tag{7.6}$$

then the difference between the two model expectations is given by

$$E[f(\Delta s, T_i)] - E^{\mathbf{Q}}[f(\Delta s, T_i)] \approx E^{H} \left[\frac{\Delta F_i}{\Delta t} \right] \Delta s. \tag{7.7}$$

Proof From Theorem 7.1.1, it follows that

$$E[f(\Delta s, T_i)] - E^{\mathbf{Q}}[f(\Delta s, T_i)] = E^H\left[\frac{\Delta F_i}{\Delta t}\right]\Delta s + \sigma_{0i}v_{0i}\Delta s. \tag{7.8}$$

From the assumption in equation (7.6), we may neglect the second term of the right-hand side to obtain an approximation. This gives equation (7.7), which completes the proof. □

The inequality (7.6) is the same as equation (6.60) in Proposition 6.5.1; this is satisfied under a large rolled trend with low volatility, as explained after the proof of Proposition 6.5.1. Naturally, this condition is not satisfied under a small rolled trend with high volatility. An example of this will be given in the LMRW (Section 10.2.1, Case A).

Choice of sample period

With respect to managing the risk of interest-rate rises, we sometimes hear the widely accepted explanation that the risk-neutral simulation implies valuation more on the safe side than the real-world simulation does. The reasoning is the following. The market price of risk might be negative, and the case of null market price of risk is equivalent to the spot measure model, so the real-world model will simulate lower interest rates than the spot measure model.

However, it is possible that $E^H[\Delta F_i/\Delta t] \gg 0$. Succinctly, interest rates may rise rapidly. In this case, the real-world model will simulate higher interest rates than the risk-neutral model, which follows from the above corollary. In fact, an example of a positive market price risk will be given in Section 10.3.

7.2 Negative Price Tendency of Market Price of Risk

In Section 4.2, we referred to the traditionally given reason for the negative market price of risk. Starting from there, we theoretically elucidate the mechanism for this, using the formula for the market price of risk.

In empirical analysis of the term structure of interest rates, we often find that the observation period is long, such as thirty years. For example, De Jong (2000), Duffee (2002), and Cheridito *et al.* (2007) typically use thirty- or forty-year observation periods in analyzing the U.S. Treasury market to estimate the term structure and the market price of risk.

When comparing the performance of short rate models, working with longer periods provides a better examination. However, for valuing a constant market price of risk, it is not clear that a long-period observation is advantageous. Indeed, it seems that long-period observation tends to imply a negative market price of risk. This section examines that tendency. To simplify the argument for clarity and convenience, we introduce some simple term structures: a flat yield model and a positive slope model.

7.2.1 Flat Yield Model

Let $x_i, i = 1, \cdots, n$ be a sequence of time lengths with $x_{i+1} - x_i = \delta > 0$, and let $F(t, x_i), i = 1, \cdots, n$ denote the forward rates observed on $t \in [0, \infty)$. We assume that the yield is always flat. Then, the forward rates $F(t, x_i), i = 1, \cdots, n$ are also flat, and so we may denote them by $F(t, x_i) = F(t)$. We call this interest rate model a *flat yield model*. This model represents sample data, but it is not assumed to be an Ito process.

Let $[0, \tau]$ be a sample period with $0 < \tau < \infty$. From PCA for the sample, we obtain an eigenvalue $(\rho_1)^2$, the principal component e^1, and the first volatility component σ^1. To distinguish according to the length of the observation period ($[0, \tau]$), we denote these values by $\rho(\tau), e(\tau)$ and $\sigma(\tau)$, respectively, and omit the superscript "1" for the order in principal components.

Let us estimate the market price of risk in the flat yield model, applying Theorem 6.2.1. By the flat yield assumption, the first principal component is also flat. From this, the condition $\sum_{i=1}^{n}(e_i(\tau))^2 = 1$ implies that

$$e_i(\tau) = \frac{1}{\sqrt{n}} \quad ; \quad i = 1, \cdots, n. \tag{7.9}$$

The volatility $\sigma_{0i}(\tau)$ is expressed as

$$\begin{aligned} \sigma_{0i}(\tau) &= \rho(\tau)e_i(\tau) \\ &= \frac{\rho(\tau)}{\sqrt{n}}, \end{aligned} \tag{7.10}$$

and we denote this by setting $\sigma(\tau) = \sigma_{0i}(\tau)$ for simplicity. From equation (4.10), $v_{0i}(\tau)$ is obtained from $v_{0i}(\tau) = -\sigma(\tau)\delta i$. The constant $\beta(\tau)$ is defined with respect to τ by equation (6.16). Taking these together with equation (6.16), $\beta(\tau)$ is represented by

$$\begin{aligned} \beta(\tau) &= \sum_{i=1}^{n} \sigma(\tau)v_{0i}(\tau)e_i = -\frac{(\sigma(\tau))^2\delta}{\sqrt{n}} \sum_{i=1}^{n} i \\ &= -\frac{1}{2}(\sigma(\tau))^2\delta\sqrt{n}(n-1). \end{aligned} \tag{7.11}$$

Because of the flatness assumption and from equation (6.55), the rolled trend coincides with the observable trend. Then, from equations (6.53) and (6.57), the first rolled trend score $R(\tau)$ is given by

$$\begin{aligned} R(\tau) &= O(\tau) = \sum_{i=1}^{n} \frac{F(\tau) - F(0)}{\sqrt{n}\tau} \\ &= \frac{\sqrt{n}(F(\tau) - F(0))}{\tau}. \end{aligned} \tag{7.12}$$

We denote by $\varphi(\tau)$ the first market price of risk implied from the sample period $[0, \tau]$. Recall that Lemma 6.4.1 presents $= E^H[\alpha]$. From this, $\varphi(\tau)$ is estimated by Theorem 6.2.1 as

$$\varphi(\tau) = \frac{R(\tau) + \beta(\tau)}{\rho(\tau)}. \tag{7.13}$$

7.2.2 Negative Price Tendency

By using equation (7.13), let us examine a sufficient condition for $\varphi(\tau) < 0$. The sign of $\varphi(\tau)$ coincides with the sign of $R(\tau) + \beta(\tau)$ in equation (7.13) because we always set $\rho(\tau) > 0$. Combining equation (7.11) with (7.12), we have

$$R(\tau) + \beta(\tau) = \frac{\sqrt{n}(F(\tau) - F(0))}{\tau} - \frac{1}{2}(\sigma(\tau))^2 \delta \sqrt{n}(n-1). \tag{7.14}$$

Then, the following theorem holds, which provides a sufficient condition for $\varphi(\tau) < 0$ in the flat yield model.

Theorem 7.2.1 (Negative price condition) *In a flat yield model, whenever*

$$\frac{F(\tau) - F(0)}{\tau} < \frac{\delta(n-1)}{2}(\sigma(\tau))^2, \tag{7.15a}$$

it holds that $\varphi(\tau) < 0$. *Conversely, if*

$$\frac{F(\tau) - F(0)}{\tau} > \frac{\delta(n-1)}{2}(\sigma(\tau))^2, \tag{7.15b}$$

then $\varphi(\tau) > 0$.

The next example shows that the inequality (7.15a) is satisfied when the observation period is sufficiently long.

Example 7.2.1

We set $\delta = 0.5$ (years), $n = 20$, and $\tau = 20$ (years). Suppose that the volatility is 5%; that is, $\sigma(20) = 0.05$. We assume that the forward rates are always positive and less than 20%; specifically, $0 < F(t) < 0.2$ for $t \in [0, 20]$. These assumptions should be sufficiently natural for our experience.

In this case, the left-hand side of equation (7.15a) is evaluated as

$$\frac{F(20) - F(0)}{\tau} < \frac{0.2 - 0}{20} = 0.01. \tag{7.16}$$

This means that the yield rises by less than 1% per year, on average. The right-hand side of equation (7.15a) is calculated as

$$\frac{19}{2} \times 0.5 \times (0.05)^2 = 0.011875, \tag{7.17}$$

which is larger than the left-hand side. These figures satisfy the inequality (7.15a), and so the market price of risk is estimated to be negative.

Specifically, the market price of risk $\varphi(20)$ is estimated as follows. The value of $\rho(20)$ is calculated from equation (7.10) as

$$\rho(20) = \sqrt{20}\sigma(20) = 4.47 \times 0.05 = 0.2236. \tag{7.18}$$

From these figures and equation (7.13), $\varphi(20)$ is calculated to be -0.0084 as follows:

$$\varphi(20) < \frac{0.01 - 0.011875}{\rho(20)} = \frac{0.01 - 0.011875}{0.2236} = -0.0084. \tag{7.19}$$

Assumptions of negative price tendency

We additionally assume that there exists a positive constant $\bar{\sigma}$ such that

$$\lim_{\tau \to \infty} \sigma(\tau) = \bar{\sigma}. \tag{7.20}$$

This means that the historical volatility $\sigma(\tau)$ converges to $\bar{\sigma}$ over long observation periods. This assumption agrees with our intuition from experience and is consistent with observed statistics.

Furthermore, we assume that there exist two constants c_l and c_h such that

$$c_l < F(t) < c_h \tag{7.21}$$

for $t \in [0, \infty]$; that is, the forward rates are bounded from above and below. For the past several decades, the forward rates in the U.S. Treasury market have been less than 20%. Additionally, the mean reversion property of the interest rates is roughly consistent with the above assumption of boundedness. Hence, the assumption (7.21) is feasible for the U.S. Treasury market and for some other interest rate markets.

The next theorem means, roughly, that long-period observation tends to imply a negative value for the first market price of risk, φ.

Theorem 7.2.2 (Negative price tendency I) *In a flat yield model, if the conditions (7.20) and (7.21) hold, then the first market price of risk $\varphi(\tau)$ converges to a negative constant as*

$$\lim_{\tau \to \infty} \varphi(\tau) = -\frac{(n-1)\delta\bar{\sigma}}{2}. \tag{7.22}$$

Proof From equation (7.13), it holds that

$$\lim_{\tau\to\infty}\varphi(\tau)=\lim_{\tau\to\infty}\frac{R(\tau)+\beta(\tau)}{\rho(\tau)}. \tag{7.23}$$

Equation (7.12) and the boundedness condition (7.21) together imply $\lim_{\tau\to\infty}R(\tau)=0$. Then, we have

$$\lim_{\tau\to\infty}\varphi(\tau)=\lim_{\tau\to\infty}\frac{\beta(\tau)}{\rho(\tau)}. \tag{7.24}$$

Substituting (7.10) and (7.11) into this, we obtain

$$\begin{aligned}\lim_{\tau\to\infty}\frac{\beta(\tau)}{\rho(\tau)} &= \lim_{\tau\to\infty}\frac{-(\sigma(\tau))^2\delta\sqrt{n}(n-1)}{2\sqrt{n}\sigma(\tau)}\\ &= -\lim_{\tau\to\infty}\frac{(n-1)\delta\sigma(\tau)}{2}\\ &= -\frac{(n-1)\delta\bar{\sigma}}{2}. \end{aligned}\tag{7.25}$$

This completes the proof. □

This theorem is immediately verified in the next example.

Example 7.2.2

Under the same conditions as in Example 7.2.1, we assume that $\bar{\sigma}=0.05$. Then, the right-hand side of (7.22) is

$$-\frac{19\times 0.5\times 0.05}{2}=-0.2375. \tag{7.26}$$

From this, the market price of risk $\varphi(\tau)$ converges to a negative constant (here, -0.2375) as τ becomes large.

Causes of negative price tendency

Theorems 7.2.1 and 7.2.2 suggest three distinct causes for the negative price tendency:

- $n\delta$—long-term forward rate curve;
- σ—high volatility; and
- τ—long-period observation.

From the argument for the Hull–White model in Section 4.4, the mean reversion property implies that the HJM volatility $\sigma(t,T)$ will become lower as T becomes larger (cf. equation (4.48)), which is shown by the narrow line in Fig. 7.2. Let us consider how to approximate a volatility function $\sigma(t,T)$ by a flat volatility σ. When $n\delta = x_1$, the volatility is approximated by the flat volatility σ_1, the bold line in Fig. 7.2. Taking $n\delta$ to be larger, as $n\delta = x_2$, the volatility $\sigma(t,T)$ is approximated by σ_2, shown as the dashed line in the figure. Naturally, we see that $0 < \sigma_2 < \sigma_1$. Succinctly, the flat volatility σ will tend to become smaller as $n\delta$ becomes longer. Then, in a practical sense, the right-hand side of equation (7.15a),

$$\frac{(n-1)\delta}{2}(\sigma(\tau))^2, \tag{7.27}$$

does not always becomes large when $(n-1)\delta$ becomes large. Hence, we may reasonably adopt the view that the impact of $n\delta$ is relatively small.

Next, suppose that we calculate the volatility for each period length, letting $\tau = 10, 20, 30$ (years); we denote these volatilities by $\sigma(10)$, $\sigma(20)$, and $\sigma(30)$, respectively. Empirically, the long period of observation suggests that these values do not have much difference in meaning. The right-hand side of (7.15a) supports this as well. Along these lines, we may reasonably assert that the impact of $\sigma(\tau)$ on the negative price tendency is limited.

The left-hand side of (7.15a) tends toward 0 as τ becomes large. Thus, it is accepted here that the impact of τ on the negative price tendency is stronger than the impacts of $n\delta$ and $\sigma(\tau)$.

There are many empirical studies about term structures of interest rates that work with long-period samples, and many of these estimate the market price of risk to be negative. Theorems 7.2.1 and 7.2.2 suggest that the price might be negative because of the long period used for observation. Indeed, short-period observation might imply a positive value for the market price of risk. Some actual examples of this will be presented in Chapter 10.

7.2.3 Positive Slope Model

We next consider the case in which the forward rate curve has a positive slope during the sample period. This type of case is more commonly observed rather than a flat yield.

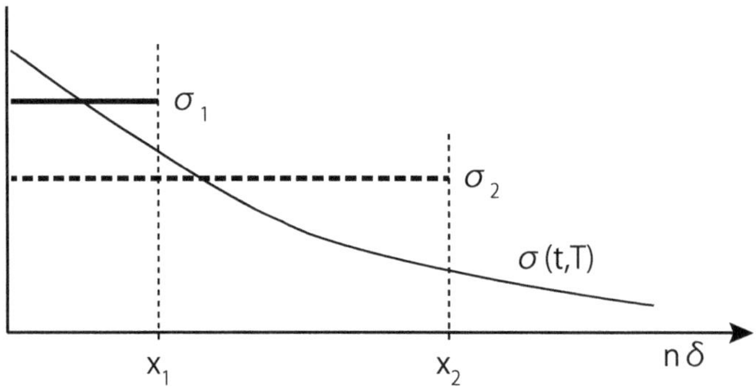

Figure 7.2: Large $n\delta$ implies small σ

For simplicity, we assume that the forward rate is observed to have the form $F(t,x) = F(t,0) + ax$ for a positive constant a. Then, the volatility is flat in x, which is denoted by $\sigma(\tau)$ for a observation period $[0,\tau]$. We call this model a "positive slope model." We recall the rolled trend in equation (6.55) as

$$\begin{aligned} E^H\left[\frac{\Delta F_i(t_k)}{\Delta t}\right] &= E^H\left[\frac{F(t_{k+1},x_i) - F(t_k,x_i)}{\Delta t}\right] \\ &\quad -E^H\left[\frac{F(t_{k+1},x_i) - F(t_{k+1},x_i - \Delta t)}{\Delta t}\right]. \end{aligned} \tag{7.28}$$

In the positive slope model, it holds that

$$\frac{F(t_k,x_i) - F(t_k,x_i - \Delta t)}{\Delta t} = a \tag{7.29}$$

for all k and i. Then, we have

$$E^H\left[\frac{\Delta F_i(t_k)}{\Delta t}\right] = E^H\left[\frac{F(t_{k+1},x_i) - F(t_k,x_i)}{\Delta t}\right] - a. \tag{7.30}$$

By applying the argument used with the flat yield model to the positive slope model, we obtain the following theorem.

Theorem 7.2.3 (Negative price tendency II) *In a positive slope model, when* $\lim_{\tau\to\infty}\sigma(\tau) = \bar{\sigma}$ *and there exist constants* c_l *and* c_h *such that* $c_l < F(t) < c_h$ *for* $t \in [0,\infty]$*, it follows that*

$$\lim_{\tau\to\infty}\varphi(\tau) = -\frac{a}{\bar{\sigma}} - \frac{(n-1)\delta\bar{\sigma}}{2}. \tag{7.31}$$

Proof By the same argument as in Section 7.2.1, it follows that $e_i(\tau) = 1/\sqrt{n}$ for all i, and

$$\beta(\tau) = -\frac{1}{2}(\sigma(\tau))^2\delta\sqrt{n}(n-1). \tag{7.32}$$

From the proof for Theorem 7.2.3, we have

$$\lim_{\tau\to\infty}\frac{\beta(\tau)}{\rho(\tau)} = -\frac{(n-1)\delta\bar{\sigma}}{2}. \tag{7.33}$$

Since the first term of equation (7.30) is equal to the observable trend, it holds that $R(\tau) = O(\tau) - a\sqrt{n}$. The boundedness condition implies that $\lim_{\tau\to\infty} O(\tau) = 0$. Then, we have $\lim_{\tau\to\infty} R(\tau) = -a\sqrt{n}$. From Theorem 6.2.1 and equation (7.33), it follows that

$$\begin{aligned}\lim_{\tau\to\infty}\varphi(\tau) &= \lim_{\tau\to\infty}\frac{R(\tau)+\beta(\tau)}{\rho(\tau)} \\ &= -\lim_{\tau\to\infty}\frac{R(\tau)}{\sigma(\tau)\sqrt{n}} + \lim_{\tau\to\infty}\frac{\beta(\tau)}{\rho(\tau)} \\ &= -\frac{a}{\bar{\sigma}} + -\frac{(n-1)\delta\bar{\sigma}}{2}. \end{aligned} \tag{7.34}$$

This completes the proof. □

By comparing equation (7.22) with equation (7.31), we see that the positive slope model admits a stronger negative tendency than the flat yield model does.

In actual markets, the forward rate curve is typically positively sloped or (sometimes) roughly flat, although a negatively slope forward rate curve is occasionally observed. Following along these lines, Theorems 7.2.2 and 7.2.3 imply that *the negative market price of risk is caused by adopting a long period for observation.*

Naturally, Theorem 7.2.3 holds even when $a < 0$, this represents a negative slope model.

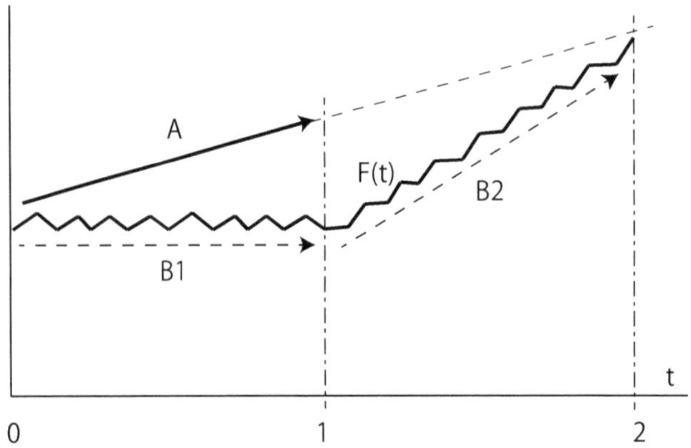

Figure 7.3: $F(t)$ indicates an example path of the forward rate. Three arrows indicate the drifts in real-world models for different cases.

7.3 Assumption of Constant Market Price of Risk

Throughout this book, the market price of risk is estimated under the assumption that it is constant over the sampled period. A market price of risk estimated under this condition is here referred to as a *constant market price of risk.*

Naturally, there is another approach: adopt a time-varying setup for estimating the market price of risk. We call a price estimated in this way a *time-varying market price of risk.* The market price of risk was originally defined as a stochastic process in Section 3.3. Because of this, a time-varying setup might be more legitimate than a constant setup. However, assuming a constant market price of risk is considered suitable for risk management by reasoning coming from engineering observations and explained as follows.

Two cases

Suppose that we intend to use a real-world model for risk valuation when considering a one-year scenario for interest rate, and we have to use a two-year observation period for this objective. Let $[0, 2]$ be a two-year sample period for estimating the market price of risk; we examine the following two cases.

In Case A, we estimate the constant market price of risk φ_A for the period $[0, 2]$. In Case B, we adopt a time-varying approach and divide the observation period into subperiods $[0,1]$ and $[1,2]$. In Case B, we estimate the market prices of risk φ_{B1} and φ_{B2} for the periods $[0,1]$ and $[1,2]$ respectively, assuming that they are constant for each period. Case B thus represents a simple model for a time-varying market price of risk. Case B is split into cases B1 and B2, defined as the constant case for the periods $[0,1]$ and $[1,2]$, respectively.

For simplicity, we use the flat yield model, which was introduced in Section 7.2. Suppose that the polyline in Fig. 7.3 represents a sample path of the forward rate $F(t)$, where $F(t)$ is almost unchanged in the earlier period $[0,1]$, and rising rapidly in the later period $[1,2]$. The first rolled trend scores are denoted R_A, R_{B1}, and R_{B2} for cases A, B1, and B2, respectively; the observable trend scores for each period are denoted O_A, O_{B1}, and O_{B2} analogously. Accordingly, for case A, the first eigenvalue is ρ_A, β_1 of equation (7.11) is β_A, and the market price of risk is φ_A. The values ρ_{B1}, β_{B1}, and φ_{B1} are defined likewise for case B1, and the values ρ_{B2}, β_{B2}, and φ_{B2} for case B2.

Market price of risk

From Fig. 7.2, we can see that $O_{B2} > O_A > O_{B1} \approx 0$. In the flat yield model, the first rolled trend score is equal to the first observable trend score. From this, we have $R_A = O_A, R_{B1} = O_{B1}$ and $R_{B2} = O_{B2}$. Accordingly, we have

$$R_{B2} > R_A > R_{B1} \approx 0. \tag{7.35}$$

We may assume for simplicity that volatility is constant over the whole period $[0,2]$, and so it follows that $\rho_A = \rho_{B1} = \rho_{B2}$. Accordingly, we have $\beta_A = \beta_{B1} = \beta_{B2}$. We recall equation (7.13) as

$$\varphi_X = \frac{R_X + \beta_X}{\rho_X} \quad ; \quad X = A, B_1, B_2. \tag{7.36}$$

Here, the subscript X indicates the case (A, B_1, or B_2). In our setting, φ_X depends on only the rolled trend score R_X. Then, we have from equation (7.35) that $\varphi_{B2} > \varphi_A > \varphi_{B1} = 0$.

When we use the time-varying market price of risk, $\varphi_B(t)$ is given by

$$\varphi_B(t) = \left(\begin{array}{ll} \varphi_{B1} & ; \quad t \in [0,1] \\ \varphi_{B2} & ; \quad t \in (1,2] \end{array} \right). \tag{7.37}$$

Drift in simulation

Theorem 6.8.1 states that the real-world model admits a historical trend. From this start, we qualitatively examine the drifts in each model as follows.

In case A, the expectation of the real-world simulation for a one-year period results in the drift exhibited by the arrow A in Fig. 7.3, which corresponds to the average speed of change in the forward rate over the whole period $[0, 2]$.

In case B, we have two market prices of risk, φ_{B1} and φ_{B2}. Therefore, we have to determine which we choose for a one-year simulation. If we adopt φ_{B1}, then the real-world simulation results in a flat drift, as illustrated by the arrow B_1 in Fig. 7.3. However, this does not make sense for considering interest rate shocks in the two-year period.

If, instead, we adopt φ_{B2}, the simulation results in the rapid rise of the forward rate, illustrated by the arrow B_2 in Fig. 7.3. This model is equivalent to a model that uses only the one-year period $[1, 2]$, and so the interest rate shock is too large for the two-year observation. Consequently, case B effectively means that we are not using the two-year observation.

Even when we subdivide the period into shorter intervals, it is still meaningless by the same reasoning as above. Thus, we may see that, in the sense of engineering, case A provides a reasonable interest rate shock given the requirement to use a two-year observation. This reasoning applies equally to other lengths of observation period. Along these lines, assuming a constant market price of risk is more suitable for risk management than assuming a time-varying price.

CHAPTER 8

REAL-WORLD MODEL IN THE HULL–WHITE MODEL

Abstract: This chapter studies construction of a Hull–White-type real-world model, using the results of Section 6 to do so.

First, we briefly summarize some approaches to volatility estimation in the short rate model. Next, we present two methods for calibrating the Hull–White model. One is to analyze the short rate dynamics. The other is to analyze the forward rate dynamics, working within the HJM framework. Additionally, we remark on some practical aspects of volatility estimation with respect to the mean reversion rate.

Accordingly, we present a method for constructing a Hull–White model under the real-world measure. The chief benefit of this is that the real-world Hull–White model is simple to compute; Section 8.6 summarizes the numerical procedures necessary to construct the real-world model. Further, some numerical examples will be presented in Chapter 10.

Keywords: Historical volatility, Hull–White model, Hull–White volatility, Humped volatility, Implied volatility, Market price of risk, Mean reversion, Monte Carlo simulation, Negative mean reversion, Nelson–Siegel model, Norm-invariant condition, Numerical procedure, One-factor model, Principal component analysis, Real-world model, Risk-neutral model, Rolled trend score, short rate model, Volatility estimation

Takashi Yasuoka

The Hull–White model is simple to use and comprehensive enough for many practitioners, which has led to this model being widely used in financial institutions for derivatives pricing. To study the real-world model in this framework, we begin with a discussion of estimating the volatility structure for risk management in the short rate model.

8.1 Volatility Estimation

Volatility estimation is a traditional subject in analyzing interest rate markets, and so it has been studied in many works. For a review of those works, see, for example, Poon and Granger (2003).

Proceeding from the viewpoint of risk management, this section summarizes three approaches to estimate the volatility structure in the short rate model:

1. implied volatility;
2. historical volatility: short rates; and
3. historical volatility: entire forward rates.

To compare these methods, we consider the evolutions of short-, middle-, and long-term interest rates.

Implied volatility

For option pricing, the volatility is estimated such that the model explains the market prices of caps, floors, and swaptions. Volatility estimated in this way is referred to as *implied volatility.* In this line of investigation, tree models are used for calibration: a binomial tree in the Ho–Lee model (Ho and Lee, 1986) and a trinomial tree in the Hull–White model (Hull and White, 1994). Since these tree models admit a recombined structure, they are convenient for the use in calibration and they have been widely used for option pricing since its early days. For details of these, see those works or later works such as Hull (2009) and Rebonato (1996).

As stated in Section 4.3, this approach models future volatility as forecast by market participants. A consequence of this is that it is not certain whether implied volatility explains the future or historical dynamics of interest rates.

Because of this uncertainty, this approach is not thought to be suitable for use in risk management.

Historical volatility: Short rates

The volatility derived from historical data is referred to as *historical volatility*. For calibration of the short rate model, we can take either of two approaches to estimating historical volatility. One approach requires observing the short rate dynamics; the other requires observing the dynamics of an entire forward rate curve. A great many papers have studied the performance of short rate models in capturing the stochastic behavior of the short rate. For example, Chan *et al.* (1992) compares the performance of a number of affine models of Merton (1973), Brennan and Schwartz (1977, 1979), Vasicek (1977), and Cox *et al.* (1985), among others. These models are calibrated such that the model explains the distribution of the short rate for the sample period. In Section 8.2, we will introduce a calibration method that takes this approach in the Hull–White model.

Let us consider a portfolio such that short rate risk accounts for the majority of the interest rate risk. In such a portfolio, the short rate approach may be a valid approach to risk management. In practice, the interest rate risk at many financial institutions consists of short-, middle-. and long-term interest rate risk. This means that the short rate approach is of quite limited usefulness for our objective.

Historical volatility: Entire forward rates

For the reasons discussed above, it is better in the context of risk management to construct the volatility such that it explains the entire evolution of the forward rates. Fortuitously, some types of short rate models are described as a special case of the HJM model. For example, the Ho–Lee model and the Hull–White model are well known as special cases of a Gaussian HJM model. Indeed, we represented the Hull–White model in the HJM framework in Section 4.4.

And so, in Section 8.3, we will introduce a calibration method with regard to the forward rate dynamics for the Hull–White model. Naturally, it is not certain that historical volatility will be duplicated in future periods. However, this is a problem better addressed in economics or financial engineering, and beyond the scope of this book.

8.2 Historical Volatility of the Short Rate

This section presents a method for estimating volatility in the Hull–White model from the short rate distribution.

Short rate process in the Hull–White model

As introduced in Section 4.4, the short rate process in the Hull–White model is represented by

$$dr(t) = \kappa \left\{ \theta(t) - r(t) + \frac{\sigma}{\kappa}\varphi_t \right\} dt + \sigma dW_t, \tag{8.1}$$

where W_t is the one-dimensional Brownian motion under the real-world measure $\mathbf{P}$, $\kappa > 0$ is the mean reversion rate, $\sigma > 0$ is the diffusion coefficient of the short rate, φ_t is the market price of risk, and $\theta(t)$ is a positive process determined by equation (4.46).

Setting $Z_t = \int_0^t \varphi_s ds + W_t$, we know that there exists a risk-neutral measure $\mathbf{Q}$ equivalent to $\mathbf{P}$ such that Z_t is a Brownian motion under $\mathbf{Q}$. The short rate process $r(t)$ is represented under $\mathbf{Q}$ as

$$dr(t) = \kappa\{\theta(t) - r(t)\}dt + \sigma dZ_t. \tag{8.2}$$

Short rate distribution

To estimate the parameters κ and σ, we recall the following properties of the short rate distribution. From equation (4.58), the expectation of $r(t)$ under $\mathbf{Q}$ is given by

$$E^{\mathbf{Q}}[r(t)] = f(0,t) + \frac{\sigma^2}{2\kappa^2}(1 - e^{-\kappa t})^2. \tag{8.3}$$

From equation (4.59), the variance of $r(t)$ is represented by

$$Var[r(t)] = \frac{\sigma^2}{2\kappa}(1 - e^{-2\kappa t}). \tag{8.4}$$

By calculating the variance of changes in the historical short rate, we can estimate κ and σ by comparing the calculated variance with $Var[r(t)]$. The algorithm for this is as follows.

Historical volatility

Let $t_k, k = 1, \cdots, J+1$ be a sequence of observation times, with $t_{k+1} - t_k = \Delta t$, where Δt is a sampling interval. For a sample period $[t_1, t_{J+1}]$, let $r(t_k)$ be the instantaneous short rate observed at t_k for every k. We assume that the evolution of $r(t_k)$ follows equation (8.1). We use $V_{\Delta t}$ to denote the variance of the multiset whose elements are of the form $r(t_{i+1}) - r(t_i)$; thus,

$$V_{\Delta t} = \frac{1}{J-1} \sum_{i=1}^{J} \{r(t_{i+1}) - r(t_i)\}^2. \tag{8.5}$$

From equation (8.4), it follows that

$$\begin{aligned} V_{\Delta t} &= Var[r(\Delta t)] \\ &= \frac{\sigma^2}{2\kappa}(1 - e^{-2\kappa\Delta t}), \end{aligned} \tag{8.6}$$

for an arbitrary interval Δt.

Let us consider another interval Δs, with $\Delta t \neq \Delta s$, and calculate $V_{\Delta s}$. From this, we have two equations, equation (8.6) and $V_{\Delta s} = \frac{\sigma^2}{2\kappa}(1 - e^{-2\kappa\Delta s})$. Solving this system of nonlinear equations for κ and σ, we formally obtain them. However, equation (8.6) does not hold for arbitrary intervals when we use actual market data. To overcome this, we approximately estimate the parameters κ and σ. We set at least three intervals $\Delta t_i, i = 1, \cdots, m$, $(m \geq 3)$ and then calculate $V_{\Delta t_i} x$ for each $i = 1, \cdots, m$.

To obtain an approximation such that

$$V_{\Delta t_i} \approx \frac{\sigma^2}{2\kappa}\{1 - \exp(-2\kappa\Delta t_i)\} \tag{8.7}$$

for all i, we apply a least squares approach to the variance, as

$$\sum_{i=1}^{m} \left\{ V_{\Delta t_i} - \frac{\sigma^2}{2\kappa}\{1 - \exp(-2\kappa\Delta t_i)\} \right\}^2. \tag{8.8}$$

Alternatively, we may solve a different least squares problem for the standard deviation, as

$$\sum_{i=1}^{m} \left\{ \sqrt{V_{\Delta t_i}} - \sigma\sqrt{\frac{1 - \exp(-2\kappa\Delta t_i)}{2\kappa}} \right\}^2. \tag{8.9}$$

From this, we obtain estimates of κ and σ as the solutions that minimize the above.

We remark that the variance $V_{\Delta t}$ is increasing in Δt almost linearly, and so the former form (8.8) is more subject to terms with a large i than the latter form, equation (8.9). Succinctly, the latter formulation is considered to be suitable for approximation. Additionally we remark that this method is limited to cases with positive mean reversion.

Example 8.2

As an example of calibration, we examine the Japanese LIBOR swap rates from 16 June 2008 to 31 August 2009. For convenience, we regard the six-month LIBOR as the instantaneous spot rate $r(t)$. We set $\Delta t_1 = 1$, $\Delta t_2 = 5$, $\Delta t_3 = 10$, $\Delta t_4 = 20$, and $\Delta t_5 = 40$ (days).

Solving the least squares problem for the standard deviation (8.9), we obtain $\sigma = 0.0318$ and $\kappa = 0.00492$. Fig. 8.1 compares the observation and the approximation, where the dots represents $\sqrt{V_{\Delta t_i}}$ for each i, and the bold line represents the volatility of equation (8.6) in the Hull–White model with the above parameters.

Naturally, this approach is limited to cases with positive mean reversion and restricted to using a short interval Δt in the sampling interval. Indeed if we set $\Delta t = 10$ (years), we need data from a very long period (more than a century). From this, the short rate approach is restricted in its ability to estimate the volatility for the short-term structure.

8.3 Historical Volatility of Forward Rate

This section studies volatility estimation for the Hull–White model within the HJM framework.

The Hull–White model in the HJM framework

Section 4.4 showed that the Hull–White model with parameters σ and κ is represented by the HJM model with the volatility

$$\sigma(t, T) = \sigma \exp\{-\kappa(T - t)\}. \tag{8.10}$$

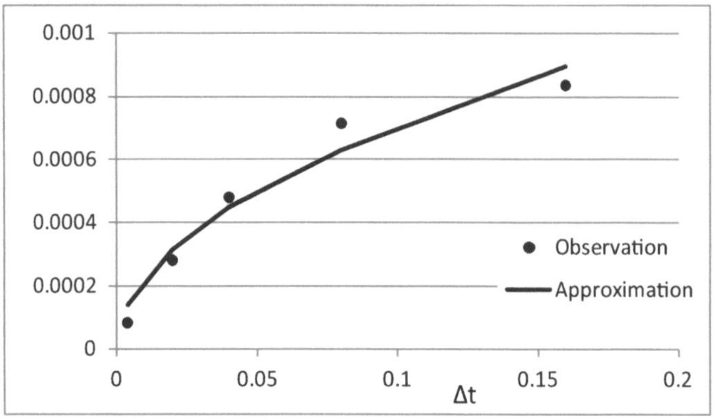

Figure 8.1: Volatility structure in the Hull–White model. "Observation" represents $\sqrt{V_{\Delta t}}$, and "approximation" represents $\sqrt{Var[r(\Delta t)]}$. The LIBOR/swap rates were provided by Mizuho Information and Research Institute.

For convenience, we refer to this volatility structure as the *Hull–White volatility*. And so the forward rate process $f(t,T)$ is described under $\mathbf{P}$, from equations (4.50) and (8.10), as

$$\begin{aligned} f(t,T) &= f(0,T) + \int_0^t \frac{\sigma^2}{\kappa} e^{-\kappa(T-s)}[1 - e^{-\kappa(T-s)}]ds \\ &\quad +\sigma \int_0^t e^{-\kappa(T-s)}\varphi_s ds + \sigma \int_0^t e^{-\kappa(T-s)} dW_s. \end{aligned} \tag{8.11}$$

We here study construction of the volatility structure by working with this form. The corresponding market price of risk will be estimated in Section 8.4.

Volatility fitting

We determine the parameters κ and σ such that the Hull–White volatility approximates the first principal volatility component. For this, we use least squares approximation for fitting.

We set a time-length sequence $x_i,\ i = 1, \cdots, n$ with $x_i < x_{i+1}$. Let $\Delta t > 0$ be fixed and $t_k = \Delta t k, k = 1, \cdots, J+1$ be a sequence of observation dates. For an observation dataset $F(t_k, x_i)$, we set

$$\Delta F_i(t_k) = F(t_{k+1}, x_i - \Delta t) - F(t_k, x_i). \tag{8.12}$$

From the covariance of $\Delta F_i(t_k)$, PCA identifies the principal components e^l and the eigenvalues ρ_l for $l = 1, \cdots, n$.

We approximate the first volatility component $\rho_1 e_i^1$ by $\sigma \exp(-\kappa x_i)$, with σ and κ chosen such that

$$\rho_1 e_i^1 \approx \sigma \exp(-\kappa x_i). \tag{8.13}$$

Consider the least squares problem

$$\sum_{i=1}^{n} \{\rho_1 e_i^1 - \sigma \exp(-\kappa x_i)\}^2 \tag{8.14}$$

under the restriction

$$(\rho_1)^2 = \sigma^2 \sum_{i=1}^{n} \exp(-2\kappa x_i). \tag{8.15}$$

Solving this yields σ and κ.

The condition (8.15) is referred to as the *norm-invariant condition*; it ensures that the implied Hull–White volatility has the same norm as that of the first volatility component. If we do not impose this condition, then the implied Hull–White volatility may have a norm different from that of the first volatility component ρ_1. This difference makes the numerical procedure unnecessarily complicated for real-world modeling. To avoid this, we assume the norm-invariant condition, which will be successfully applied for the estimation of the market price of risk in Section 8.4

Once we have determined σ and κ, we obtain the Hull–White volatility by setting $\sigma(0, x_i) = \sigma \exp(-\kappa x_i)$ for each i.

Humped volatility

The volatility structure $\sigma(0, x_i)$ is not always observed to be exponentially decaying on i. Sometimes, we observe a humped volatility structure; that is, the volatility increases from the spot rate to the middle-term forward rate and decreases in the long term. Using an actual example, we give some remarks about the calibration.

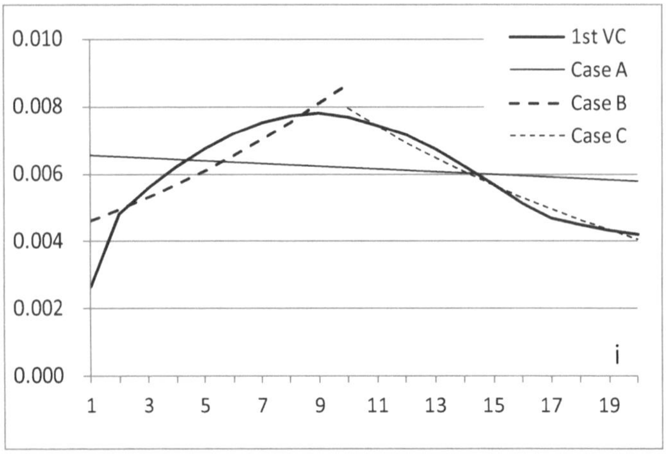

Figure 8.2: Approximation of the first volatility component by the Hull–White volatility "1st VC" represents the first volatility component. Implied forward rates are obtained from the Japanese LIBOR swap market from 16 June 2008 to 31 August 2009. Interest rate data are the same as in Fig. 8.1. The forward rates and the principal volatility component were calculated by the author.

Example 8.3.1 (Humped volatility)

Set $\delta = 0.5$ (year) and $i = 1, \cdots, 20$. From the same data as in Example 8.2, we obtain the implied six-month forward rates, which we regard as the instantaneous forward rates.

The bold line in Fig. 8.2 shows the first volatility component, which is humped—increasing up to $i = 9$ and decreasing from $i = 9$ to $i = 20$. This is troublesome when modeling the Hull–White volatility $\sigma \exp(-\kappa x)$ because this function is monotone on x. The second column in Table 8.2 shows the first principal component of the historical data, as derived by PCA.

Example 8.3.2 (Calibration for humped volatility)

To fit the Hull–White volatility to the humped structure, we consider three calibration styles, as follows. In Case A, we estimate the parameters σ and κ from the principal component for $i = 1, \cdots, 20$, which corresponds to entire evolution of the forward rates. In Case B, we estimate the parameters with $i = 1, \cdots, 10$, which corresponds to the dynamics of the short- and middle-term forward rates. In Case C, we estimate the parameters with $i = 10, \cdots, 20$, which corresponds to the evolution of the middle- and long-term forward rates.

Table 8.1: Volatility fitting in the Hull–White model. "1st VC" represents the first volatility component. Forward rates and the volatility component are the same as in Fig. 8.2.

		$\sigma \exp(-\kappa x_i)$		
		Case A	Case B	Case C
i	1st VC	$i = 1, \cdots, 20$	$i = 1, \cdots, 10$	$i = 10, \cdots, 20$
1	0.00264	0.00656	0.00461	
2	0.00481	0.00651	0.00495	
3	0.00558	0.00647	0.00531	
4	0.00620	0.00643	0.00569	
5	0.00676	0.00639	0.00611	
6	0.00720	0.00635	0.00655	
7	0.00753	0.00630	0.00703	
8	0.00774	0.00626	0.00754	
9	0.00779	0.00622	0.00809	
10	0.00767	0.00618	0.00868	0.00795
11	0.00744	0.00614		0.00743
12	0.00715	0.00610		0.00695
13	0.00675	0.00606		0.00649
14	0.00623	0.00602		0.00607
15	0.00566	0.00598		0.00567
16	0.00512	0.00595		0.00530
17	0.00471	0.00591		0.00496
18	0.00449	0.00587		0.00463
19	0.00433	0.00583		0.00433
20	0.00421	0.00579		0.00405

The results are shown in Fig. 8.2 and Table 8.1. The third column in Table 8.1 and the narrow solid line in Fig. 8.2 show the Hull–White volatility estimated in Case A, with σ and κ shown in Table 8.2, where the mean reversion rate is seen to be slightly positive, at 0.0130. Thus, the volatility is modeled with weakly positive mean reversion for the entire forward rates.

In Case B, the Hull–White volatility is shown as the fourth column in Table 8.1 and the bold dashed line in Fig. 8.2. From Table 8.2, the mean reversion rate is seen to be remarkably negative, at -0.1405; that is, the volatility is modeled so as to represent a negative mean reversion for short- and middle-term forward rates.

The rightmost column of Table 8.1 and the narrow dashed line in Fig. 8.2 show the Hull–White volatility in Case C. From Table 8.2, we see that the mean reversion rate is obviously positive, at 0.1350. Thus, the volatility is modeled so as to represent a positive mean reversion for middle- and long-term forward rates.

This humped structure is typically observed, rather than being a rare event, and so we reasonably hesitate over which method to choose. Although we work with the Hull–White model here, which method for calibration is reasonable depends on the properties of the interest rate risk specific to each financial institution and each portfolio. When a financial institution (or portfolio) has mostly short-term interest rate risk, the method of Case B is appropriate. However, when a financial institution has both short- and long-term interest rate risk, the method of Case A may be appropriate. Making this choice is a financial engineering matter.

For comparison, the rightmost column in Table 8.2 exhibits the parameter obtained in Section 8.2, that is, the volatility implied by the short rate distribution. This result is quite different from all those of Cases A, B, and C.

Humped volatility model

Furthermore, if we intend to model the humped volatility structure in its entirety, it might be better to depart from the Hull–White model. The humped volatility is modeled in Bhar *et al.* (2002), Mercurio and Moraleda (2000), and Moraleda and Vorst (1997), among others, in the form

$$\sigma(t,T) = \sigma\{\gamma(T-t)+1\}\exp\{-\kappa(T-t)\}, \tag{8.16}$$

where σ, γ, and κ are positive constants. This function is humped when $\gamma > \kappa$. For details, readers should consult Brigo and Mercurio (2007) and Nawalkha

Table 8.2: Parameters in the Hull–White model for three cases. The column labeled "Short rate" represents the results from Section 8.2.

	Case A	Case B	Case C	Short rate
σ	0.0066	0.0043	0.0156	0.0318
κ	0.0130	-0.1405	0.1350	0.0049

et al. (2007). It might be possible to construct the real-world model with this volatility as an application of the argument in the next section.

However, when working with non parametric models, there is a way to work with the first principal component as the volatility in the HJM model such that $\sigma(0, x_i) = \rho_1 e_i^1$ for $i = 1, \cdots, n$, where $(\rho_1)^2$ is the first eigenvalue and e^1 is the first principal component; that is, we would be considering a one-factor HJM model. For that case, the real-world model can be built as shown in Section 6.9.

8.4 Real-world Modeling

In this section, we present a method of calculating the market price of risk in a one-factor Hull–White model, applying Theorem 6.3.2. The approach here is basically taken with reference to real-world modeling in the Gaussian HJM model.

First, we note an important difference between the Hull–White model and the Gaussian HJM model in real-world modeling. For this, we recall the simulation form (6.87) in a full-factor Gaussian HJM model, which is

$$f(\Delta s, T_i) = f(0, T_i) + E^H \left[\frac{\Delta F_i}{\Delta t} \right] \Delta s + \sqrt{\Delta s} \sigma_{0i} W_1. \tag{8.17}$$

Here, the second term is determined from the observed rolled trend for each i, and we can use an arbitrary volatility structure for σ_{0i}.

In the Hull–White model, the volatility is parametrically given by the function $\sigma \exp\{-\kappa(T - t)\}$, and the drift term is determined from this volatility and the market price of risk. From this, the drift term is different from the observed rolled trend due to the use of one-dimensional modeling.

First volatility component

Let $t_k, k = 1, \cdots, J + 1$ and $x_i, i = 1, \cdots, n$ be the same as in Section 8.3. Suppose that we have already obtained the first eigenvalue $(\rho)^2$ and the first principal component $(e_1, \cdots, e_n)^T$. For clarity, we denote ρ_1 as ρ in this section and do the same with other variables.

To determine the parameters κ and σ, recall the least squares problem

(8.14),

$$\sum_{i=1}^{n} \{\rho e_i - \sigma \exp(-\kappa x_i)\}^2. \tag{8.18}$$

We determine σ and κ by finding the solution that minimizes the above equation and satisfies the norm-invariant condition (8.15),

$$(\rho)^2 = \sigma^2 \sum_{i=1}^{n} \exp(-2\kappa x_i). \tag{8.19}$$

From these parameters, we set the volatility σ_{0i} from the Hull–White volatility such that

$$\sigma_{0i} = \sigma \exp(-\kappa x_i) \quad ; \quad i = 1, \cdots, n. \tag{8.20}$$

We may also call $(\sigma_{01}, \cdots, \sigma_{0n})^T$ the Hull–White volatility. Next, we define an n-dimensional vector $(\tilde{e}_1, \cdots, \tilde{e}_n)^T$ by

$$\tilde{e}_i = \frac{\sigma}{\rho} \exp(-\kappa x_i) \quad ; \quad i = 1, \cdots, n. \tag{8.21}$$

From equation (8.19), we see that

$$\sum_{i=1}^{n} (\tilde{e}_i)^2 = 1. \tag{8.22}$$

Hence, we may regard $(\tilde{e}_1, \cdots, \tilde{e}_n)^T$ as the first principal component. Since it holds that

$$\sigma_{0i} = \rho \tilde{e}_i \quad ; \quad i = 1, \cdots, n, \tag{8.23}$$

the Hull–White volatility $(\sigma_{01}, \cdots, \sigma_{0n})^T$ can be regarded as the first volatility component. Thus, the volatility structure σ_{0i} is determined by equation (8.20) or, equivalently, by equation (8.23).

Norm-invariant condition

A remark on the norm-invariant condition, which we imposed on the least squares problem (8.18), might help here. In numerical analysis, the norm of the minimizing solution might be slightly different from that of the original first volatility component, $(\rho e_1, \cdots, \rho e_n)^T$. For this reason, equation (8.22) does not necessary hold, and so we impose the condition (8.19) on the approximation. This means that we obtain the Hull-White volatility as a new volatility component, and this setup makes it easy to calculate the market price of risk, which we will see later.

Calculation of β

By equation (4.49), we have

$$\begin{aligned} \sigma_{0i}v_{0i} &= \sigma(0, x_i)v(0, x_i) \\ &= -\frac{\sigma^2}{\kappa}\exp(-\kappa x_i)\{1 - \exp(-\kappa x_i)\} \;\; ; \;\; i = 1, \cdots, n. \end{aligned} \tag{8.24}$$

From this relation, we obtain the constant β, defined in equation (6.16) by

$$\beta = \sum_{i=1}^{n} \sigma_{0i}v_{0i}\tilde{e}_i. \tag{8.25}$$

Drift term

It is not trivial to apply Theorem 6.3.2 to the Hull–White model because of the use of one-dimensional modeling with parametric volatility. So we must carefully develop our argument, which follows.

To estimate the market price of risk within the Gaussian HJM framework, we recall $\alpha_l(t_k)$, defined in equation (6.15) as

$$\alpha_l(t_k) = \frac{1}{\Delta t}\sum_{i=1}^{n} \Delta F_i(t_k)e_i^l \;\; ; \;\; l = 1, \cdots, d, k = 1, \cdots, J. \tag{8.26}$$

We note that this equation is valid for a multi-factor model where the principal volatility components are employed and the rank of the covariance is equal to d. If the observed data $\Delta F_i(t_k)$ follow the one-factor Hull–White model, then we may assume that this is the case in which $d = 1$. In reality, market data do not typically satisfy this assumption. Therefore, we artificially determine $\alpha(t_k)$ as

$$\alpha(t_k) = \sum_{i=1}^{n} \frac{\Delta F_i(t_k)}{\Delta t}\tilde{e}_i \;\; ; \;\; k = 1, \cdots, J. \tag{8.27}$$

Fortunately, we can regard $\tilde{e}$ as the first principal component, and so Proposition B.2.1 implies that the above $\alpha(t_k)$ is the solution to the approximation

$$\frac{\Delta F_i(t_k)}{\Delta t} \approx \alpha(t_k)\tilde{e}_i. \tag{8.28}$$

This means that the change in the forward rates $(\Delta F_1(t_k), \cdots, \Delta F_n(t_k))^T$ are approximated by a simple scaling of the Hull-White volatility. In fact, from the following argument, we shall see that we do not need to compute $\alpha(t_k)$ for each t_k.

Market price of risk

Note that we are working in the one-dimensional principal component space determined by the Hull–White volatility. Theorem 6.3.2 implies that

$$\varphi = \frac{1}{\rho}\sum_{i=1}^{n}\left\{E^H\left[\frac{\Delta F_i}{\Delta t}\right] + \sigma_{0i}v_{0i}\right\}\tilde{e}_i. \tag{8.29}$$

Substituting equations (8.25) and (8.27) into the above, we obtain an alternative expression of φ as $\varphi = \frac{1}{\rho}(E^H[\alpha] + \beta)$.

From the definition (6.58), we calculate the first rolled trend score R as

$$R = \sum_{i=1}^{n} E^H\left[\frac{\Delta F_i}{\Delta t}\right]\tilde{e}_i. \tag{8.30}$$

Lemma 6.4.1 asserts that $E^H[\alpha] = R$. From this, we have

$$\varphi = \frac{R+\beta}{\rho}. \tag{8.31}$$

This means that we can obtain φ without needing $\alpha(t_k), k = 1, \cdots, J$, which is the reason that we do not need to calculate them (as stated above).

We note that there might be a more elegant method to derive the form (8.31).

8.5 Simulation Model

We finally present a form for simulation under $\mathbf{P}$. Set $T_i = x_i$ for $i = 1, \cdots, n$; here, T_i indicates the date and x_i indicates the time length. Let $f(0, T_i), i = 1, \cdots, n$ be an initial forward rate.

We remark that we cannot use the form (6.87),

$$f(\Delta s, T_i) = f(0, T_i) + E^H\left[\frac{\Delta F_i}{\Delta t}\right]\Delta s + \sqrt{\Delta s}\sigma_{0i}W_1, \tag{8.32}$$

because this is valid for only the full-factor model. From the argument for the drift term in the previous section, it is practical to work with the form (6.74) for simulation in the Hull–White model, as

$$f(\Delta s, T_i) = f(0, T_i) + \{-\sigma_{0i}v_{0i} + \sigma_{0i}\varphi\}\Delta s + \sqrt{\Delta s}\sigma_{0i}W_1. \tag{8.33}$$

Substituting equations (8.20) and (8.24) into the above, we obtain

$$\begin{aligned} f(\Delta s, T_i) &= f(0, T_i) + \left\{\frac{\sigma^2}{\kappa}e^{-\kappa x_i}(1 - e^{-\kappa x_i}) + \sigma_{0i}\varphi\right\}\Delta s + \sqrt{\Delta s}\sigma_{0i}W_1 \\ &= f(0, T_i) + \sigma e^{-\kappa x_i}\left\{\frac{\sigma}{\kappa}(1 - e^{-\kappa x_i}) + \varphi\right\}\Delta s \\ &\quad + \sqrt{\Delta s}\sigma e^{-\kappa x_i}W_1. \end{aligned} \tag{8.34}$$

This is the form of the real-world simulation in the Hull–White model. From this and equation (8.31), we obtain the following theorem.

Theorem 8.5.1 (1) *In a one-factor Hull–White model, the market price of risk is estimated by* $\varphi = (R + \beta)/\rho$, *where* R *and* β *are obtained by equations (8.30) and (8.25), respectively, and* $(\rho)^2$ *is the first eigenvalue.*
(2) *A single-period simulation for a short time period* Δs *is given by*

$$\begin{aligned} f(\Delta s, T_i) &= f(0, T_i) + \sigma e^{-\kappa x_i}\left\{\frac{\sigma}{\kappa}(1 - e^{-\kappa x_i}) + \varphi\right\}\Delta s \\ &\quad + \sqrt{\Delta s}\sigma e^{-\kappa x_i}W_1. \end{aligned} \tag{8.35}$$

Similarly to Theorem 7.1.1, the following corollary specifies the distributions of $f(\Delta s, T_i)$ under $\mathbf{P}$ and $\mathbf{Q}$, for which the proof is obvious.

Corollary 8.5.2 *In a one-factor Hull–White model, let us consider two simulation forms for* $f(\Delta s, T_i)$*: by equation (8.35) under* $\mathbf{P}$*, and by equation (8.11) under* $\mathbf{Q}$.

(1) *$f(\Delta s, T_i)$ is normally distributed under $\mathbf{P}$ and $\mathbf{Q}$, and the expectations under each measures are given by*

$$E[f(\Delta s, T_i)] = f(0, T_i) + \sigma e^{-\kappa x_i} \left\{ \frac{\sigma}{\kappa}(1 - e^{-\kappa x_i}) + \varphi \right\} \Delta s, \tag{8.36}$$

$$E^{\mathbf{Q}}[f(\Delta s, T_i)] = f(0, T_i) + \frac{\sigma^2}{\kappa} e^{-\kappa x_i} \{1 - e^{-\kappa x_i}\} \Delta s. \tag{8.37}$$

The variance of $f(\Delta s, T_i)$ in both models is equal to $\Delta s \sigma^2 \exp(-2\kappa x_i)$.
(2) *The expected difference in $f(\Delta s, T_i)$ between the real-world model and the risk-neutral model is given by*

$$E[f(\Delta s, T_i)] - E^{\mathbf{Q}}[f(\Delta s, T_i)] = \sigma e^{-\kappa x_i} \varphi \Delta s. \tag{8.38}$$

From the second result, the real-world model simulates higher (resp., lower) forward rates than the risk-neutral model under $\mathbf{Q}$ when the market price of risk is positive (resp., negative).

We remark that the dimensional reduction to a one-factor model cannot avoid introducing model risk when C_d is not sufficiently close to 1. This is a typical problem in financial engineering for one-dimensional modeling.

Nelson–Siegel model

Although this book does not study real-world modeling by using the Nelson–Siegel term structure, this term structure is sometimes employed in the study of economics. Here, we briefly address ourselves to the real-world modeling of the Nelson–Siegel term structure model.

By a method analogous to the argument in Section 8.4, it is possible to construct a two- or three-factor model using the Nelson–Siegel function.

Let T_i and x_i be the same as above, and let a two-dimensional volatility be given by the Nelson–Siegel function as

$$\sigma^1(0, T) = 1 \tag{8.39a}$$

$$\sigma^2(0, T) = e^{-c_1 T} - c_2, \tag{8.39b}$$

where c_1 and c_2 are positive constants; $\sigma^1(0, T)$ represents a parallel shift in the forward rate curve, which corresponds to the first principal component; and $\sigma^2(0, T)$ represents a slope change in the curve, which corresponds to the second principal component. In particular, c_1 corresponds somewhat to the mean reversion rate in the Hull–White model.

Next, for some integers i and j with $1 \le i < j \le n$, we determine c_2 by

$$c_2 = \frac{1}{2}(e^{-c_1 x_i} + e^{-c_1 x_j}). \tag{8.40}$$

Here, i and j are chosen such that the volatility structure (8.39b) adequately explains the historical term structure.

For example, we may set $i = 1$ and $j = n$. From this, it follows that

$$\sigma^1 = (\sigma^1_{01}, \sigma^1_{0n}) = (1, 1) \tag{8.41a}$$

$$\sigma^2 = (\sigma^2_{01}, \sigma^2_{0n}) = (e^{-c_1 x_1} - c_2, e^{-c_1 x_n} - c_2). \tag{8.41b}$$

A direct calculation from equation (8.40) implies that

$$\begin{aligned} \sigma^1\sigma^2 &= \sigma^1_{01}\sigma^2_{01} + \sigma^1_{0n}\sigma^2_{0n} \\ &= (e^{-c_1 x_1} - c_2) + (e^{-c_1 x_n} - c_2) \\ &= 0. \end{aligned} \tag{8.42}$$

Then, σ^1 is orthogonal to σ^2 when we consider only two grid points, at x_1 and x_n.

We may regard σ^1 and σ^2 as volatility components obtained by PCA. Combining this with the argument in Section 8.4 for the Hull–White model, the market price of risk is estimated in the manner developed in Section 6.2. The rest is entrusted to readers.

8.6 Numerical Procedure

We already see that the Hull–White model is simple to construct as a real-world model. This section summarizes a numerical procedure for estimating the market price of risk and constructs a Monte Carlo simulation model. Since the calculation is completed in a one-dimensional model, the subscript "1" for vectors to indicate that they are the first factor number is omitted. Numerical examples will be shown in Sections 10.3 and 10.4.

Let x_i, t_k, and $\Delta F_i(t_k)$ be the same as in Section 6.9; here, $i = 1, \cdots, n$ and $k = 1, \cdots, J+1$.

Market price of risk

1) $F(t_{k+1}, x_i - \Delta t)$ is obtained by the interpolation (6.93), and $\Delta F_i(t_k)$ is given by equation (6.92) for $i, k,\ i = 1, \cdots, n,\ k = 1, \cdots, J$.

2) The eigenvalue $(\rho)^2$ and the principal component $e = (e_1, \cdots, e_n)^T$ are obtained by PCA for the covariance $Cov(\Delta F_i(t_k), \Delta F_j(t_k))/\Delta t$. Here, we set ρ such that $\rho > 0$.

3) We determine the parameters σ and κ by solving the least squares problem (8.14),

$$\sum_{i=1}^{n} \{\rho e_i - \sigma \exp(-\kappa x_i)\}^2, \tag{8.43}$$

under the norm-invariant condition, $(\rho)^2 = \sum_{i=1}^{n} \sigma^2 \exp(-2\kappa x_i)$.

4) We define the n-dimensional vector $(\tilde{e}_1, \cdots, \tilde{e}_n)$ by

$$\tilde{e}_i = \frac{\sigma}{\rho} \exp(-\kappa x_i) \quad ; \quad i = 1, \cdots, n, \tag{8.44}$$

and set the Hull–White volatility from $\sigma_{0i} = \rho \tilde{e}_i$ for $i = 1, \cdots, n$.

5) From equations (8.24) and (8.25), we calculate $\sigma_{0i} v_{0i}$ as

$$\sigma_{0i} v_{0i} = -\frac{\sigma^2}{\kappa} \exp(-\kappa x_i)\{1 - \exp(-\kappa x_i)\}. \tag{8.45}$$

6) The constant β is calculated from equations (8.44) and (8.45) as $\beta = \sum_{i=1}^{n} \sigma_{0i} v_{0i} \tilde{e}_i$.

7) We calculate the rolled trend $E^H[\Delta F_i/\Delta t]$ from $\Delta F_i(t_k)$ for all i.

8) By equation (8.30), the first rolled trend score is obtained by

$$R = \sum_{i=1}^{n} E^H\left[\frac{\Delta F_i}{\Delta t}\right] \tilde{e}_i. \tag{8.46}$$

9) The market price of risk is estimated from equation (8.31) as $\varphi = (R + \beta)/\rho$.

Monte Carlo simulation

1) Set $x_i = T_i$ for $i = 1, \cdots, n$.

2) Let $f(0, T_i), i = 1, \cdots, n$ be an initial forward rate.

3) Determine the volatility structure and estimate the market price of risk according to the previous procedures, from 1) to 9).

4) From equation (8.35), a single-period simulation for a short time interval Δs under $\mathbf{P}$ is represented by

$$\begin{aligned} f(\Delta s, T_i) &= f(0, T_i) + \sigma e^{-\kappa x_i} \left\{ \frac{\sigma}{\kappa}(1 - e^{-\kappa x_i}) + \varphi \right\} \Delta s \\ &\quad + \sqrt{\Delta s} \sigma e^{-\kappa x_i} W_1, \end{aligned} \tag{8.47}$$

with $i = 1, \cdots, n$. Here, W_1 is a one-dimensional standard normal distribution.

CHAPTER 9

REAL-WORLD MODEL IN THE LIBOR MARKET MODEL

Abstract: This section of the book develops the theory of simulation in the LMRW. Although the theory for this is developed similarly to that for the Gaussian HJM model, the results here are somewhat more complicated than those. In particular, the drift term in the LMRW has an additional feature that makes it different from that in the Gaussian model. Moreover, the methods for reducing dimensionality and constructing the drift term for use in simulation are different from those for the Gaussian model. Readers are recommended to review the corresponding results in Chapter 6 to more deeply understand the properties of the LMRW.

Most of the arguments in this chapter are based on Yasuoka (2013a); Section 9.2 is newly written to describe maximum likelihood estimation for the market price of risk.

Some numerical examples will be shown in Chapter 10, using the same historical data as in the example for the Gaussian HJM model.

Keyword: Complete market, Dimensionality reduction, Eigenvalue, Full-factor model, Interpretation of the market price of risk, Least squares problem, LIBOR market model, LMRW, Log-scale observable trend, Log-scale rolled trend, Market price of risk, Monte Carlo simulation, Maximum likelihood estimation, MPR score, Negative price tendency, PCA, Principal component score, Properties of simulation, Real-world measure, Real-world simulation, State space setup, Volatility component

Takashi Yasuoka

We have already studied a real-world model, the Gaussian HJM model, in Chapter 6. The drawback of the Gaussian model is that it generates negative interest rates. To allow satisfying the practical requirement of a positive interest rate model, this section develops a theory of simulation in the LMRW. The structure of the arguments used to develop this model are parallel to those applied to the Gaussian HJM model, following Yasuoka (2013a).

9.1 Discretization of LIBOR Process

In this section, we introduce a basic setup to describe the observation of LIBOR data in the framework of the LMRW.

Setup of LIBOR processes

Let $\tau > 0$ be a time horizon, and let $0 < T_1 < \cdots < T_{n+1} = \tau$ be a sequence of maturity dates such that $T_{i+1} - T_i = \delta_i > 0$ for all i. Then, x_i is defined as the time length to T_i at $t = 0$ for all i. In this chapter, we assume that the market is complete and arbitrage-free, meaning that the market price of risk is determined uniquely.

We denote by $L_i(t)$ the forward LIBOR observed at t over the period $[T_i, T_{i+1}]$, and by $\lambda_i(t)$ a d-dimensional deterministic volatility of $L_i(t)$, where we assume that $0 < d \leq n$. A d-dimensional process $\chi_i(t)$ is defined in equation (5.9) as

$$\chi_i(t) = \frac{\lambda_i(t)\delta_i L_i(t)}{1 + \delta_i L_i(t)}. \tag{9.1}$$

We remark that we sometimes use L_i, λ_i, and χ_i instead of $L_i(t)$, $\lambda_i(t)$, and $\chi_i(t)$, respectively, for the sake of brevity. Other variables are treated the same.

In the LMRW, the LIBOR process is expressed from equation (5.10) as

$$L_i(t) = L_i(0) \exp\left\{ \int_0^t \left(\lambda_i \sum_{j=m(t)}^{i} \chi_j + \lambda_i \varphi - \frac{|\lambda_i|^2}{2} \right) dt + \int_0^t \lambda_i dW_t \right\}, \tag{9.2}$$

for $i = 1, \cdots, n$, where W_t is a d-dimensional Brownian motion under $\mathbf{P}$.

Let $\{t_k\}_{k=1,\cdots,J+1}$ be a sequence of observation times with $t_{k+1} - t_k = \Delta t > 0$, where $J + 1$ $(J > 0)$ is the number of observation times and $\Delta t > 0$ is a

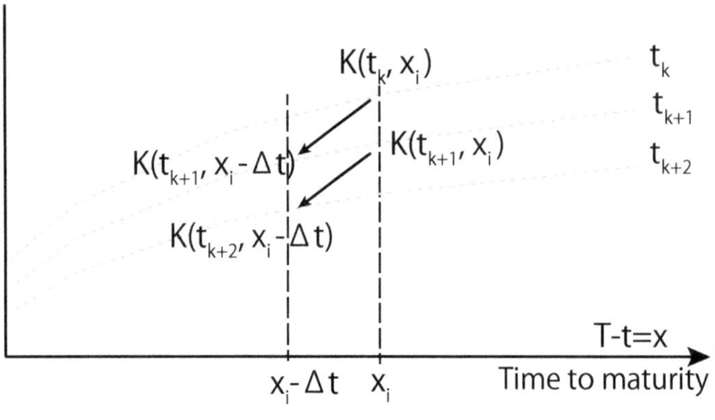

Figure 9.1: Observation of forward LIBOR. The forward LIBOR is observed in the form $K(t, x_i)$, for a fixed value of x_i, at t_k, t_{k+1}, and t_{k+2}.

constant. The Euler approximation of equation (9.2) implies

$$\begin{aligned} \log L_i(t + \Delta t) &= \log L_i(t) + \left\{ \lambda_i \sum_{j=m(t)}^{i} \chi_j(t) + \lambda_i \varphi - \frac{|\lambda_i|^2}{2} \right\} \Delta t \\ &\quad + \sqrt{\Delta t} \lambda_i W_1, \end{aligned} \tag{9.3}$$

where $W_1 = \int_0^1 dW$ is a d-dimensional standard normal distribution.

Observation of forward LIBOR

For simplicity, we assume in the following that $T_{i+1} - T_i = \delta > 0$ for all i with $T_1 = \delta$. Setting $T - t = x$ and $x_i = \delta i$ for all i, we denote by $K(t_k, x_i)$ the implied forward LIBOR on the period $[t_k + x_i, t_k + x_{i+1}]$ as observed at time t_k. Further, we assume that $K(t_k, x_i)$ is continuously extended to $K(t, x)$ for arbitrary t and x. Then, it holds that

$$L_i(t) = K(t, x_i - t) \ ; \ \ i = 1, \cdots, n. \tag{9.4}$$

We usually obtain the forward LIBOR from the LIBOR/swap rates in the form $K(t, \delta i)$, rather than in the form $L_i(t)$, because we observe the term structure of the LIBOR/swap rates with respect to the term length x_i. Fig. 9.1 visually illustrates this observation. The dashed lines exhibit forward LIBOR curves observed at times $t_k, t_{k+1},$ and t_{k+2}, and the forward LIBOR is written in the form $K(t_1, x_i), \cdots, K(t_{J+1}, x_i)$ for a fixed x_i.

We assume that the volatility corresponding to the process $K(t_k - t, \delta i - t)$ with $t \in [0, \Delta t]$ is given by $\lambda_i(0)$ for all k. Additionally, we write $\lambda_{0i} = \lambda_i(0)$ for convenience. With this, we define a sequence[1] $\kappa_j(t_k), k = 1, \cdots, J+1$ as

$$\kappa_j(t_k) = \frac{\lambda_{0j}\delta K(t_k, \delta j)}{1 + \delta K(t_k, \delta j)} \quad ; \quad k = 1, \cdots, J+1. \tag{9.5}$$

Replacing $\chi_j(t)$ of equation (9.1) with $\kappa_j(t_k)$, equation (9.3) becomes

$$\begin{aligned} \log K(t_k + \Delta t, x_i - \Delta t) &= \log K(t_k, x_i) + \left\{ \lambda_{0i} \sum_{j=1}^{i} \kappa_j(t_k) \right. \\ &\quad \left. + \lambda_{0i}\varphi - \frac{|\lambda_{0i}|^2}{2} \right\} \Delta t + \sqrt{\Delta t}\lambda_{0i} W_1, \end{aligned} \tag{9.6}$$

where we set $m(t_k) = 1$ in equation (9.3) for all k with $t_k = 0+0$. For this, we remark that if $t_k = 0$ then it originally holds that $m(t) = 0$. However, equation (9.6) is obtained from integration of $t \in (0, \Delta t]$, where $m(t) = 1$. Then, we may substitute $m(t_k) = 1$ into the term $\sum_{j=m(t_k)}^{i} \kappa_j(t_k)$ in equation (9.6).

9.2 Estimation of the Market Price of Risk

This section presents the maximum likelihood estimation of the market price of risk in the LIBOR market model.

PCA

In the manner developed in Section 6.2, we represent the LIBOR process in a principal component space.

A sample covariance matrix V is obtained from

$$\begin{aligned} V_{ij} &= \frac{1}{\Delta t} Cov\left(\log K(t_k + \Delta t, x_i - \Delta t) - \log K(t_k, x_i),\right. \\ &\quad \left. \log K(t_k + \Delta t, x_j - \Delta t) - \log K(t_k, x_j)\right), \end{aligned} \tag{9.7}$$

[1] We note that the symbol κ_j here does not indicate the mean reversion rate from the Hull–White model.

for $i, j = 1, \cdots, n$. We assume that the covariance matrix V has rank $d \leq n$. Similarly to the approach in Section 6.2, V is decomposed into

$$V_{ij} = \sum_{l=1}^{d} e_i^l (\rho_l)^2 e_j^l \quad ; \quad 1 \leq i \leq n, 1 \leq j \leq n, \tag{9.8}$$

where $(\rho_l)^2$ is the lth eigenvalue, and $e^l = (e_1^l, \cdots, e_n^l)$ is the lth principal component. Here, we always assume that

$$e_1^l > 0, \ \rho_l > 0 \ ; \quad l = 1, \cdots, d, \tag{9.9}$$

and that all eigenvalues are distinct. This assumption is the same as that used in the real-world model for the Gaussian HJM model.

Since V is a symmetric matrix, the set of principal components $e^1, \cdots, e^d$ is orthonormal by Proposition A.2.2; specifically,

$$\sum_{i=1}^{n} e_i^l e_i^h = \delta_{lh} \quad ; \quad 1 \leq l, \leq d, 1 \leq h \leq d. \tag{9.10}$$

Principal component space

We set the principal volatility component as

$$\lambda_{0i}^l = \rho_l e_i^l \quad ; \quad i = 1, \cdots, n, \ l = 1, \cdots, d. \tag{9.11}$$

Next, we represent the dynamics of the forward LIBOR by using PCA. Similarly to that approach in Section 6.2, we call $\lambda^l = (\lambda_{01}^l, \cdots, \lambda_{0n}^l)^T$ the *lth principal volatility component*, or the *lth volatility component* for short. It follows that

$$\begin{aligned} |\lambda^l|^2 &= \sum_{i=1}^{n} (\rho_l e_i^l)^2 = |\rho_l|^2 \sum_{i=1}^{n} (e_i^l)^2 \\ &= (\rho_l)^2. \end{aligned} \tag{9.12}$$

From this, ρ_l indicates the magnitude of the lth volatility component λ^l.

Since the rank of V is d, the $n \times d$ matrix $(\lambda^1, \cdots, \lambda^d)$ has rank d. We set $\Delta \tilde{K}_i(y_k)$ as

$$\Delta \tilde{K}_i(t_k) = \log K(t_{k+1}, x_i - \Delta t) - \log K(t_k, x_i). \tag{9.13}$$

With this, equation (9.6) becomes

$$\begin{aligned}\Delta\tilde{K}_i(t_k) &= \left\{\lambda_{0i}\sum_{j=1}^{i}\kappa_j(t_k)+\lambda_{0i}\varphi-\frac{|\lambda_{0i}|^2}{2}\right\}\Delta t+\sqrt{\Delta t}\lambda_{0i}W_1\\ &= \left\{\lambda_{0i}\sum_{j=1}^{i}\kappa_j(t_k)+\sum_{m=1}^{d}\lambda_{0i}^m\varphi_m-\frac{|\lambda_{0i}|^2}{2}\right\}\Delta t\\ &\quad +\sqrt{\Delta t}\sum_{m=1}^{d}\lambda_{0i}^m W_1^m \ ; \quad i=1,\cdots,n. \end{aligned}\tag{9.14}$$

Consider a d-dimensional principal component space spanned by $e^1,\cdots,e^d$. Regarding

$$\left(\frac{\Delta\tilde{K}_1(t_k)}{\Delta t},\cdots,\frac{\Delta\tilde{K}_n(t_k)}{\Delta t}\right)^T \tag{9.15}$$

as an n-dimensional vector in $\mathbf{R}^n$, we define a sequence $\tilde{\alpha}_l(t_k), k=1,\cdots,J$ as the *lth projection* of the vector by setting

$$\tilde{\alpha}_l(t_k)=\sum_{i=1}^{n}\frac{\Delta\tilde{K}_i(t_k)}{\Delta t}e_i^l \ ; \quad l=1,\cdots,d. \tag{9.16}$$

Similarly, we define a d-dimensional sequence $\tilde{\beta}_l(t_k)$ as

$$\tilde{\beta}_l(t_k)=\sum_{i=1}^{n}\left\{\lambda_{0i}\sum_{j=1}^{i}\kappa_j(t_k)-\frac{|\lambda_{0i}|^2}{2}\right\}e_i^l \ ; \quad l=1,\cdots,d. \tag{9.17}$$

We remark that the constant vector $(\beta_1,\cdots,\beta_d)^T$ was defined in the Gaussian HJM model by equation (6.15). In contrast, $\kappa_j(t_k)$ in the right-hand side of equation (9.17) depends on t_k, and $\tilde{\beta}_l(t_k)$, too, is defined as depending on t_k.

Dividing equation (9.14) by Δt, and projecting the result into e^l, we have, from (9.16), that

$$\tilde{\alpha}_l(t_k)=\tilde{\beta}_l(t_k)+\sum_{i=1}^{n}\sum_{m=1}^{d}\lambda_{0i}^m\varphi_m e_i^l+\frac{1}{\sqrt{\Delta t}}\sum_{i=1}^{n}\sum_{m=1}^{d}\lambda_{0i}^m W_1^m e_i^l. \tag{9.18}$$

From equation (9.11) and the orthonormality expressed in equation (9.10), we have

$$\begin{aligned}\tilde{\alpha}_l(t_k) &= \tilde{\beta}_l(t_k) + \sum_{m=1}^{d} \rho_m \varphi_m \sum_{i=1}^{n} e_i^m e_i^l + \frac{1}{\sqrt{\Delta t}} \sum_{m=1}^{d} \rho_m W_1^m \sum_{i=1}^{n} e_i^m e_i^l \\ &= (\tilde{\beta}_l(t_k) + \rho_l \varphi_l) + \frac{1}{\sqrt{\Delta t}} \rho_l W_1^l. \qquad (9.19)\end{aligned}$$

This is an expression of equation (9.14) in the principal component space. This form differs from the corresponding equation (6.17) in the Gaussian HJM model as follows:

- $\tilde{\alpha}_l(t_k)$ is measured in a logarithmic scale; and
- $\tilde{\beta}_l(t_k), k = 1, \cdots, J$ is a sequence in t_k, and involves the term $-|\lambda_{0i}|^2/2$.

Maximum likelihood estimation

The last term in the right-hand side of equation (9.19) is normally distributed. From Proposition C.0.1, the maximum likelihood estimation of the market price of risk φ_l is obtained as the solution to the least squares problem of $\theta_l(\varphi_l)$:

$$\theta_l(\varphi_l) = \sum_{k=1}^{J} |\tilde{\alpha}_l(t_k) - \{\tilde{\beta}_l(t_k) + \rho_l \varphi_l\}|^2 \quad ; \quad l = 1, \cdots, d. \qquad (9.20)$$

Note that this formulation is basically the same as the least squares problem (6.19) in the Gaussian HJM framework, and each $\theta_l(\varphi_l)$ is a one-variable function of φ_l. We can solve d minimizing problems for each $\theta_l(\varphi_l)$, $l = 1, \cdots, d$, independently, to obtain $\varphi = (\varphi_1, \cdots, \varphi_d)^T$. We have the following theorem, which is similar to Theorem 6.2.1.

Theorem 9.2.1 *For the LIBOR market model, we assume that the volatility corresponding to $K(t_k + t, \delta i - t)$ with $t \in [0, \Delta t]$ is given by the principal volatility component such that λ_{0i}^l is defined by equation (9.11). Then, the lth market price of risk, φ_l, is uniquely given by*

$$\varphi_l = \frac{1}{\rho_l} \left\{ E^H[\tilde{\alpha}_l] - E^H[\tilde{\beta}_l] \right\} \quad ; \quad l = 1, \cdots, d, \qquad (9.21)$$

where

$$\tilde{\alpha}_l(t_k) = \sum_{i=1}^{n} \frac{\Delta \tilde{K}_i(t_k)}{\Delta t} e_i^l \quad ; \quad l = 1, \cdots, d, \tag{9.22}$$

$$\tilde{\beta}_l(t_k) = \sum_{i=1}^{n} \left\{ \lambda_{0i} \sum_{j=1}^{i} \kappa_j(t_k) - \frac{|\lambda_{0i}|^2}{2} \right\} e_i^l \quad ; \quad l = 1, \cdots, d. \tag{9.23}$$

Proof By direct calculation,

$$\frac{\partial \theta(\varphi_l)}{\partial \varphi_l} = -2 \sum_{k=1}^{J} [\tilde{\alpha}_l(t_k) - \{\tilde{\beta}_l(t_k) + \rho_l \varphi_l\}] \rho_l, \tag{9.24}$$

and $\partial^2 \theta / \partial \varphi_l^2 = 2(\rho_l)^2 J > 0$ for all $l = 1, \cdots, d$. Since $\theta(\varphi_l)$ is a one-variable function of φ_l and $\rho_l \neq 0$, $\theta(\varphi_l)$ is strictly convex with respect to φ_l. The least squares solution then exists uniquely, and can be written as the root of the equation

$$\frac{\partial \theta(\varphi_l)}{\partial \varphi_l} = -2\rho_l \sum_{k=1}^{J} \{\tilde{\alpha}_l(t_k) - (\tilde{\beta}_l(t_k) + \rho_l \varphi_l)\} = 0. \tag{9.25}$$

Since $\rho_l \neq 0$, the above equation is reduced to

$$\begin{aligned} 0 &= \sum_{k=1}^{J} \{\tilde{\alpha}_l(t_k) - (\tilde{\beta}_l(t_k) + \rho_l \varphi_l)\} \\ &= \rho_l \varphi_l J + \sum_{k=1}^{J} \{\tilde{\alpha}_l(t_k) - \tilde{\beta}_l(t_k)\}. \end{aligned} \tag{9.26}$$

The sample means of $\tilde{\alpha}_l(t_k)$ and $\tilde{\beta}_l(t_k)$ are represented by $E^H[\tilde{\alpha}_l] = \frac{1}{J} \sum_{k=1}^{J} \tilde{\alpha}_l(t_k)$ and $E^H[\tilde{\beta}_l] = \frac{1}{J} \sum_{k=1}^{J} \tilde{\beta}_l(t_k)$, respectively. Substituting these into equation (9.26), the term $\rho_l \varphi_l$ is represented as

$$\begin{aligned} \rho_l \varphi_l &= \frac{1}{J} \sum_{k=1}^{J} \{\tilde{\alpha}_l(t_k) - \tilde{\beta}_l(t_k)\} \\ &= E^H[\tilde{\alpha}_l] - E^H[\tilde{\beta}_l]. \end{aligned} \tag{9.27}$$

Then, the lth market price of risk φ_l is formulated as $\varphi_l = \frac{1}{\rho_l}\{E^H[\tilde{\alpha}_l] - E^H[\tilde{\beta}_l]\}$. This completes the proof. □

From this formulation of φ_l, we can develop a theory of simulation in the LMRW analogous to that developed in the Gaussian HJM model.

Comparison with the Gaussian HJM model

We here give a remark on the expression of the market price of risk in the LMRW in comparison with that in the Gaussian HJM model.

In the LMRW, the market price of risk is formulated as equation (9.21), in which we can see that the sign for the term $E^H[\tilde{\beta}_l]$ is negative. In contrast, the market price of risk for the Gaussian HJM model is formulated, in equation (6.20), as $\varphi_l = \frac{1}{\rho_l}\{E^H[\alpha_l] + \beta_l\}$, in which we see the sign for the constant term β_l is positive, and so opposite that in the LMRW.

To verify this difference, we recall the forward rate process (4.17) in the HJM model as

$$df(t,T) = \{-\sigma(t,T)v(t,T) + \sigma(t,T)\varphi(t)\}\,dt + \sigma(t,T)dW_t. \tag{9.28}$$

Here, the process $v(t,T)$ was defined by equation (4.10), which includes a negative sign, as

$$v(s,T) = -\int_s^T \sigma(s,u)du. \tag{9.29}$$

From this, the constant β_l is defined, by equation (6.16), as $\beta_l = \sum_{i=1}^n \sigma_{0i} v_{0i} e_i^l$, and so the sign of β_l is opposite that of the HJM volatility $\sigma(t,T)$.

In the LMRW, the LIBOR process is given, in (5.10), as

$$\frac{dL_i(t)}{L_i(t)} = \left\{\lambda_i(t)\sum_{j=m(t)}^{i} \chi_j(t) + \lambda_i(t)\varphi_t\right\} dt + \lambda_i(t)dW_t. \tag{9.30}$$

With this, the observation of the LIBOR is represented, in (9.6), as

$$\begin{aligned}\log K(t_k+\Delta t, x_i-\Delta t) &= \log K(t_k, x_i) + \left\{\lambda_{0i}\sum_{j=1}^{i}\kappa_j(t_k)\right.\\ &\quad \left. + \lambda_{0i}\varphi - \frac{|\lambda_{0i}|^2}{2}\right\}\Delta t + \sqrt{\Delta t}\lambda_{0i}W_1, \end{aligned} \tag{9.31}$$

where

$$\kappa_j(t_k) = \frac{\lambda_{0j}\delta K(t_k,\delta j)}{1+\delta K(t_k,\delta j)}. \tag{9.32}$$

Taking this as given, the sequence $\tilde{\beta}(t_k)$ is defined, by equation (9.17), as

$$\tilde{\beta}_l(t_k) = \sum_{i=1}^{n} \left\{ \lambda_{0i} \sum_{j=1}^{i} \kappa_j(t_k) - \frac{|\lambda_{0i}|^2}{2} \right\} e_i^l. \tag{9.33}$$

Then, the sign of $\tilde{\beta}_l(t_k)$ coincides with that of the LIBOR volatility, λ.

Along these lines, the sign of $E^H[\tilde{\beta}_l]$ in equation (9.21) is opposite to that of β_l in equation (6.20). In this sense, the formulation (9.21) in the LMRW is consistent with the formulation (6.20) in the Gaussian HJM model.

9.3 State Space Setup

This section estimates the market price of risk in a state space setup, corresponding to the argument in the Gaussian HJM framework in Section 6.3. Here, we denote the market price of risk by $\varphi' = (\varphi'_1, \cdots, \varphi'_d)^T$ to avoid confusion with the results from the previous section.

We suppose the same conditions as in Section 9.2, where the principal volatility components are employed. Substituting $\Delta\tilde{K}_i(t_k)$ from equation (9.13) into equation (9.6), we have

$$\Delta\tilde{K}_i(t_k) = \left\{ \lambda_{0i} \sum_{j=1}^{i} \kappa_j(t_k) + \lambda_{0i}\varphi' - \frac{|\lambda_{0i}|^2}{2} \right\} \Delta t + \sqrt{\Delta t}\lambda_{0i} W_1, \tag{9.34}$$

for all k and i.

We denote by $\epsilon(\varphi')$ the sum of the squared differences between both sides of the above equation in the time series and cross sections, neglecting the random part, such that

$$\begin{aligned} \epsilon(\varphi') &= \frac{1}{J} \sum_{k=1}^{J} \sum_{i=1}^{n} \left\{ \Delta\tilde{K}_i(t_k) - \left(\lambda_{0i} \sum_{j=1}^{i} \kappa_j(t_k) \right.\right. \\ &\quad \left.\left. + \lambda_{0i}\varphi' - \frac{|\lambda_{0i}|^2}{2} \right) \Delta t \right\}^2. \end{aligned} \tag{9.35}$$

Let φ' be the solution that minimizes $\epsilon(\varphi')$. According to Chapter 6, we call this setting the *state space setup*, and we call the setting in the previous section the *PCA setup*. The differences between φ' and φ (as defined in the previous section) are as follows.

- φ is the solution that minimizes $\theta(\varphi)$ from equation (9.20) in the PCA setup, and is the maximum likelihood estimate of the market price of risk.

- φ' is the solution that minimizes $\epsilon(\varphi')$ of equation (9.35) in the state space setup.

As it was in the study of the Gaussian HJM model, the derivation of $\epsilon(\varphi')$ is immediate; further, it is more comprehensive than that of $\theta(\varphi)$, because $\epsilon(\varphi')$ is defined without the use of PCA. Accordingly, φ' is defined more directly than the PCA setup. However, it is not trivial in this setup to obtain φ' as the maximum likelihood estimate because the structure of equation (9.34), needed for maximum likelihood estimation, is quite complicated.

With respect to the minimizing problem of $\epsilon(\varphi')$, we obtain the following theorem, which is analogous to Theorem 6.3.2.

Theorem 9.3.1 *The solution to the least squares problem for $\epsilon(\varphi')$ is uniquely given by*

$$\varphi'_l = \frac{1}{\rho_l}\sum_{i=1}^{n}\left\{E^H\left[\frac{\Delta\tilde{K}_i}{\Delta t}\right] - \lambda_{0i}E^H\left[\sum_{j=1}^{i}\kappa_j\right] + \frac{|\lambda_{0i}|^2}{2}\right\}e^l_i, \tag{9.36}$$

for $l = 1, \cdots, d$.

Proof From the definition of the sample mean, it holds that

$$\frac{1}{J}\sum_{k=1}^{J}\Delta\tilde{K}_i(t_k) = E^H[\Delta\tilde{K}_i] \tag{9.37}$$

and

$$\frac{1}{J}\sum_{k=1}^{J}\sum_{j=1}^{i}\kappa_j(t_k) = E^H\left[\sum_{j=1}^{i}\kappa_j\right]. \tag{9.38}$$

Substituting these into equation (9.35), we have

$$\epsilon(\varphi') = \sum_{i=1}^{n}\left(E^H[\Delta\tilde{K}_i] - \left\{\lambda_{0i}E^H\left[\sum_{j=1}^{i}\kappa_j\right] + \lambda_{0i}\varphi' - \frac{|\lambda_{0i}|^2}{2}\right\}\Delta t\right)^2. \tag{9.39}$$

To avoid confusion, the subscripts i and l express the length of time x_i to the maturity T_i and the ordering index of the Brownian motion W_l, respectively.

From $\lambda_{0i}\varphi' = \sum_{l=1}^{d} \lambda_{0i}^{l}\varphi'_l$, it follows that

$$\frac{\partial \lambda_{0i}\varphi'}{\partial \varphi'_l} = \lambda_{0i}^{l} \;\; ; \;\; l = 1, \cdots, d, \; i = 1, \cdots, n. \tag{9.40}$$

With this, the partial derivative of $\epsilon(\varphi')$ in φ'_l is given by

$$\begin{aligned} \frac{\partial \epsilon(\varphi')}{\partial \varphi'_l} &= 2\sum_{i=1}^{n} \left(E^H[\Delta\tilde{K}_i] - \left\{ \lambda_{0i} E^H \left[\sum_{j=1}^{i} \kappa_j \right] \right.\right. \\ &\qquad \left.\left. + \lambda_{0i}\varphi' - \frac{|\lambda_{0i}|^2}{2} \right\} \Delta t \right) \lambda_{0i}^{l} \Delta t \;\; ; \;\; l = 1, \cdots, d. \end{aligned} \tag{9.41}$$

Also, it holds that

$$\frac{\partial^2 \epsilon(\varphi')}{\partial \varphi'_l \partial \varphi'_m} = 2\sum_{i=1}^{n} \lambda_{0i}^{l}\lambda_{0i}^{m}\Delta t^2 \;\; ; \;\; l, m = 1, \cdots, d. \tag{9.42}$$

We recall that the lth volatility component is given, by equation (9.11), as

$$\lambda_{0i}^{l} = \rho_l e_i^l \;\; ; \;\; l = 1, \cdots, d, \; i = 1, \cdots, n. \tag{9.43}$$

From the orthonormality in equation (9.10), we have

$$2\sum_{i=1}^{n} \lambda_{0i}^{l}\lambda_{0i}^{m}\Delta t^2 = 2\rho_l\rho_m\delta_{lm}\Delta t^2. \tag{9.44}$$

Thus, the Hessian matrix of $\epsilon(\varphi')$ is diagonal because

$$\frac{\partial^2 \epsilon(\varphi')}{\partial \varphi'_l \partial \varphi'_m} = 2(\Delta t \rho_l)^2 \delta_{lm}. \tag{9.45}$$

The assumption (9.9) ensures that the Hessian is positive definite. Then, $\epsilon(\varphi')$ is strictly convex with respect to φ'. Hence, the solution $\varphi' = (\varphi'_1, \cdots, \varphi'_d)^T$ to the least squares problem is uniquely determined by solving $\nabla\epsilon(\varphi') = 0$.

For simplicity of expression, we define a constant vector $\gamma = (\gamma_1, \cdots, \gamma_n)^T$ as

$$\gamma_i = E^H\left[\frac{\Delta\tilde{K}_i}{\Delta t}\right] - \lambda_{0i}E^H\left[\sum_{j=1}^{i}\kappa_j\right] + \frac{|\lambda_{0i}|^2}{2} \;\; ; \;\; i = 1, \cdots, n. \tag{9.46}$$

Note that γ is completely determined from the historical data. Substituting equation (9.46) into equation (9.41), the equation $\nabla\epsilon(\varphi') = 0$ can be decomposed to

$$\sum_{i=1}^{n}(\gamma_i - \lambda_{0i}\varphi')\lambda_{0i}^l = 0 \;\; ; \;\; l = 1, \cdots, d. \tag{9.47}$$

By equation (9.43), we have the following.

$$\begin{aligned}\sum_{i=1}^{n}\lambda_{0i}\varphi'\lambda_{0i}^l &= \sum_{i=1}^{n}\lambda_{0i}^l\sum_{m=1}^{d}\varphi'_m\lambda_{0i}^m \\ &= \sum_{i=1}^{n}\rho_l e_i^l\sum_{m=1}^{d}\varphi'_m\rho_m e_i^m \\ &= \rho_l\sum_{m=1}^{d}\varphi'_m\rho_m\sum_{i=1}^{n}e_i^l e_i^m \end{aligned} \tag{9.48}$$

The principal components e^l and e^m are orthonormal to each other for all l and m, and so the above equation can be reduced to

$$\begin{aligned}\sum_{i=1}^{n}\lambda_{0i}\varphi'\lambda_{0i}^l &= \rho_l\sum_{m=1}^{d}\varphi'_h\rho_h\delta_{lm} \\ &= (\rho_l)^2\varphi'_l \;\; ; \;\; l = 1, \cdots, d. \end{aligned} \tag{9.49}$$

Additionally, it holds that

$$\begin{aligned}\sum_{i=1}^{n}\gamma_i\lambda_{0i}^l &= \sum_{i=1}^{n}\gamma_i\rho_l e_i^l \\ &= \rho_l\sum_{i=1}^{n}\gamma_i e_i^l \;\; ; \;\; l = 1, \cdots, d. \end{aligned} \tag{9.50}$$

Substituting these into equation (9.47), we have $\rho_l\varphi'_l = \sum_{i=1}^{n}\gamma_i e_i^l$. From this, we obtain

$$\varphi'_l = \frac{1}{\rho_l}\sum_{i=1}^{n}\gamma_i e_i^l \;\; ; \;\; l = 1, \cdots, d. \tag{9.51}$$

Substituting equation (9.46) into γ_i in the above, we have

$$\varphi'_l = \frac{1}{\rho_l}\sum_{i=1}^{n}\left\{E^H\left[\frac{\Delta\tilde{K}_i}{\Delta t}\right] - \lambda_{0i}E^H\left[\sum_{j=1}^{i}\kappa_j\right] + \frac{|\lambda_{0i}|^2}{2}\right\}e_i^l. \tag{9.52}$$

This completes the proof. □

We have the following corollary, as an analogue of Corollary 6.3.3.

Corollary 9.3.2 *Under the same conditions as in Theorem 9.3.1, the solution for φ' that minimizes $\epsilon(\varphi')$ coincides with the maximum likelihood estimate of the market price of risk φ; that is, $\varphi'_l = \varphi_l$ for $l = 1, \cdots, d$.*

Proof By equation (9.21) in Theorem 9.2.1, φ is given by $\varphi_l = \frac{1}{\rho_l}\{E^H[\tilde{\alpha}_l] - E^H[\tilde{\beta}_l]\}$ for each l. Substituting equations (9.16) and (9.17) into this, we have that

$$\begin{aligned}\varphi_l &= \frac{1}{\rho_l}\sum_{i=1}^{n}\left\{E^H\left[\frac{\Delta \tilde{K}_i}{\Delta t}\right] - E^H\left[\lambda_{0i}\sum_{j=1}^{i}\kappa_j(t_k) - \frac{|\lambda_{0i}|^2}{2}\right]\right\}e_i^l \\ &= \frac{1}{\rho_l}\sum_{i=1}^{n}\left\{E^H\left[\frac{\Delta \tilde{K}_i}{\Delta t}\right] - \lambda_{0i}E^H\left[\sum_{j=1}^{i}\kappa_j\right] + \frac{|\lambda_{0i}|^2}{2}\right\}e_i^l, \end{aligned} \tag{9.53}$$

for $l = 1, \cdots, d$. The right-hand side is equal to φ'_l in Theorem 9.3.1. This completes the proof. □

9.4 Historical Trends of LIBOR

This section examines the numerical meaning of the market price of risk in connection with the average change in the forward LIBOR. For this, we make some definitions to describe the average change of the forward LIBOR in a manner similar to that introduced in Section 9.4.

Log-scale observable trend

Let $t_k, k = 1, \cdots, J+1$, $x_i, i = 1, \cdots, n$ and $K(t_k, x_i)$ be as defined in Section 9.1. The *log-scale observable trend* of forward LIBOR $K(\cdot, x_i)$ is defined as

$$E^H\left[\frac{1}{\Delta t}\log\frac{K(t_{k+1}, x_i)}{K(t_k, x_i)}\right]. \tag{9.54}$$

It holds that

$$E^H\left[\frac{1}{\Delta t}\log\frac{K(t_{k+1}, x_i)}{K(t_k, x_i)}\right] = \frac{1}{\Delta t J}\log\frac{K(t_{J+1}, x_i)}{K(t_1, x_i)}. \tag{9.55}$$

Then, the log-scale observable trend for x_i is positive when $K(t_{J+1}, x_i) - K(t_1, x_i) > 0$. Conversely, this trend is negative when $K(t_{J+1}, x_i) - K(t_1, x_i) < 0$.

The log-scale observable trend represents an average change in the log-scale forward LIBOR for a fixed x_j during the sample period $[t_1, t_{J+1}]$. Precisely speaking, this trend indicates the averaged speed of log-scale change of the forward LIBOR. The fundamental property of this trend is basically the same as that explained in Fig. 6.2 for the HJM framework.

Log-scale rolled trend

We set $\Delta\tilde{K}_i(t_k)$ as

$$\Delta\tilde{K}_i(t_k) = \log K(t_{k+1}, x_i - \Delta t) - \log K(t_k, x_i), \tag{9.56}$$

and define the *log-scale rolled trend* of $K(\,\cdot, x_i)$ as $E^H[\Delta\tilde{K}_i/\Delta t]$. Immediately, it holds that

$$E^H\left[\frac{\Delta\tilde{K}_i}{\Delta t}\right] = \frac{1}{\Delta t}E^H\left[\log\frac{K(t_{k+1}, x_i - \Delta t)}{K(t_k, x_i)}\right]. \tag{9.57}$$

Then, we have

$$\begin{aligned} E^H\left[\frac{\Delta\tilde{K}_i}{\Delta t}\right] &= -\frac{1}{\Delta t}E^H\left[\log K(t_k, x_i) - \log K(t_{k+1}, x_i - \Delta t)\right] \\ &\quad + E^H\left[\frac{1}{\Delta t}\log\frac{K(t_{k+1}, x_i)}{K(t_k, x_i)}\right]. \end{aligned} \tag{9.58}$$

The first term nearly represents the sample mean of the slope of the forward LIBOR curve in log-scale, and the second one is equal to the log-scale observable trend. Similarly to the rolled trend in the Gaussian HJM model, the log-scale rolled trend corresponds to the roll-down or roll-up of the forward LIBOR in log-scale.

In the LMRW, we always work with the trends and the scores in log-scale, and so we will sometimes omit the term "log-scale" for convenience in the following. The next definition is analogous to Definition 6.4 in the Gaussian HJM framework.

Definition 9.4 The *lth principal component score of the observable trend* $\tilde{O}_l$ is defined as

$$\tilde{O}_l = \sum_{i=1}^{n} E^H \left[\frac{1}{\Delta t} \log \frac{K(t_{k+1}, x_i)}{K(t_k, x_i)} \right] e_i^l \ ; \ l = 1, \cdots, d. \tag{9.59}$$

Similarly, the *lth principal component score of the rolled trend* $\tilde{R}_l$ is defined as

$$\tilde{R}_l = \sum_{i=1}^{n} E^H \left[\frac{\Delta \tilde{K}_i}{\Delta t} \right] e_i^l \ ; \ l = 1, \cdots, d. \tag{9.60}$$

We refer to $\tilde{O}_l$ and $\tilde{R}_l$ as the *lth observable trend score* and the *lth rolled trend score*, respectively, for short.

According to the argument in Sections 4.3 and 6.4, we see that $\tilde{O}_1, \tilde{O}_2$, and $\tilde{O}_3$ respectively represent the level, slope, and curvature factors of the observable trend. Similarly, $\tilde{R}_1, \tilde{R}_2$, and $\tilde{R}_3$ respectively represent the level, slope, and curvature factors of the rolled trend.

Examples for $\tilde{R}_1$ and $\tilde{R}_2$

The value of $\tilde{R}_1$ is explained similarly to the explanation in Section 6.4. From equation (9.58), it roughly holds that

$$\tilde{R}_1 \approx \tilde{O}_1 - \{\text{Mean of the slope of forward LIBOR curve}\}. \tag{9.61}$$

From this, Table 9.1 qualitatively estimates the value of $\tilde{R}_1$ with respect to the slope of the forward LIBOR curve and the observable trend. Naturally, this table exhibits the same characteristics that Table 6.1 does.

Table 9.1: Qualitative estimate of $\tilde{R}_1$ with respect to the slope of the forward LIBOR curve and the log-scale observable trend.

Slope of forward LIBOR curve	Log-scale observable trend		
	Fast fall	Stable	Fast rise
Upward sloping	Negative	Negative	Positive
Flat	Negative	Near zero	Positive
Downward sloping	Negative	Positive	Positive

The second rolled trend, too, is explained in the manner given in Section 6.4. Table 9.2 roughly estimates the values $\tilde{R}_1$ and $\tilde{R}_2$ with respect to the observable trend. Furthermore, the rolled trend scores of higher orders are explained in the same manner.

9.5 Qualitative Estimate of Market Price of Risk

In this section, we investigate the meaning of the market price of risk with respect to a term structure of the rolled trend. The next proposition is an analogue of Proposition 6.5.1.

Proposition 9.5.1 *Under the assumptions of Theorem 9.2.1, if it holds that*

$$\left|\lambda_{0i} E^H\left[\sum_{j=1}^{i} \kappa_j\right]\right| + \frac{|\lambda_{0i}|^2}{2} \ll \left|E^H\left[\frac{\Delta K_i}{\Delta t}\right]\right| \tag{9.62}$$

for all i, then the market price of risk φ_l is approximated by $\varphi_l \approx \tilde{R}_l/\rho_l$ for every $l = 1, \cdots, d$.

Proof From Theorem 9.3.1, the lth market price of risk is represented by

$$\varphi_l = \frac{1}{\rho_l}\sum_{i=1}^{n}\left\{E^H\left[\frac{\Delta\tilde{K}_i}{\Delta t}\right] - \lambda_{0i}E^H\left[\sum_{j=1}^{i}\kappa_j\right] + \frac{|\lambda_{0i}|^2}{2}\right\} e_i^l. \tag{9.63}$$

By the assumption (9.62), we can approximate this as

$$\varphi_l \approx \frac{1}{\rho_l}\sum_{i=1}^{n} E^H\left[\frac{\Delta\tilde{K}_i}{\Delta t}\right] e_i^l. \tag{9.64}$$

Table 9.2: $\tilde{R}_1$ and $\tilde{R}_2$ with respect to log-scale observable trends. Forward LIBOR curves are assumed to be upward-sloping during the sample period.

Observable trend	$\tilde{R}_1$	$\tilde{R}_2$
Bull steep	Negative	Negative
Steep	Negative	Negative
Bear steep	Near zero	Negative
Bull flat	Negative	Positive
Flat	Negative	Positive
Bear flat	Near zero	Positive

Table 9.3: Qualitative estimate for the first market price of risk φ_1 with respect to the observable trend.

Slope of forward LIBOR curve	Observable trend		
	Fast fall	Stable	Fast rise
Upward-sloping	Negative	Negative	Positive
Flat	Negative	Near zero	Positive
Downward-sloping	Negative	Positive	Positive

Substituting equation (9.60) into the above, we obtain $\varphi_l \approx \tilde{R}_l/\rho_l$. This completes the proof. □

In Section 10.2, we will show an actual example that satisfies the inequality (9.62).

However, the market data do not always satisfy this inequality. For example, let us suppose an interest rate market where the LIBOR volatility is lower than 0.2 (20%) when taking the long-range view. Then, we may assume that $|\lambda_i| < 0.2$ for all i. Recall that χ_j was replaced by κ_j in Section 9.1. From equation (5.12), $\sum_{j=1}^{i} \kappa_j$ indicates the volatility of the ith bond price, which would be absolutely lower than the LIBOR volatility. Then, we may assume that $\left|\sum_{j=1}^{i} \kappa_j\right| = 0.01$.

With these, the left-hand side in equation (9.62) is estimated by

$$\begin{aligned} \left|\lambda_{0i} E^H\left[\sum_{j=1}^{i} \kappa_j(t_k)\right]\right| + \frac{|\lambda_{0i}|^2}{2} &\ll 0.2 \times 0.01 + \frac{0.2^2}{2} \\ &= 0.002 + 0.02 \\ &= 0.022 \ (2.2\%). \end{aligned} \tag{9.65}$$

However, the right-hand side of equation (9.62) represents an average speed of the rolled trend. It is not usual for the forward LIBOR to change more than 2% in a year.

Therefore, the assumption (9.62) requires that the volatility is low and the forward LIBOR changes by a large amount. Although this condition is not always satisfied, Proposition 9.5.1 is useful to qualitatively explain the meaning of the market price of risk.

Table 9.4: Qualitative estimates for φ_1 and φ_2. Forward LIBOR curves are assumed to be upward-sloping in the sample period.

Observable trend	φ_1	φ_2
Bull steep	Negative	Negative
Steep	Negative	Negative
Bear steep	Near zero	Negative
Bull flat	Negative	Positive
Flat	Negative	Positive
Bear flat	Near zero	Positive

Rolled trend and the market price of risk

From equation (9.12), ρ_l indicates the magnitude of the lth volatility component λ^l. As stated in Section 6.5, we may say that ρ_l indicates the lth volatility risk. With this, Proposition 9.5.1 states that *the lth market price of risk φ_l means, roughly, the rolled trend score corresponding to the lth volatility risk*; that is,

$$\{l^{th} \text{ market price of risk}\} \approx \frac{\{\text{Magnitude of } l^{th} \text{ rolled trend}\}}{\{l^{th} \text{ volatility risk}\}}. \tag{9.66}$$

Assuming that $\tilde{O}_l \approx \tilde{R}_l$, the above estimate is roughly dependent on the observable trend. Replacing $\tilde{R}_1$ with φ_1 in Table 9.1, we obtain Table 9.3, which shows a qualitative estimate of the first market price of risk φ_1.

In the manner described in Section 6.5, we obtain Table 9.4. This table shows rough estimates of φ_1 and φ_2 with respect to the observable trend, where the forward LIBOR curves are assumed to be upward-sloping in the sample period, and the condition (9.62) is assumed to hold.

The market price of risk and investment

Similarly to the argument in Section 6.6, we infer the meaning of the market price of risk in connection with a bond investment strategy. Here, the deduction follows the pattern of deduction in the Gaussian HJM model, we list only the results. For details, see the observation in Section 6.6.

- The first market price of risk φ_1 is a risk-adjusted measure for the roll-down return of the entire forward LIBOR curve.

- The second market price of risk φ_2 is a risk-adjusted measure for the steepening strategy.
- The third market price of risk φ_3 is a risk-adjusted measure for the butterfly trading strategy.

Negative price tendency

When the inequality (9.62) fails to hold, the market price of risk is not necessarily well-approximated by Proposition 9.5.1. In such a case, there is a possibility that the second term in equation (9.36) will be larger than the first term (the rolled trend).

In this respect, long-period observation would indicate a negative price tendency for the first market price of risk in the LIBOR market model, as in Theorem 7.2.2.

Remark

The observations in this section were presented in Yasuoka (2013a) earlier than the analogous observation in the Gaussian HJM framework, which was given in Yasuoka (2015). If the market price of risk was calculated by statistical software, then we could obtain a numerical value only and might not consider these issues. Along these lines, we may say that quantitative estimation of the market price of risk makes studying real-world modeling theoretically feasible. Because of this, we continue to develop the theoretical foundation for real-world simulation in the following sections.

9.6 Fundamental Properties of Simulation

This section investigates the properties of simulation in the LMRW. Let the time interval $\Delta s > 0$ be fixed, and let $\lambda_i(t)$ and $\gamma_i(t)$ be constant for $t \in [0, \Delta s]$. Let $L_i(0)$ be an initial forward LIBOR. From equation (9.2), we have

$$\begin{aligned} L_i(\Delta s) &= L_i(0) \exp\left\{ \int_0^{\Delta s} \left(\lambda_i(t) \sum_{j=m(t)}^{i} \chi_j(t) + \lambda_i(t)\varphi - \frac{|\lambda_i(t)|^2}{2} \right) dt \right. \\ &\quad \left. + \int_0^{\Delta s} \lambda_i(t) dW_t \right\} \quad ; \quad i = 1, \cdots n, \end{aligned} \tag{9.67}$$

where W_t is a d-dimensional Brownian motion under $\mathbf{P}$. We assume a full-factor model—specifically, that $d = n$ and the $n \times n$ matrix λ_i has rank n—and examine the properties of real-world simulation.

By the Euler approximation, $L_i(\Delta s)$ can be expressed as

$$\begin{aligned}\log L_i(\Delta s) &= \log L_i(0) + \left\{ \lambda_{0i} \sum_{j=m(t)}^{i} \chi_{0j} + \lambda_{0i}\varphi - \frac{|\lambda_{0i}|^2}{2} \right\} \Delta s \\ &\quad + \sqrt{\Delta s}\lambda_{0i} W_1 \ \ ; \ \ i = 1, \cdots, n. \end{aligned} \tag{9.68}$$

Here, we let $\lambda_{0i} = \lambda_i(0)$ and $\chi_{0i} = \chi_i(0)$. Then, the single-period simulation for $L_i(\Delta s)$ is executed with this form.

Projection to principal component space

We assume that the principal volatility components are used for the volatility, such that λ_{0i}^l is defined by equation (9.11).

Then, the market price of risk is given by Theorem 9.2.1.

In the manner introduced in Section 6.7, we examine the properties of equation (9.68) in the principal component space. The lth projection of equation (9.68) is represented as

$$\begin{aligned}\sum_{i=1}^{n} \log L_i(\Delta s) e_i^l &= \sum_{i=1}^{n} \log L_i(0) e_i^l \\ &\quad + \sum_{i=1}^{n} \left\{ \lambda_{0i} \sum_{j=m(t)}^{i} \chi_{0j} e_i^l + \lambda_{0i}\varphi e_i^l - \frac{|\lambda_{0i}|^2}{2} e_i^l \right\} \Delta s \\ &\quad + \sum_{i=1}^{n} \sqrt{\Delta s}\lambda_{0i} W_1 e_i^l. \end{aligned} \tag{9.69}$$

We set constants $b_l, l = 1, \cdots, d$ by letting

$$b_l = \sum_{i=1}^{n} \left\{ \lambda_{0i} \sum_{j=1}^{i} \chi_{0j} - \frac{|\lambda_{0i}|^2}{2} \right\} e_i^l. \tag{9.70}$$

With this, equation (9.69) becomes

$$\begin{aligned}\sum_{i=1}^{n} \log L_i(\Delta s) e_i^l &= \sum_{i=1}^{n} \log L_i(0) e_i^l + \left(b_l + \sum_{i=1}^{n} \lambda_{0i} \varphi e_i^l \right) \Delta s \\ &\quad + \sum_{i=1}^{n} \sqrt{\Delta s} \lambda_{0i} W_1 e_i^l. \end{aligned} \tag{9.71}$$

By the definition of λ_{0i} and the orthonormality of the principal components, we have

$$\begin{aligned}\sum_{i=1}^{n} \lambda_{0i} \varphi e_i^l &= \sum_{i=1}^{n} \sum_{m=1}^{n} \rho_m e_i^m \varphi_m e_i^l \\ &= \rho_l \varphi_l \ ; \quad l = 1, \cdots, n \end{aligned} \tag{9.72}$$

and

$$\begin{aligned}\sum_{i=1}^{n} \lambda_{0i} W_1 e_i^l &= \sum_{i=1}^{n} \sum_{m=1}^{n} \rho_m e_i^m W_1^m e_i^l \\ &= \rho_l W_1^l \ ; \quad l = 1, \cdots, n. \end{aligned} \tag{9.73}$$

Substituting these into equation (9.71), we obtain

$$\sum_{i=1}^{n} \log L_i(\Delta s) e_i^l = \sum_{i=1}^{n} \log L_i(0) e_i^l + (b_l + \rho_l \varphi_l) \Delta s + \sqrt{\Delta s} \rho_l W_1^l. \tag{9.74}$$

From Theorem 9.2.1, we already have that $\rho_l \varphi_l = E^H[\tilde{\alpha}_l] - E^H[\tilde{\beta}_l]$. Here, $\tilde{\alpha}_l(t_k)$ and $\tilde{\beta}_l(t_k)$ are given by

$$\tilde{\alpha}_l(t_k) = \sum_{i=1}^{n} \frac{\Delta \tilde{K}_i(t_k)}{\Delta t} e_i^l, \tag{9.75}$$

$$\tilde{\beta}_l(t_k) = \sum_{i=1}^{n} \left\{ \lambda_{0i} \sum_{j=1}^{i} \kappa_j(t_k) - \frac{|\lambda_{0i}|^2}{2} \right\} e_i^l. \tag{9.76}$$

From these, equation (9.74) becomes

$$\begin{aligned}\sum_{i=1}^{n} \log L_i(\Delta s) e_i^l &= \sum_{i=1}^{n} \log L_i(0) e_i^l + \left(b_l + E^H[\tilde{\alpha}_l] - E^H[\tilde{\beta}_l] \right) \Delta s \\ &\quad + \sqrt{\Delta s} \rho_l W_1^l \ ; \quad l = 1, \cdots, n. \end{aligned} \tag{9.77}$$

This represents a simulation model in the principal component space.

Real-world simulation model

Further. we modify the above equation to examine the properties of the drift term. From equations (9.70) and (9.76), it follows that

$$\begin{aligned} b_l - E^H[\tilde{\beta}_l] &= \sum_{i=1}^{n}\left\{\lambda_{0i}\sum_{j=1}^{i}\chi_{0j} - \frac{|\lambda_{0i}|^2}{2}\right. \\ &\quad \left. - \lambda_{0i}E^H\left[\sum_{j=1}^{i}\kappa_j\right] + \frac{|\lambda_{0i}|^2}{2}\right\} e_i^l \\ &= \sum_{i=1}^{n}\left\{\lambda_{0i}\sum_{j=1}^{i}\chi_{0j} - \lambda_{0i}E^H\left[\sum_{j=1}^{i}\kappa_j\right]\right\} e_i^l \\ &= \sum_{i=1}^{n}\lambda_{0i}\left\{\sum_{j=1}^{i}\chi_{0j} - E^H\left[\sum_{j=1}^{i}\kappa_j\right]\right\} e_i^l. \end{aligned} \tag{9.78}$$

Substituting this into equation (9.77), we have

$$\begin{aligned} \sum_{i=1}^{n}\log L_i(\Delta s)e_i^l &= \sum_{i=1}^{n}\log L_i(0)e_i^l + \left\{E^H\left[\tilde{\alpha}_l\right]\right. \\ &\quad \left. + \sum_{i=1}^{n}\lambda_{0i}\left(\sum_{j=1}^{i}\chi_{0j} - E^H\left[\sum_{j=1}^{i}\kappa_j\right]\right) e_i^l\right\}\Delta s \\ &\quad + \sqrt{\Delta s}\rho_l W_1^l \ ; \ \ l = 1, \cdots, d. \end{aligned} \tag{9.79}$$

Note that $E^H[\tilde{\alpha}_l]$ and $E^H[\sum_{j=1}^{i}\kappa_j]$ are calculated from the sample data, and the values of $\log L_i(0)$, λ_{0j}, and χ_{0j} are determined from the initial data. Along these lines, equation (9.79) practically specifies the real-world simulation model in the principal component space.

Remark on $\tilde{\beta}_l(t_k)$ and b_l

Here, we give a supplementary explanation about the subtle difference between two similar variables, $\tilde{\beta}_l(t_k)$ and b_l. Initially, $\chi_i(t)$ is defined by equation (5.9) for introducing the LIBOR process in Section 5.3 as

$$\chi_i(t) = \frac{\lambda_i(t)\delta_i L_i(t)}{1+\delta_j L_i(t)} \quad ; \quad i = 1, \cdots, n. \tag{9.80}$$

Here, we set the constant χ_{0i} by letting

$$\chi_{0i} = \chi_(0) = \frac{\lambda_{0j}\delta_i L_i(0)}{1+\delta_j L_i(0)} \tag{9.81}$$

for the initial LIBOR $L_i(0)$. Then, the constant b_l is determined by equation (9.70) with the initial LIBOR and the given volatility, resulting in

$$b_l = \sum_{i=1}^{n} \left\{ \lambda_{0i} \sum_{j=1}^{i} \chi_{0j} - \frac{|\lambda_{0i}|^2}{2} \right\} e_i^l \quad ; \quad l = 1, \cdots, d. \tag{9.82}$$

The sequences $\kappa_j(t_k)$ and $\tilde{\beta}_l(t_k)$ are calculated by equations (9.5) and (9.76), respectively, for all sampled days t_k as

$$\kappa_j(t_k) = \frac{\lambda_{0j}\delta K(t_k, \delta j)}{1+\delta K(t_k, \delta j)} \quad ; \quad j = 1, \cdots, n, \ k = 1, \cdots, J \tag{9.83}$$

and

$$\tilde{\beta}_l(t_k) = \sum_{i=1}^{n} \left\{ \lambda_{0i} \sum_{j=1}^{i} \kappa_j(t_k) - \frac{|\lambda_{0i}|^2}{2} \right\} e_i^l \ ; \qquad l = 1, \cdots, d, \ k = 1, \cdots, J. \tag{9.84}$$

Hence, b_l is a constant, but $\tilde{\beta}_l(t_k)$ is defined as a sequence in t_k.

Approximation of simulation model

In the LMRW, the properties of the simulation model are not simple to explain in the way that the properties of the Gaussian HJM model are. Keeping this in mind, we begin by working with a case chosen for the simplicity of examining it: We take the case where the initial LIBOR is equal to the historical mean. Specifically,

$$L_j(0) = E^H[K(\,\cdot, \delta j)]. \tag{9.85}$$

This assumption may seem somewhat general for studying the properties of the simulation. Indeed, we can find this as an initial condition in Geiger (2011, pp. 52–53).

For this case, we expect that the following approximation holds:

$$\frac{\lambda_{0j}\delta L_j 0)}{1+\delta L_j(0)} \approx E^H\left[\frac{\lambda_{0j}\delta K(\,\cdot,\delta j)}{1+\delta K(\,\cdot,\delta j)}\right] \quad ; \quad j=1,\cdots,n. \tag{9.86}$$

From this and equation (9.1), we have

$$\begin{aligned}\sum_{j=1}^{i}\chi_{0j} &= \sum_{j=1}^{i}\frac{\lambda_{0j}\delta L_j(0)}{1+\delta L_j(0)} \\ &\approx E^H\left[\sum_{j=1}^{i}\frac{\lambda_{0j}\delta K(\,\cdot,\delta j)}{1+\delta K(\,\cdot,\delta j)}\right] \quad ; \quad i=1,\cdots,n. \end{aligned}\tag{9.87}$$

Substituting equation (9.5) into the above, we obtain

$$\sum_{j=1}^{i}\chi_{0j} \approx E^H\left[\sum_{j=1}^{i}\kappa_j\right] \quad ; \quad i=1,\cdots,n. \tag{9.88}$$

From this, the simulation having the form given in equation (9.79) is approximately reduced to

$$\sum_{i=1}^{n}\log L_i(\Delta s)e_i^l \approx \sum_{i=1}^{n}\log L_i(0)e_i^l + E^H\left[\tilde{\alpha}_l\right]\Delta s + \sqrt{\Delta s}\rho_l W_1^l. \tag{9.89}$$

Recalling the definitions of $\tilde{\alpha}_l$ and $\tilde{R}_l$, by equations (9.75) and (9.60), respectively, we have

$$\begin{aligned} E^H\left[\tilde{\alpha}_l\right] &= E^H\left[\frac{\sum_{i=1}^{n}\Delta\tilde{K}_i(t_k)e_i^l}{\Delta t}\right] = \sum_{i=1}^{n}E^H\left[\frac{\Delta\tilde{K}_i}{\Delta t}\right]e_i^l \\ &= \tilde{R}_l \quad ; \quad l=1,\cdots,n. \end{aligned}\tag{9.90}$$

This relation is an analogue to the result from Lemma 6.4.1 in the Gaussian HJM framework. Substituting this into (9.89), we obtain

$$\sum_{i=1}^{n}\log L_i(\Delta s)e_i^l \approx \sum_{i=1}^{n}\log L_i(0)e_i^l + \tilde{R}_l\Delta s + \sqrt{\Delta s}\rho_l W_1^l. \tag{9.91}$$

Properties of simulation model

The above approximation (9.91) admits the same structure as the real-world model (6.80) in the Gaussian HJM model:

$$\sum_{i=1}^{n} f(\Delta s, T_i)e_i^l = \sum_{i=1}^{n} f(0, T_i)e_i^l + R_l\Delta s + \sqrt{\Delta s}\rho_l W_1^l. \tag{9.92}$$

Both models are characterized by the lth rolled trend score for the drift term and historical volatility for the diffusion term. The difference between them is that the form (9.91) is an approximation represented in log-scale, while the initial condition is set by equation (9.85).

On the basis of this observation, we may say that *the simulation model approximately consists of historical drift and historical volatility in the principal component space representation*, while the initial LIBOR is given by the sample mean as equation (9.85). To make a more general argument, in the next section, we will examine the properties of the drift term under an arbitrary initial condition.

9.7 Real-world Model in State Space

In the previous section, we studied the properties of the simulation in the principal component space, where the initial forward LIBOR is assumed to satisfy equation (9.85). This section expands on this by allowing an arbitrary initial condition.

From equation (9.79), $L_i(\Delta s)$ is represented in the principal component space by

$$\begin{aligned}\sum_{i=1}^{n} \log L_i(\Delta s)e_i^l \quad = \quad & \sum_{i=1}^{n} \log L_i(0)e_i^l + \Big\{E^H\left[\tilde{\alpha}_l\right] \\ & + \sum_{i=1}^{n} \lambda_{0i}\left(\sum_{j=1}^{i} \chi_{0j} - E^H\left[\sum_{j=1}^{i} \kappa_j\right]\right) e_i^l\Big\}\Delta s \\ & + \sqrt{\Delta s}\rho_l W_1^l \;\; ; \;\; l = 1, \cdots, n.\end{aligned} \tag{9.93}$$

Converting this equation to an expression in the state space, the next theorem shows that a full-factor simulation is achieved in the state space, eliminating the market price of risk. This result corresponds to Theorem 6.8.1 in the Gaussian HJM model.

Theorem 9.7.1 *For a full-factor LIBOR market model, let λ^l be the lth volatility component, defined by $\lambda^l_{0i} = \rho_l e^l_i$ for $i = 1, \cdots, n$. Let φ be the market price of risk obtained by applying Theorem 9.2.1. For an arbitrary initial forward LIBOR $L_i(0)$ and a small time step $\Delta s > 0$ with $\Delta s < T_1$, $L_i(\Delta s)$ is simulated by*

$$\log L_i(\Delta s) = \log L_1(0) + \left\{ E^H\left[\frac{\Delta\tilde{K}_i}{\Delta t}\right] + \lambda_{0i}\left(\sum_{j=1}^{i}\chi_{0j} - E^H\left[\sum_{j=1}^{i}\kappa_j\right]\right)\right\}\Delta s + \sqrt{\Delta s}\lambda_{0i}W_1. \tag{9.94}$$

Proof By the same argument as in Appendix B, we can convert equation (9.93) to the corresponding expression in the state space. Specifically, left-multiplying both sides of equation (9.93) by $(e^1, \cdots, e^n)$, the left-hand side becomes

$$(e^1, \cdots, e^n)\begin{pmatrix} \sum_{i=1}^n \log L_i(\Delta s)e^1_i \\ \vdots \\ \sum_{i=1}^n \log L_i(\Delta s)e^n_i \end{pmatrix} = \begin{pmatrix} \log L_1(\Delta s) \\ \vdots \\ \log L_n(\Delta s) \end{pmatrix}, \tag{9.95}$$

and the first term in the right-hand side becomes

$$(e^1, \cdots, e^n)\begin{pmatrix} \sum_{i=1}^n \log L_i(0)e^1_i \\ \vdots \\ \sum_{i=1}^n \log L_i(0)e^n_i \end{pmatrix} = \begin{pmatrix} \log L_1(0) \\ \vdots \\ \log L_n(0) \end{pmatrix}. \tag{9.96}$$

From equation (9.16), the second term of equation (9.93) becomes

$$\begin{aligned}(e^1, \cdots, e^n)&\begin{pmatrix} E^H[\tilde{\alpha}_1] + \sum_{i=1}^n \lambda_{0i}\left(\sum_{j=1}^i \chi_{0j} - E^H\left[\sum_{j=1}^i \kappa_j\right]\right)e^1_i \\ \vdots \\ E^H[\tilde{\alpha}_n] + \sum_{i=1}^n \lambda_{0i}\left(\sum_{j=1}^i \chi_{0j} - E^H\left[\sum_{j=1}^i \kappa_j\right]\right)e^n_i \end{pmatrix} \\ &= \begin{pmatrix} E^H\left[\Delta\tilde{K}_1/\Delta t\right] + \lambda_{01}\left(\sum_{j=1}^1 \chi_{0j} - E^H\left[\sum_{j=1}^1 \kappa_j\right]\right) \\ \vdots \\ E^H\left[\Delta\tilde{K}_n/\Delta t\right] + \lambda_{0n}\left(\sum_{j=1}^n \chi_{0j} - E^H\left[\sum_{j=1}^n \kappa_j\right]\right) \end{pmatrix}.\end{aligned} \tag{9.97}$$

For the last term of (9.93), we have, from (9.73), that

$$\begin{aligned} (e^1, \cdots, e^n) \begin{pmatrix} \rho_1 W_1^1 \\ \vdots \\ \rho_n W_1^n \end{pmatrix} &= (e^1, \cdots, e^n) \begin{pmatrix} \sum_{i=1}^n \lambda_{0i} W_1 e_i^1 \\ \vdots \\ \sum_{i=1}^n \lambda_{0i} W_1 e_i^n \end{pmatrix} \\ &= \begin{pmatrix} \lambda_{01} W_1 \\ \vdots \\ \lambda_{0n} W_1 \end{pmatrix}. \end{aligned} \tag{9.98}$$

Summing each ith component separately, we obtain

$$\begin{aligned} \log L_i(\Delta s) &= \log L_i(0) + \left\{ E^H \left[\frac{\Delta \tilde{K}_i}{\Delta t} \right] \right. \\ &\quad \left. + \lambda_{0i} \left(\sum_{j=1}^{i} \chi_{0j} - E^H \left[\sum_{j=1}^{i} \kappa_j \right] \right) \right\} \Delta s + \sqrt{\Delta s} \lambda_{0i} W_1, \end{aligned} \tag{9.99}$$

for all i. This completes the proof. □

Properties of drift term

Now, we can examine the properties of the drift term in the simulation model (9.94). In the Gaussian HJM model, we see, from equation (6.87), that the drift coefficient of the real-world model is simply given by $E^H[\Delta F_i/\Delta t]$. Then, the drift is precisely the same as the rolled trend of the forward rate.

In contrast, the drift term in the LMRW is somewhat different from equation (6.87). Specifically, the drift coefficient for the process $\log L_i$ is expressed, from equation (9.94), as

$$E^H \left[\frac{\Delta \tilde{K}_i}{\Delta t} \right] + \lambda_{0i} \left(\sum_{j=1}^{i} \chi_{0j} - E^H \left[\sum_{j=1}^{i} \kappa_j \right] \right). \tag{9.100}$$

Here, the first term indicates the rolled trend of L_i in the sample period.

Let us examine the properties of the second term. To address this, we note that we have already studied the case in which the initial LIBOR is given by the sample mean, as assumed in equation (9.85),

$$L_j(0) = E^H[K(\ \cdot, \delta i)]. \tag{9.101}$$

From the approximation (9.88), specifically,

$$\sum_{j=1}^{i} \chi_j(0) \approx E^H\left[\sum_{j=1}^{i} \kappa_j\right], \tag{9.102}$$

and the second term in equation (9.100) is approximately equal to zero. Thus, the drift is approximately equal to the rolled trend of $K(\,\cdot, x_i)$. The following corollary summarizes this observation; this gives a state space expression of the form (9.91) in the PCA setup.

Corollary 9.7.2 *In a full-factor simulation model in the LMRW, if an initial forward LIBOR is equal to the sample mean of the historical forward LIBOR, as in equation (9.101), then it holds for* $i = 1, \cdots, n$ *that*

$$\log L_i(\Delta s) \approx \log L_i(0) + E^H\left[\frac{\Delta K_i}{\Delta t}\right]\Delta s + \sqrt{\Delta s}\lambda_i Z(1). \tag{9.103}$$

Since the term $E^H\left[\Delta K_i/\Delta t\right]$ represents the historical rolled trend of the forward LIBOR change, this corollary shows that real-world simulations are approximately equivalent to an empirical term structure model when the initial LIBOR is given by the sample mean.

Drift with general initial conditions

Next, let us consider a general case for the initial LIBOR and examine the properties of the drift term. For this objective, we develop our argument by using numerical approximation in a practical manner.

If the initial LIBOR is higher than the sample mean, so that $L_j(0) > E^H[K(\,\cdot, \delta i)]$, then it roughly holds that

$$\sum_{j=1}^{i} \chi_j(0) > E^H\left[\sum_{j=1}^{i} \kappa_j\right]. \tag{9.104}$$

Hence, the drift in equation (9.94) is roughly higher than the rolled trend. Conversely, if $L_j(0) < E^H[K(\,\cdot, \delta i)]$, then the drift will tend to be lower than the rolled trend. The difference from the case in the Gaussian HJM model is noteworthy. Building on this observation, we note that if the initial LIBOR curve is steeper than the sample mean of the LIBOR curve, then the simulation results in steepening drift, and similarly for higher-order observations.

It might be fruitful to investigate the meaning of this feature from the viewpoint of real-world simulation or risk management in the future.

Arbitrage pricing by simulation

For arbitrage pricing by simulation, let us recall the framework for this from Section 5.3, where the implied short rate $\bar{\mu}(t)$ was defined by $\bar{\mu}(t) = \bar{\mu}(T_{m(t)})$ such that

$$\bar{\mu}(T_i) = \frac{1}{\delta_{i-1}} \log\{1 + \delta_{i-1} L_{i-1}(T_{i-1})\} \quad ; \quad i = 1, \cdots, n \tag{9.105}$$

for each i. Here, $\bar{\mu}(t)$ is constant on each period $(T_{i-1}, T_i]$ with $i = 1, \cdots, n$.

By using the market price of risk φ and the implied short rate $\bar{\mu}(t)$, the state price deflator was given, in equation (5.24), as

$$\xi(t) = \exp\left\{ - \int_0^t \left(\bar{\mu}(s) + \frac{|\varphi|^2}{2} \right) ds - \int_0^t \varphi_s dW_s \right\}. \tag{9.106a}$$

By applying the Euler approximation, we obtain the discretization of $\xi(\Delta s)$ as

$$\xi(\Delta s) = \exp\left\{ - \left(\bar{\mu}(0) + \frac{|\varphi|^2}{2} \right) \Delta s - \sqrt{\Delta s} \varphi W_1 \right\}. \tag{9.106b}$$

Thus, arbitrage pricing can be carried out by simulation in the LMRW.

As an example, consider a security whose payoff at $T < T_1$ is given by a random variable X. The price p_t of this security at t is given by $p_t = \frac{1}{\xi(t)} E_t[\xi(T)X]$.

It is numerically possible to simulate the evolution of the LIBOR for longer periods, For this, we have two major approaches; one is using a time-homogeneous volatility, and the second is using a maturity-dependent volatility. It is a subject for future research to investigate what volatility structure is reasonable to use for long-period real-world simulation. In contrast, for a strictly numerical technique, see Norman (2009).

9.8 Dimensionality Reduction

We worked with the full-factor simulation model in the LMRW in Sections 9.6 and 9.7. For practical use, this section investigates how to reduce the number of factors needed for approximating the full-factor model.

In the Gaussian HJM model, the dimensionality could be determined by measuring the accumulated contribution rate, as stated in Section 6.8. In this way, PCA mostly provides a solution to the problem of reducing dimensionality.

However, as described in the following subsections, the simulation model in the LMRW has specific properties that PCA cannot capture. Thus, we need to introduce other measures for dimensionality reduction. Toward this objective, this section is divided into three subsections. Section 9.8.1 presents a setup that can be used to formulate the problem of dimensionality reduction. With this setup, Theorem 9.8.2 provides a fundamental result for reducing the number of dimensions. Furthermore, this theorem is modified to obtain Corollaries 9.8.3 and 9.8.4 in Section 9.8.3, which are practically useful.

The argument here is just a numerical analysis problem. The proofs of Proposition 9.8.1 and Theorem 9.8.2 are presented in Appendix D.

9.8.1 Setup of Dimensionality Reduction

This subsection formulates the problem of dimensionality reduction in the LMRW. The basic setup is the same as in Sections 9.1 and 9.2. Additionally, we assume that the eigenvalues satisfy

$$(\rho_1)^2 > (\rho_2)^2 > \cdots > (\rho_n)^2 > 0, \tag{9.107}$$

and

$$\lim_{l \to n} (\rho_l)^2 = 0. \tag{9.108}$$

Here, convergence is measured in the sense of engineering because $\{\rho_i\}_i$ is a finite sequence, and "convergence" will be used in the above sense in this section. In this context, we say that the accumulated contribution rate C_l satisfies $\lim_{l \to n} C_l = 1$.

Let us recall the formulation of LIBOR process in the LMRW, given by equation (9.2) as

$$L_i(t) = L_i(0) \exp\left\{ \int_0^t \left(\lambda_i \sum_{j=m(t)}^{i} \chi_j + \lambda_i \varphi - \frac{|\lambda_i|^2}{2} \right) dt + \int_0^t \lambda_i dW_t \right\} \tag{9.109}$$

for $i = 1, \cdots, n$, where W_t denotes the n-dimensional Brownian motion under $\mathbf{P}$.

The d-factor model

Our objective is to determine the number of factors d such that the d-factor model sufficiently approximates the full-factor model. As is conventional, let us begin our argument with the full-factor model.

For a short time interval $\Delta s > 0$, the Euler approximation implies $\log L_i(\Delta s)$ from equations (9.1) and (9.109) as

$$\begin{aligned}\log L_i(\Delta s) &= \log L_i(0) + \sum_{l=1}^{n} \lambda_{0i}^l \sum_{j=1}^{i} \frac{\delta \lambda_{0j}^l L_j(0)}{1+\delta L_j(0)} \Delta s - \sum_{l=1}^{n} \frac{(\lambda_{0i}^l)^2}{2} \Delta s \\ &\quad + \sum_{l=1}^{n} \lambda_{0i}^l \varphi_l \Delta s + \sum_{l=1}^{n} \lambda_{0i}^l \sqrt{\Delta s} W_1^l. \end{aligned} \tag{9.110}$$

To avoid confusion, in the first d-factor model we denote L_i, φ_l and γ_i by $\breve{L}_i$, $\breve{\varphi}_l$ and $\breve{\gamma}_i$, respectively. Hence, $\log \breve{L}_i(\Delta s)$ is represented as

$$\begin{aligned}\log \breve{L}_i(\Delta s) &= \log L_i(0) + \sum_{l=1}^{d} \lambda_{0i}^l \sum_{j=1}^{i} \frac{\delta \lambda_{0j}^l L_j(0)}{1+\delta L_j(0)} \Delta s - \sum_{l=1}^{d} \frac{(\lambda_{0i}^l)^2}{2} \Delta s \\ &\quad + \sum_{l=1}^{d} \lambda_{0i}^l \breve{\varphi}_l \Delta s + \sum_{l=1}^{d} \lambda_{0i}^l \sqrt{\Delta s} W_1^l. \end{aligned} \tag{9.111}$$

With these, our objective is then simplified to the problem of how to determine the lowest dimensionality d such that equation (9.111) approximates equation (9.110) sufficiently well.

9.8.2 Dimensionality Reduction

This section investigates a method to reduce the dimensionality for simulation. For this, a measure, the "MPR score" (market-price-of-risk score) is introduced. First, we show the convergence of the market price of risk in the following proposition.

Proposition 9.8.1 *If the dimensionality d is high enough that $C_d \approx 1$, then it follows that $\breve{\varphi}_l \approx \varphi_l$ for all $l = 1, \cdots, d$.*

Proof See Appendix D.1. □

This proposition means that we must ensure the dimensionality d is sufficiently high even when we calculate only the first market price of risk.

MPR score

The n-dimensional constant vector $\gamma = (\gamma_1, \cdots, \gamma_n)^T$ was defined, by equation (9.46), as

$$\gamma_i = E^H\left[\frac{\Delta \tilde{K}_i}{\Delta t}\right] - \lambda_{0i} E^H\left[\sum_{j=1}^{i} \kappa_j\right] + \frac{|\lambda_{0i}|^2}{2}. \tag{9.112}$$

By using this, the lth market price of risk was represented in equation (9.51) as $\varphi_l = \frac{1}{\rho_l}\sum_{i=1}^{n} \gamma_i e_i^l$. We define a constant vector $\zeta = (\zeta_1, \cdots, \zeta_n)^T$ by letting

$$\zeta_l = \sum_{i=1}^{n} \gamma_i e_i^l \ ; \quad l = 1, \cdots, n. \tag{9.113}$$

With these, the market price of risk is represented by $\varphi_l = \zeta_l / \rho_l$. Here, ζ_l is the lth projection of γ and also the score of its lth principal component. Along these lines, we call ζ_l the *lth MPR score*.

MPR score in d-dimensional model

The d-dimensional version of γ_i is denoted $\breve{\gamma}_i$. This is specified as

$$\breve{\gamma}_i = E^H\left[\frac{\Delta \tilde{K}_i}{\Delta t}\right] - \lambda_{0i} E^H\left[\sum_{j=1}^{i} \kappa_j\right] + \frac{|\lambda_{0i}|^2}{2} \ ; \quad i = 1, \cdots, n. \tag{9.114}$$

Here, the inner product in the second and third terms is defined in the d-dimensional Euclidean space. Additionally, the MPR score $\breve{\zeta}_l$ for the d-dimensional model is defined by

$$\breve{\zeta}_l = \sum_{i=1}^{n} \breve{\gamma}_i e_i^l \ ; \quad l = 1, \cdots, d, \tag{9.115}$$

where the inner product in the right-hand side is calculated in the same way as above. Then, the market price of risk for the d-dimensional model is represented by

$$\breve{\varphi}_l = \frac{\breve{\zeta}_l}{\rho_l} \ ; \quad l = 1, \cdots, d. \tag{9.116}$$

The following theorem shows that the MPR score acts as a measure to determine the appropriate dimensionality for the simulation.

Theorem 9.8.2 *If the factor number d is sufficiently large such that $C_d \approx 1$, and the absolute value of the MPR score $|\zeta_l|$ is sufficiently small for all l with $d < l \leq n$, then the first d-factor model (9.111) approximates the full-factor model (9.110).*

Proof See Appendix D.2. □

Thus, the dimensionality for simulation is determined from a combination of the accumulated contribution rate and the MPR score.

Remark

We assumed that the volatility risk ρ_l is strictly decreasing in l, from equation (9.107). We assumed, also, that the market price of risk has the form $\varphi_l = \zeta_l/\rho_l$; here, ρ_l appears as a denominator. This means that $|\varphi_l|$ may not be monotonically decreasing in l. Accordingly, the convergence of $\lim_{l \to n} \lambda_{0i}^l \varphi_l = 0$ holds independently from the convergence of $\lim_{d \to n} C_d = 1$. This is a feature of dimensionality reduction that is intrinsic to the LMRW.

There may be a different and simpler approach for reducing dimensionality, and study of this is suggested for future research.

9.8.3 Dimensionality Reduction in Practice

In practice, it is not feasible to compute the market price of risk φ and the MPR score ζ in the full-factor model. To accommodate practical use, we relax Theorem 9.8.2 as follows.

Corollary 9.8.3 (Dimensionality reduction) *For sufficiently large values of $\tilde{n} \leq n$, let $\breve{\zeta}_l$ $l = 1, \cdots, \tilde{n}$ denote the MPR scores in the $\tilde{n}$-factor model. If $C_d \approx 1$, and $|\breve{\zeta}_l|$ is sufficiently small for all l with $d < l \leq \tilde{n}$, then the first d-factor model (9.111) sufficiently approximates the full-factor model (9.110).*

In the following, the symbol "$\breve{\ }$" is omitted for brevity. From the same observation as above, Theorem 9.7.1 approximately holds for the d-factor model, as the following corollary asserts.

Corollary 9.8.4 *Under the assumptions of Corollary 9.8.3, the following form in the d-factor model approximates the full-factor model in the formulation (9.94):*

$$\begin{aligned}\log L_i(\Delta s) &= \log L_i(0) + E^H\left[\frac{\Delta\tilde{K}_i}{\Delta t}\right]\Delta s \\ &\quad +\lambda_{0i}\left\{\sum_{j=1}^{i}\chi_{0j} - E^H\left[\sum_{j=1}^{i}\kappa_j\right]\right\}\Delta s \\ &\quad +\sqrt{\Delta s}\lambda_{0i}W_1 \ ; \quad i=1,\cdots,n, \end{aligned} \tag{9.117}$$

where the third, fourth, and fifth terms are calculated in the d-factor model.

When we intend to simulate the interest rate scenario only without pricing, it is sufficient to use the above form. For this, we need not use the market price of risk in the formulation. In particular, the following corollary provides an approximation of equation (9.91) in the state space.

Corollary 9.8.5 *If the initial LIBOR $L_i(0)$ is equal to the sample mean of the corresponding LIBOR, that is, if*

$$L_i(0) = E^H[K(\ \cdot, \delta i)], \tag{9.118}$$

then the following approximation holds in the above d-factor model:

$$\log L_i(\Delta s) \approx \log L_i(0) + E^H\left[\frac{\Delta K_i}{\Delta t}\right]\Delta s + \sqrt{\Delta s}\lambda_{0i}Z(1) \tag{9.119}$$

for $i = 1, \cdots, n$.

This corollary states that even when we work with the d-dimensional model, the real-world simulation is approximately equivalent to a historical term structure so long as we have initial conditions satisfying equation (9.118) for each i.

9.9 Numerical Procedures in LMRW

This section describes a numerical procedure that can be used to build a simulation model in the LMRW. Let $\delta > 0$ be fixed and let x_i be a time length to the bond maturities such that $x_i = \delta i$ for $i = 1, \cdots, n$. For a fixed time interval $\Delta t > 0$, we set the sequence of observation dates by letting $t_k = \Delta t k, k = 1, \cdots, J+1$.

Numerical calculation of $\Delta \tilde{K}_i(t_k)$

$\Delta \tilde{K}_i(t_k)$ was defined in equation (9.13) by

$$\Delta \tilde{K}_i(t_k) = \log K(t_{k+1}, x_i - \Delta t) - \log K(t_k, x_i) \tag{9.120}$$

for $i = 1, \cdots, n,\ k = 1, \cdots, J$. As stated in Section 6.9 in the Gaussian HJM framework, we usually observe the forward LIBOR in the form $K(t_k, x_i)$ for a fixed time length x_i at each t_k. This means that we cannot directly observe $K(t_{k+1}, x_i - \Delta t)$, which appears in the first term of equation (9.120).

To estimate $K(t_{k+1}, x_i - \Delta t)$, the conventional method uses $K(t_{k+1}, x_i)$ as a proxy. Because the rolled trend explains the majority of the market price of risk, as mentioned in Section 9.5, it is recommended that we estimate the value by some type of interpolation. Similarly to the interpolation in equation (6.93), we here use linear interpolation, in the form

$$K(t_{k+1}, x_i - \Delta t) = \left(1 - \frac{\Delta t}{\delta}\right) K(t_{k+1}, x_i) + \frac{\Delta t}{\delta} K(t_{k+1}, x_{i-1}). \tag{9.121}$$

Naturally, spline interpolation or log-scale interpolation might provide a more reasonable estimate, but this is a matter for financial engineering.

The significance of this linear interpolation will be shown by a numerical example in Section 10.2.3, where we will see that the specific properties of the real-world simulation are easily missed if we use $K(t_{k+1}, x_i)$ instead of $K(t_{k+1}, x_i - \Delta t)$.

Calculation of the market price of risk

Assume that the covariance matrix has rank n. We describe the procedure to estimate the market price of risk in the state space setup, as follows.

1) We calculate $K(t_{k+1}, x_i - \Delta t)$ by the interpolation (9.121). By using this, $\Delta \tilde{K}_i(t_k)$ is obtained from equation (9.120) for $i = 1, \cdots, n,\ k = 1, \cdots, J$.

2) We calculate the eigenvalues $(\rho_l)^2$, the principal components e^l, and the volatilities σ^l for $l = 1, \cdots, n$ by PCA on the covariance

$Cov(\Delta\tilde{K}_i,\ \Delta\tilde{K}_j)/\Delta t.$

3) The lth volatility component λ^l is determined by $\lambda_i^l = \rho_l e_i^l$ for $i, l = 1, \cdots, n$.

4) $E^H\left[\Delta\tilde{K}_i\right]$ is obtained from the sample data for $i = 1, \cdots, n$.

5) We fix a sufficiently large integer $\tilde{n}$ with $\tilde{n} \leq n$, and then calculate the values in further steps in the $\tilde{n}$-factor model.

6) We calculate the sequence $\kappa_j(t_k), k = 1, \cdots, J$ of equation (9.5) from the observation $K(t_k, \delta i)$ as

$$\kappa_j^l(t_k) = \frac{\lambda_{0j}^l \delta K(t_k, \delta j)}{1 + \delta K(t_k, \delta j)} \quad ; \quad l = 1, \cdots, \tilde{n},\ j = 1, \cdots, n. \tag{9.122}$$

7) We calculate $E^H\left[\sum_{j=1}^i \kappa_j^l\right]$ for $l = 1, \cdots, \tilde{n}$ and $i = 1, \cdots, n$ from the above.

8) From equation (9.114) for the $\tilde{n}$-factor model, γ_i is obtained for $i = 1, \cdots, n$ by

$$\begin{aligned} \gamma_i &= E^H\left[\frac{\Delta\tilde{K}_i}{\Delta t}\right] - \lambda_{0i} E^H\left[\sum_{j=1}^{i} \kappa_j\right] + \frac{|\lambda_{0i}|^2}{2} \\ &= E^H\left[\frac{\Delta\tilde{K}_i}{\Delta t}\right] - \sum_{l=1}^{\tilde{n}} \lambda_{0i}^l E^H\left[\sum_{j=1}^{i} \kappa_j^l\right] + \frac{\sum_{l=1}^{\tilde{n}} (\lambda_{0i}^l)^2}{2}, \end{aligned} \tag{9.123}$$

where the inner product in the second and third terms is calculated in the $\tilde{n}$-factor model.

9) The MPR score ζ_l is obtained from equation (9.115) as $\zeta_l = \sum_{i=1}^n \gamma_i e_i^l$ for $l = 1, \cdots, \tilde{n}$.

10) From equation (9.116), the market price of risk is obtained in the $\tilde{n}$-factor model as $\varphi_l = \zeta_l / \rho_l$ for $l = 1, \cdots, \tilde{n}$.

The differences between this procedure and that in the Gaussian HJM framework are the following.

- The dimensionality $\tilde{n}$ is prefixed to estimate the market price of risk and the MPR score.

- The procedures from steps 6) to 8) above are more complicated than the corresponding procedures for the Gaussian HJM model.

Real-world simulation

We next summarize the procedure to build a single-period simulation model by using Corollary 9.8.4, where the market price of risk does not appear explicitly. Additionally, we show a simulation model in the original form (9.68), which involves the market price of risk.

1) The procedures from steps 1) to 9) in the above are the same.

2) We calculate the accumulated contribution rate C_d by letting

$$C_d = \frac{\sum_{l=1}^{d}(\rho_l)^2}{\sum_{l=1}^{n}(\rho_l)^2} \quad ; \quad d = 1, \cdots, \tilde{n}. \tag{9.124}$$

3) By Corollary 9.8.3, the dimensionality d, $d \le \tilde{n}$ is determined such that $C_d \approx 1$ and the MPR score $|\zeta_l|$ is sufficiently small for all l with $d < l \le \tilde{n}$.

4) We set the initial LIBOR $L_i(0)$ and generate the d-dimensional sequence of standard normal random numbers.

5) From equation (5.9), we compute $\chi_j(0)$ by letting

$$\chi_j^l(0) = \frac{\lambda_{0j}^l \delta L_j(0)}{1 + \delta L_j(0)} \quad ; \quad l = 1, \cdots, d, \ j = 1, \cdots, n. \tag{9.125}$$

6) For a time period Δs with $\Delta s < x_1$, $L_i(\delta)$ is simulated in a d-factor model by using Corollary 9.8.4. Specifically,

$$\begin{aligned} \log L_i(\Delta s) &= \log L_i(0) + E^H\left[\frac{\Delta \tilde{K}_i}{\Delta t}\right]\Delta s + \sum_{l=1}^{d}\lambda_{0i}^l\left\{\sum_{j=1}^{i}\chi_{0j}^l\right. \\ &\quad \left. -E^H\left[\sum_{j=1}^{i}\kappa_j^l\right]\right\}\Delta s + \sqrt{\Delta s}\sum_{l=1}^{d}\lambda_{0i}^l W_1^l \end{aligned} \tag{9.126}$$

for $i = 1, \cdots, n$.

7) Alternatively, we may use, from equation (9.3), the following form instead of the above:

$$\begin{aligned}\log L_i(\Delta s) &= \log L_i(0) + \left\{ \lambda_{0i} \sum_{j=m(t)}^{i} \chi_{0j} + \lambda_{0i}\varphi - \frac{|\lambda_{0i}|^2}{2} \right\} \Delta s \\ &\quad + \sqrt{\Delta s}\lambda_{0i} W_1 \\ &= \log L_i(0) + \left\{ \sum_{l=1}^{d} \lambda_{0i}^l \sum_{j=m(t)}^{i} \chi_{0j}^l + \sum_{l=1}^{d} \lambda_{0i}^l \varphi_l \right. \\ &\quad \left. - \sum_{l=1}^{d} \frac{|\lambda_{0i}^l|^2}{2} \right\} \Delta s + \sqrt{\Delta s} \sum_{l=1}^{d} \lambda_{0i}^l W_1^l, \end{aligned} \tag{9.127}$$

for $i = 1, \cdots, n$.

On the one hand, the formulation (9.126) is convenient because it highlights the features of the drift in the simulation. On the other hand, the formulation (9.127) is simple to use because it is immediately constructed from the spot LIBOR model.

Arbitrage pricing

Arbitrage pricing in the LMRW was addressed at the end of Section 9.7, where the implied short rate $\bar{\mu}(0)$ at $t = 0$ was given by $\bar{\mu}(0) = \frac{1}{\delta}\log\{1 + \delta L_0(0)\}$. From this, the state price deflator is obtained from equation (9.106b) as

$$\xi(\Delta s) = \exp\left[- \left\{ \bar{\mu}(0) + \frac{|\varphi|^2}{2} \right\} \Delta s - \sqrt{\Delta s}\varphi W_1 \right]. \tag{9.128a}$$

Specifically,

$$\xi(\Delta s) = \exp\left[- \left\{ \bar{\mu}(0) + \frac{\sum_{l=1}^{d}(\varphi_l)^2}{2} \right\} \Delta s - \sqrt{\Delta s} \sum_{l=1}^{d} \varphi_i^l W_1^l \right]. \tag{9.128b}$$

By using this, arbitrage pricing can be executed.

Long-term simulation

By repeatedly carrying out single-period simulations, it is possible to simulate long-term evolution of the forward LIBOR and the state price deflator. Naturally, we may change the volatility structure and the market price of risk with the passage of time. This might be an interesting subject for future research.

CHAPTER 10

NUMERICAL EXAMPLES

Abstract: This chapter presents numerical examples of real-world modeling using actual market data. First, we show examples within the Gaussian HJM model, working with the Japanese LIBOR swap market data. We calculate the market price of risk from the data, referring to the interpretation of the market price of risk given in Chapter 6. After that, we show numerical examples in the LMRW in parallel to the above. Since the simulation model in the LMRW is more complicated than that of the Gaussian HJM model, we consider four different cases in the LMRW to clearly illustrate the properties of the real-world model. In these, Sections 10.1 and 10.2 present detailed examinations of the examples given in Yasuoka (2015) and Yasuoka (2012, 2013a), respectively.

Additionally, we present an actual example that admits a positive market price of risk. For this, we employ the Hull–White model, working with data on U.S. Treasury yields. Finally, working with long-period observations of U.S. Treasury yields, we calculate the market prices of risk in the Hull–White model. With this, we verify that long-period observation tends to cause a negative market price of risk. These examples, in Sections 10.3 and 10.4, are original to this book.

Keywords: Dimension reduction, Drift term, Flat yield model, Full-factor model, Gaussian HJM model, Historical trend, Hull–White model, Implied forward LIBOR, Implied forward rate, LIBOR, LIBOR market model, LMRW, Long-period observation, Market price of risk, Mean reversion, Monte Carlo simulation, Negative price tendency, PCA, Real-world model, Real-world simulation, Swap rate, U.S. Treasury

Takashi Yasuoka

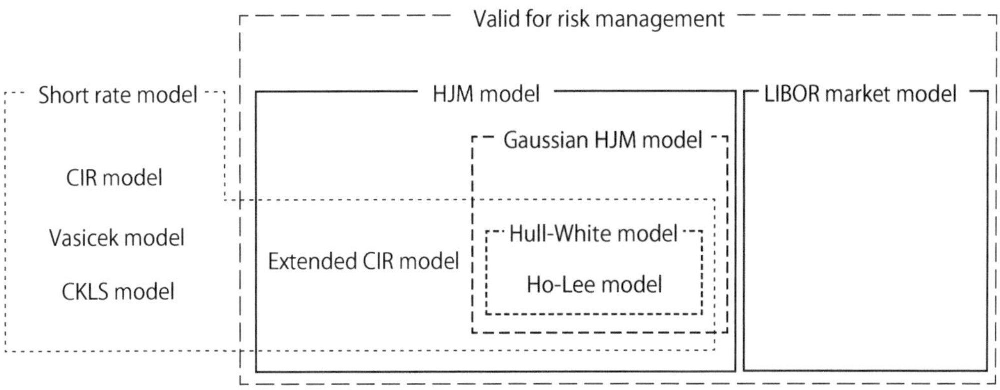

Figure 10.1: Inclusion relation among term structure models. A framework for real-world modeling has been developed for the models listed in the shaded regions.

Fig. 10.1 illustrates the inclusion relation among term structure models from the viewpoint of mathematical modeling[1]. Some of the short rate models are not arbitrage-free in the sense of Section 4.4; that is, it is impossible to fit a term structure with arbitrary initial forward rates to those models. This figure shows that the HJM model and the LIBOR market model are appropriate for use in risk management. In the HJM model, what we can construct as a real-world model is restricted to the Gaussian HJM model. Along this line, we will use the same set of historical data to exemplify the real-world modeling of these types in Sections 10.1 and 10.2.

The Ho–Lee model is a special case of the Hull–White model, in which the mean reversion rate vanishes. Specifically, the Ho–Lee model cannot be used when it is necessary to represent the mean reversion property. Because of this, the model has not been successfully used in recent practice. Here, we do not work with the Ho–Lee model when showing numerical examples. As the simplest model in this context, the Hull–White model is used in presenting an instance of a positive market price of risk and an instance of negative price tendency in Sections 10.3 and 10.4, respectively.

[1]For details of the extended CIR model, see Hull and White (1990) or Munk (2011).

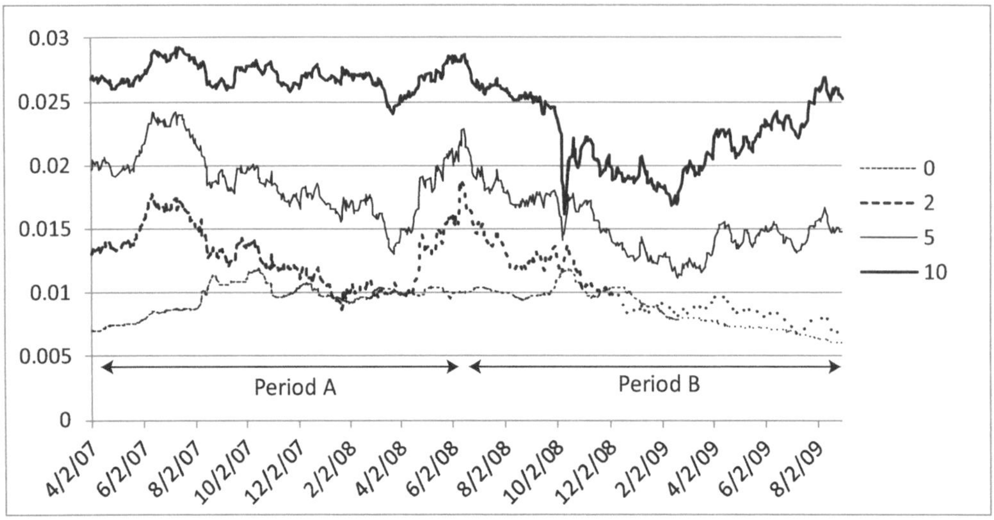

Figure 10.2: Forward rates in the Japanese LIBOR swap market. The implied six-month forward rate is regarded as the instantaneous forward rate. Period A is from 2 April 2007 to 16 June 2008, and Period B is form 16 June 2008 to 31 August 2009. Swap rate data were provided by Mizuho Information and Research Institute. LIBOR data were obtained from Riskmatrix (2014). Implied forward rates were calculated by the author.

10.1 Real-world Model in the Gaussian HJM Model

This section presents numerical examples of real-world modeling within the Gaussian HJM framework. We verify the numerical properties of the market price of risk and the drift in the simulation, referring to the results in Chapter 6.

10.1.1 Estimation of Market Price of Risk

Sample data description

We use the Japanese LIBOR swap rates for April 2007 through August 2009 and apply the cubic spline algorithm to interpolate the interest rates at semi-annual intervals. We set $\delta = 0.5$ (year) and solve for the six-month forward rate by bootstrapping. For convenience, we regard the six-month forward rate as the instantaneous forward rate.

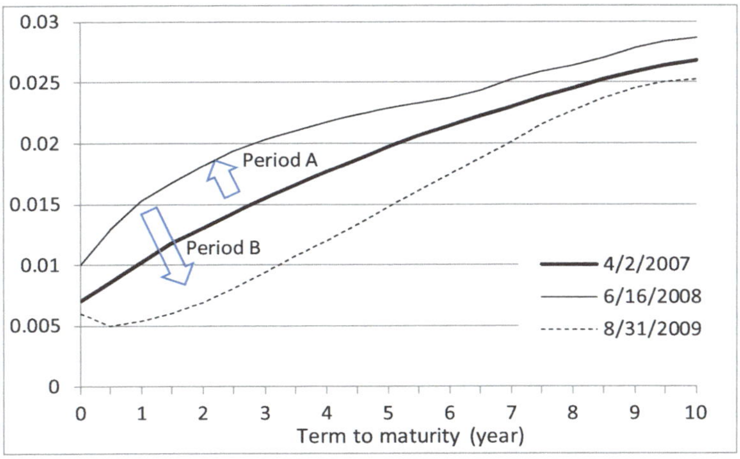

Figure 10.3: Forward rate curves at 2 April 2007, 16 June 2008, and 31 August 2009. Period A is from 2 April 2007 to 16 June 2008, and Period B is from 16 June 2008 to 31 August 2009.

Fig. 10.2 exhibits a historical chart of the forward rates with maturities of 0, 2, 5, and 10 years. This chart shows a sudden fall of the forward rates in early October 2008; that fall was related to the huge decline in the stock market as a consequence of the 2008 global financial crisis. Proposition 6.5.1 states that the market price of risk is basically determined by the rolled trend, and so from this observation it is expected that this sudden change would have little influence on the market price of risk.

To examine the numerical properties of the market price of risk, we split the sample period into two periods. Period A is earlier and covers 2 April 2007 to 16 June 2008 (297 data points), where the forward rates show an upward trend. Period B is later and covers 16 June 2008 to 31 August 2009 (298 data points), where the forward rates show a downward trend. Fig. 10.3 presents the forward rate curves of three specific days (2 April 2007, 16 June 2008, and 31 August 2009). These curves show that the observable trend is bear-flattening in period A and bull-steepening in period B.

Fig. 10.4 presents the sample mean of the forward rates in each period, where "mean $\pm$ σ" represents the mean plus/minus one standard deviation of the sample rates. We can see that the forward rate curve is mostly upward-sloping in Period A.

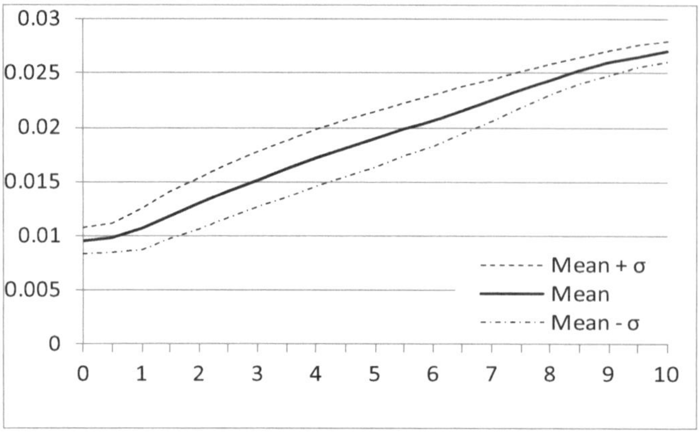

Period A

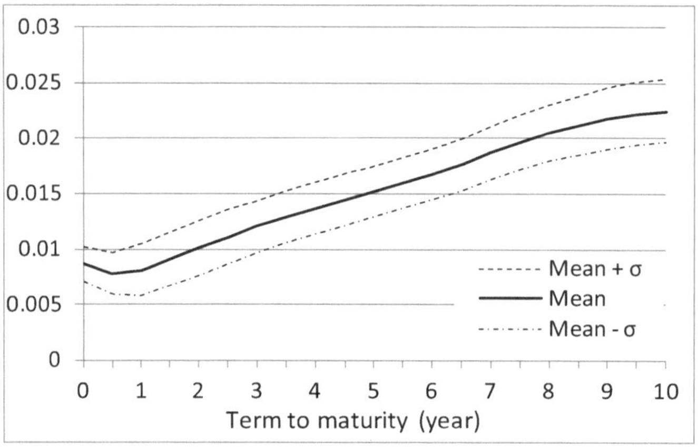

Period B

Figure 10.4: Mean and standard deviation of sample forward rates

In Period B, however, the forward rate curve is downward-sloping at the short end[2], and upward-sloping at maturity of 1 to 10 years. Because of this, the forward rates roughly admit a roll-up tendency at the short end and a roll-down tendency for maturity of 2 to 10 years.

[2]Precisely speaking, the spot LIBOR refers to the LIBOR itself, and the forward rate is implied from the LIBOR and swap rates. Because of this relation, this negative slope at the short end might be due to a difference of markets rather than due to the term structure of the interest rates.

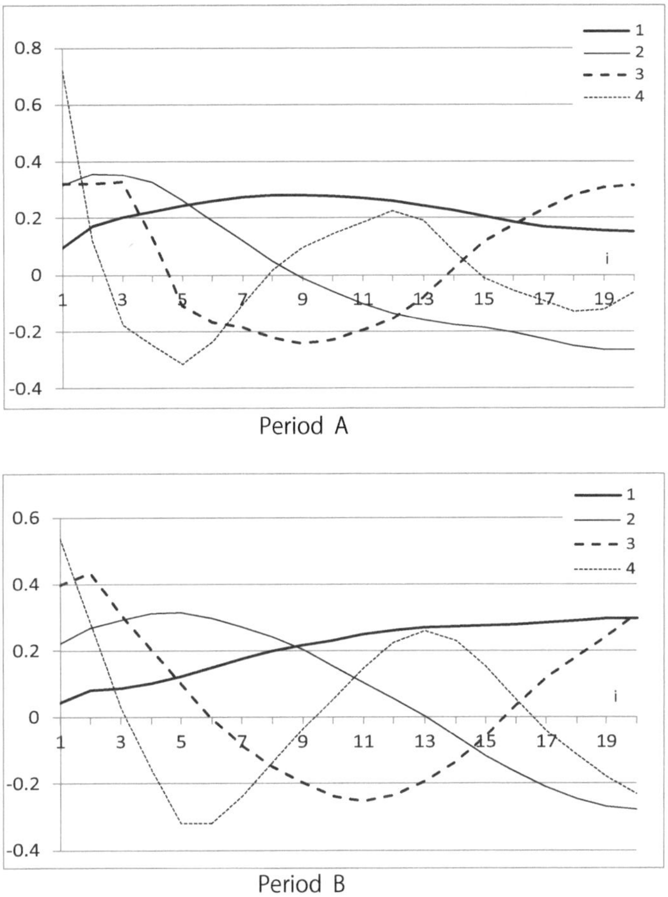

Figure 10.5: First four principal components for Period A and Period B

Calculation of the market price of risk

We set $\Delta t = 0.08$ (equivalent to 20 days). According to the procedure in Section 6.9, we compute the market price of risk. The value $\sigma_{0i} v_{0i}$ in equation (6.97) is approximately calculated in the eight-factor model. Table 10.1 shows the eigenvalues $(\rho_l)^2$, the contribution rates, and the market prices of risk φ_l for each component. We can verify that the size of φ_l is not decreasing in l, as remarked in the proof of Theorem 9.8.2[3]. Specifically, $|\varphi_l|$ attains a maximum at $l = 6$ in Period A and at $l = 5$ in Period B.

The accumulated contribution rate shows that the first three components

[3]Although this remark was made in regard to the LMRW, it is obviously valid for the Gaussian HJM model as well.

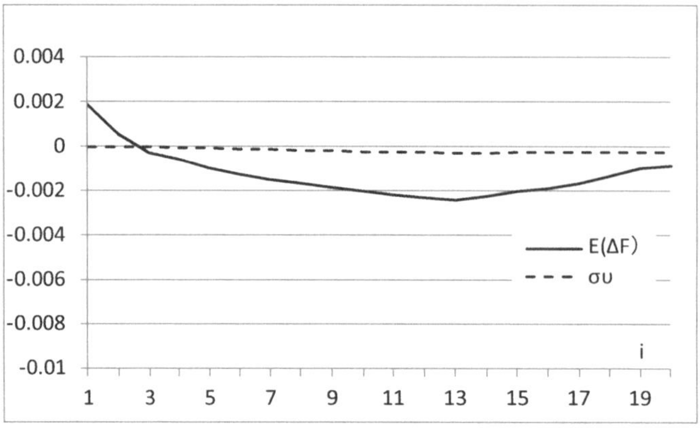

Period A

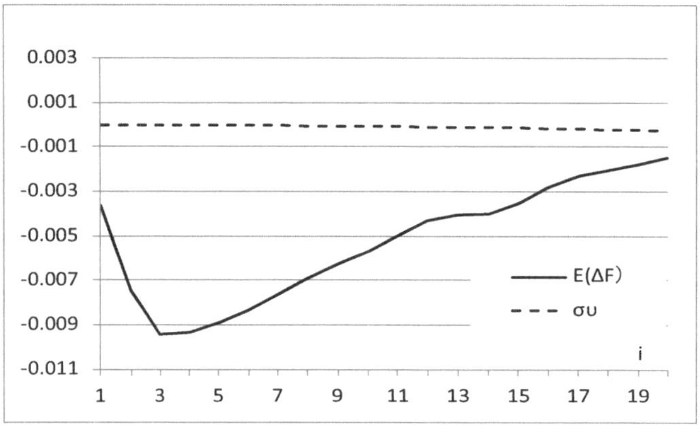

Period B

Figure 10.6: Two component terms of γ for Period A and B. γ is represented by $\gamma_i = E^H[\Delta F_i/\Delta t] + \sigma_{0i}v_{0i}$. In the graph, $E(\Delta F)$ and σv denote $E^H[\Delta F_i/\Delta t]$ and $\sigma_{0i}v_{0i}$, respectively, and $E(\Delta F)$ shows the term structure of the rolled trend.

explain more than 98% of the covariance. Fig. 10.5 exhibits the first four principal components for both periods. As mentioned in Section 4.3, the first three components represent, respectively, parallel shifts, steepness changes, and curvature changes of the forward rate curve.

Table 10.1: Eigenvalues and the market price of risk. Real-world modeling in the Gaussian HJM model.

Period A (3 April 2007 to 16 June 2008)

	Eigenvalue	Contribution rate	Accumulated contribution rate	Market price of risk
l	$(\rho_l)^2$		C_l	φ_l
1	7.61E-04	0.9305	0.9305	-0.256
2	4.53E-05	0.0554	0.9859	0.532
3	5.44E-06	0.0067	0.9926	0.598
4	3.29E-06	0.0040	0.9966	0.495
5	1.22E-06	0.0015	0.9981	0.896
6	5.86E-07	0.0007	0.9988	-1.049
7	3.22E-07	0.0004	0.9992	-0.011
8	2.45E-07	0.0003	0.999	0.311

Period B (16 June 2008 to 31 August 2009)

	Eigenvalue	Contribution rate	Accumulated contribution rate	Market price of risk
l	$(\rho_l)^2$		C_l	φ_l
1	4.77E-04	0.8082	0.8082	-0.884
2	8.35E-05	0.1413	0.9495	-1.886
3	2.38E-05	0.0402	0.9897	-0.816
4	3.14E-06	0.0053	0.995	1.113
5	1.31E-06	0.0022	0.9972	2.445
6	5.57E-07	0.0009	0.9982	-0.557
7	3.36E-07	0.0006	0.9988	1.746
8	2.55E-07	0.0004	0.9992	-0.709

Market price of risk and the historical trend

Let us verify the interpretation of the market price of risk that was given in Section 6.5. In equation (6.29), γ_i was defined as

$$\gamma_i = E^H[\Delta F_i/\Delta t] + \sigma_{0i}\upsilon_{0i}. \tag{10.1}$$

Additionally, Proposition 6.5.1 assumes that the greater part of γ_i is from $E^H[\Delta F_i/\Delta t]$, and specifically $|\sigma_{0i}\upsilon_{0i}| \ll E^H[\Delta F_i/\Delta t]$. In this respect, Fig. 10.6 shows the behavior of $E^H[\Delta F_i/\Delta t]$ and $\sigma_i\upsilon_i$ (abbreviated as $E(\Delta F)$ and $\sigma\upsilon$, respectively, in the figure). We see that $|E^H[\Delta F_i/\Delta t]|$ is considerably larger than $|\sigma_i v_i|$ in both periods. From this, it is reasonable to accept that the above inequality is almost satisfied in these cases. Along these lines, the market price of risk is approximately explained by the rolled trend from Proposition 6.5.1, as well as roughly explained by the observable trend in both cases.

The observable trend is almost bear-flattening in period A, and the row labeled "bear flat" in Table 6.4 shows that φ_1 ought to be near zero and φ_2 should be positive. Table 10.1 shows that

$$\varphi_1 = -0.256, \qquad \varphi_2 = 0.532 \tag{10.2}$$

in this period, and so they are roughly explained by Table 6.4 .

The observable trend of period B is bull-steepening. For this, Table 6.4, in the row labeled "bull steep," shows that φ_1 and φ_2 should both be negative. Table 10.1 shows that, in Period B,

$$\varphi_1 = -0.884, \qquad \varphi_2 = -1.886. \tag{10.3}$$

These values are also consistent with Table 6.4. From these, the market price of risk is mostly determined by the historical trend, rather than as an impact from the sudden fall of the interest rates in 2008.

If possible to perform, the t-test for this estimate might provide useful information about these estimates (this is left as a future subject). We node that both Period A and Period B have a time length of around 300 business day, which is relatively short in the sense of a negative price tendency. Because of this, it is not asserted that the condition (6.60) is always satisfied.

10.1.2 Observation on Simulation

Dimension reduction

Next let us determine the dimensionality such that the simulation model approximates the full-factor model. In the manner described in Section 6.8, it is sufficient to determine the number of factors d such that the accumulated contribution rate C_d is close to 1. Table 10.1 shows that C_3 is greater than 0.98 for both periods. Hence, we work with a three-factor model for both Period A and Period B.

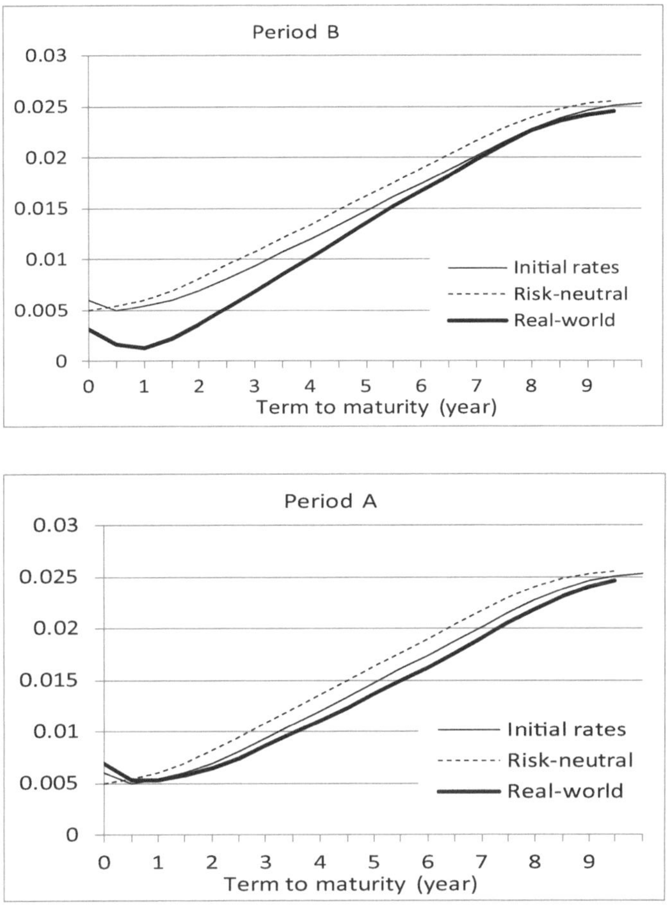

Figure 10.7: Mean of real-world simulation and risk-neutral simulation at $t = 0.5$ (year)

Drift in the real-world simulation

Here, we consider a single-period simulation, using equation (6.91) in the three-factor model. The forward rate observed of 31 August 2009 is taken as the initial forward rate, which was shown in Fig. 10.3.

The rolled trend $E^H[\Delta F_i/\Delta t]$ is exhibited in Fig. 10.6, where Period B shows a remarkable roll-down of short-term forward rates. In both cases, the negative slope of the forward rate curve is observed at the short end. To examine this feature further, let us compare real-world simulation with risk-neutral simulation for the two cases. In this, the simulation associated with Period A (resp., Period A) will be called Case A (resp., Case B).

Fig. 10.7 presents the means of the forward rate at $t = \delta$ for Case A and

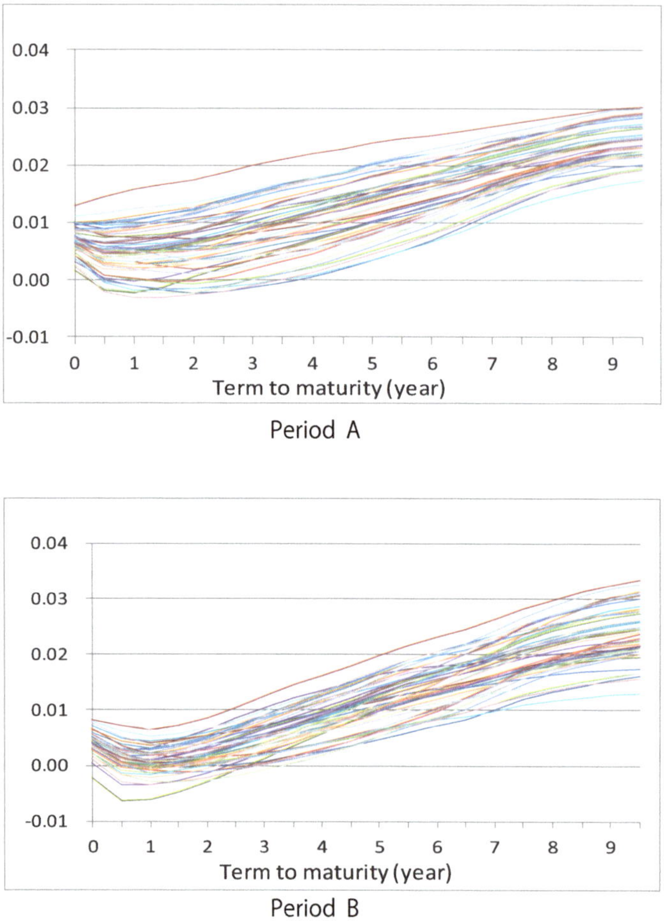

Figure 10.8: Simulated forward rates at $t = 0.5$ years; 50 simulations with a three-factor model

Case B. As explained by Fig. 7.1 in Section 7.1, the risk-neutral simulation shows that the mean of $f(\delta, T_i)$ is almost equal to the parallel shift to the left in the initial rate $f(0, T_i)$ for Δs in both cases. This feature is typical of arbitrage-free term structure models.

In contrast, the mean of the real-world simulation shows a different property, and so reproduces the rolled trend, as shown in Fig. 10.6. Along these lines, Fig. 10.7 provides a visualization of the difference between the real-world simulation and the risk-neutral one. A more detailed examination within the LMRW will be presented in Section 10.2.

Monte Carlo simulation

Following the numerical procedure described in Section 6.9, a Monte Carlo simulation is executed. Fig. 10.8 shows 50 simulations of $f(\delta, x_i)$ for each case, partially showing the negative values of short-term forward rates. Although the possibility of a negative interest rate is a drawback of the Gaussian model, the Gaussian HJM framework provides a perspective on the real-world model.

However, negative yields have been recently[4] observed in the government bond market of some European countries and of Japan. The HJM model may be valid for such markets.

10.2 LIBOR Market Model

This section presents numerical examples of simulation in the LMRW that parallel those in Section 10.1. In the modeling, the number of factors is determined to approximate the full-factor model by using Corollary 9.8.3, and the simulation model is constructed by using Corollary 9.8.4. We examine the simulation properties with a particular focus on the drift feature near the short end of the forward rate curve.

10.2.1 Estimation of Market Price of Risk

Sample data description

We again use the Japanese LIBOR swap rates, as we did in Section 10.1. Accordingly, the earlier Period A covers 2 April 2007 to 16 June 2008, where the forward LIBOR shows a tendency to rise. The later Period B covers 16 June 2008 to 31 August 2009, where the forward LIBOR shows a tendency to fall, as seen in Fig. 10.2. We recall that the observable trend is bear-flattening in Period A and bull-steepening in Period B, as shown in Fig. 10.3.

Market price of risk

We set $\Delta t = 0.08$ (equivalent to 20 days). The procedure described in Section 9.9 is used to construct the covariance matrix $Cov(\Delta\tilde{K}_i, \Delta\tilde{K}_j)$ from the sample data. Table 10.2 shows the eigenvalues $|\rho_l|^2$, the accumulated contribution

[4] This book was written over the period from summer 2014 to spring 2015.

Table 10.2: Eigenvalues and the market price of risk in the LIBOR market model. ρ^2, C_l, ζ_l, and φ_l indicate the eigenvalue, the accumulated contribution rate, the MPR score, and the market price of risk, respectively. For comparison, φ_{HJM} indicates the market price of risk as obtained from the Gaussian HJM model for the same period.

Period A (3 April 2007 to 16 June 2008)

l	ρ^2	C_l	ζ_l	φ_l	φ_{HJM}
1	2.615	0.8999	0.061	0.038	-0.256
2	0.2366	0.9813	0.369	0.758	0.532
3	0.0284	0.9911	0.126	0.746	0.598
4	0.0146	0.9961	0.014	0.114	0.495
5	0.0059	0.9982	0.016	0.205	0.896
6	0.0024	0.999	0.061	1.226	-1.049
7	0.0011	0.9994	-0.034	-1.017	-0.011
8	0.0005	0.9996	0.004	0.155	0.311

Period B (16 June 2008 to 31 August 2009)

l	ρ^2	C_l	ζ_l	φ_l	φ_{HJM}
1	1.756	0.7191	-1.449	-1.094	-0.884
2	0.4904	0.9199	-1.203	-1.718	-1.886
3	0.1481	0.9805	0.082	0.213	-0.816
4	0.024	0.9904	0.398	2.57	1.113
5	0.01	0.9945	0.209	2.089	2.445
6	0.0091	0.9982	0.053	0.55	-0.557
7	0.0014	0.9988	-0.004	-0.115	1.746
8	0.0011	0.9992	0.071	2.113	-0.709

rates, the MPR scores ζ_l, and the market prices of risk φ_l for each component, where ζ_l and φ_l are calculated in the 8-factor model. Additionally, the rightmost column contains the market prices of risk that were estimated in the Gaussian HJM model for the same sample period and appeared in the rightmost column of Table 10.1.

Table 10.2 shows that $\varphi_1 = 0.038$ and $\varphi_2 = 0.758$ in Period A. Since the observable trend is bear-flattening in this period, these values are consistent with Table 9.4 (in the row labeled "bear flat"), where φ_1 is predicted to be near zero and φ_2 is predicted to be positive.

Period B in Table 10.2 shows that $\varphi_1 = -1.094$ and $\varphi_2 = -1.718$. Since the observable trend in this period is bull-steepening, these results are also explained by Table 9.4 (in the row labeled "bull steep"), where φ_1 and φ_2 are predicted to be negative.

10.2.2 Four Cases: Cases B1 to B4

This section begins with determining the dimensionalities for Period A and Period B. From this, we investigate the properties of the simulation for Period B, setting four cases for this period.

Dimension Reduction

Fig. 10.9 shows the first four principal components e^l, $l = 1, \cdots, 4$ for periods A and B. Similarly to Section 10.1.1, the first three components explain the changes in the level, slope, and curvature, respectively, of the forward LIBOR curve. In both periods, the fourth component seems to affect the movement of the short-term forward rates. This observation is consistent with that in Longstaff et al. (2002).

We determine the number of factors to use to approximate the full-factor model by applying Corollary 9.8.3. In Table 10.2, the accumulated contribution rate shows that the first three components explain more than 98% of the covariance for the two periods. Furthermore, both periods show a non-decreasing market price of risk in l, as mentioned in Section 9.8. Indeed, $|\varphi_l|$ attains a maximum at $l = 6$ in Period A, and at $l = 5$ in Period B.

In Period A, the MPR score ζ_l is relatively small for $l > 3$. Hence, a three-factor model is sufficient for a simulation. In Period B, the MPR score ζ_l is quite small for $l > 6$. Hence, a four- or five-factor model is necessary for simulations in Period B.

From this, Period B is a distinct example of a case where the number of factors is determined by the MPR score, rather than by the PCA.

Approximation of market price of risk

We recall the definition of γ_i in equation (9.46) as

$$\gamma_i = E^H\left[\frac{\Delta\tilde{K}_i}{\Delta t}\right] - \lambda_{0i}E^H\left[\sum_{j=1}^{i}\kappa_j\right] + \frac{|\lambda_{0i}|^2}{2}. \tag{10.4}$$

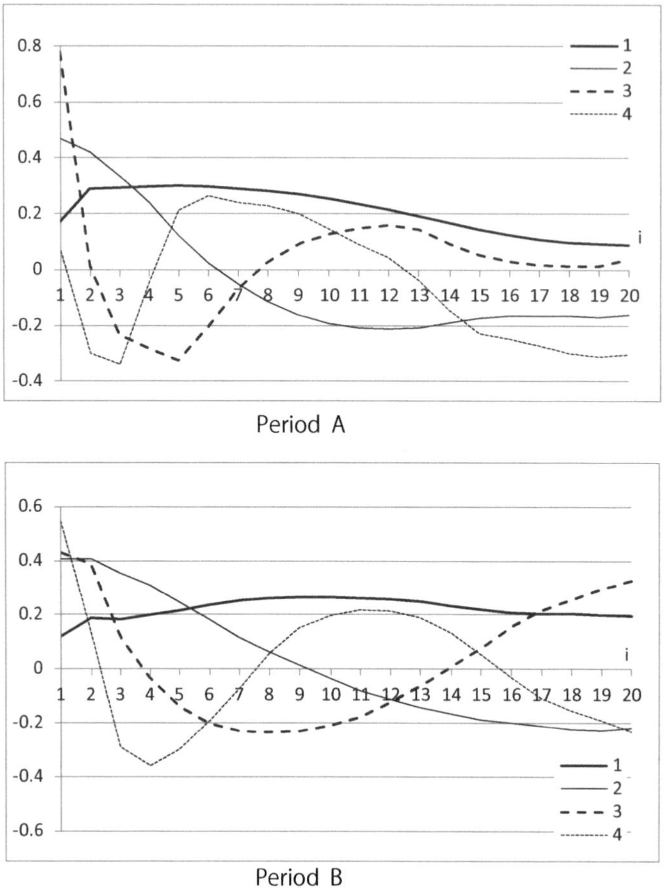

Figure 10.9: The first four principal components

Fig. 10.10 presents γ_i and three terms from the right-hand side of the above. We see that the second term, $\lambda_i E^H[\sum_{j=1}^{i} \kappa_j]$, is negligibly small in both cases. In period A, $|\lambda_i|^2/2$ does not seem to be smaller than the term $E^H[\Delta \tilde{K}_i/\Delta t]$ for some i. Hence, the inequality (9.62) in Proposition 9.5.1 does not hold for this case.

In contrast, it roughly holds for period B in Fig. 10.10, with

$$\frac{|\lambda_i|^2}{2} \ll E^H\left[\frac{\Delta \tilde{K}_i}{\Delta t}\right], \tag{10.5}$$

for almost all i, so the inequality (9.62) is almost satisfied. Then, the approximation of the market price of risk in Proposition 9.5.1 holds for Period B, as

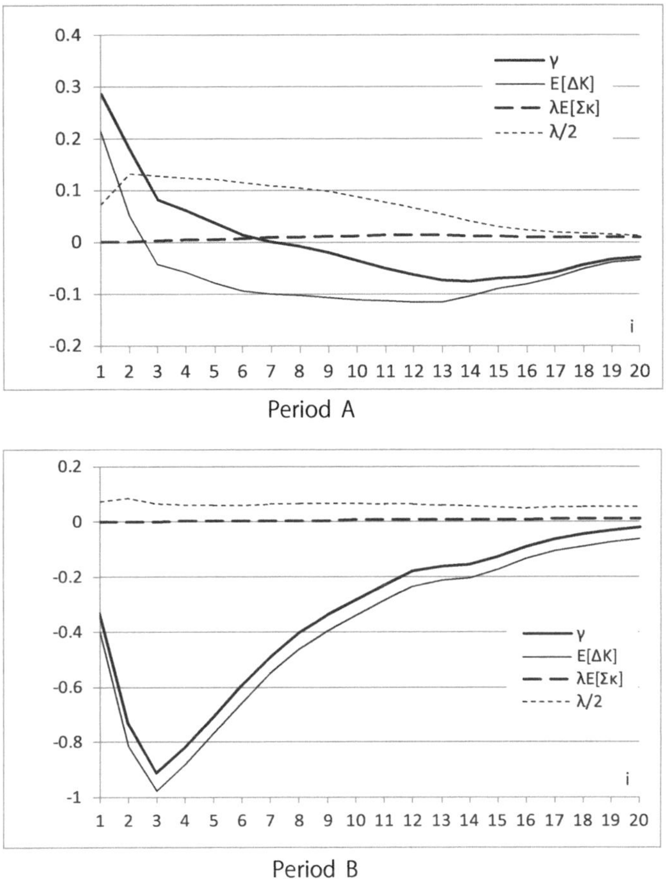

Figure 10.10: γ and its components for Period A and Period B. $E[\Delta K]$, $\lambda E[\sum \kappa]$, and $\lambda/2$ are abbreviations of $E^H[\Delta \tilde{K}_i/\Delta t]$, $\lambda_i E^H[\sum_{j=1}^{i} \kappa_j]$, and $|\lambda_i|^2/2$, respectively.

$\varphi_l \approx \tilde{R}_l/\rho_l.$

Case B1 to B4

Since Period B requires higher dimensional modeling than Period A does, it is expected that Period B will exhibit a characteristic particular to simulation in the LMRW. Because of this, we examine the simulation for Period B, working with the following four cases.

- Case B1: Four-factor real-world simulation according to the numerical procedure in Section 9.9.

Table 10.3: Summary of cases for Period B

Case	Dimensionality	Measure	$K(t_{k+1}, \delta i - \Delta t)$
B1	4	real-world	interpolation
B2	4	risk-neutral	interpolation
B3	3	real-world	interpolation
B4	4	real-world	$K(t_{k+1}, \delta i)$

- Case B2: Four-factor simulation under the spot LIBOR measure, executed by setting $\varphi = 0$ for Case B1.
- Case B3: Three-factor real-world simulation based on Case B1.
- Case B4: Four-factor real-world simulation, where $K(t_{k+1}, \delta i)$ is used as a proxy of $K(t_{k+1}, \delta i - \Delta t)$ to compute $\Delta\tilde{K}_i(t_k)$.

Case B1 mostly approximates the full-factor model, and is carried out in the manner described for modeling in Section 9.9. Then, we may regard Case B1 as a standard for comparison with other cases. Case B2 compares the risk-neutral simulation of the standard case of Case B1. Case B3 highlights things missed by the three-factor model. Case B4 examines the effect of the interpolation (9.121). Table 10.3 summarizes these cases to clarify the differences among them.

10.2.3 Examination of Four Cases

The implied forward LIBOR observed on 31 August 2009 is taken as the initial LIBOR, as in Section 10.1. In the four cases, $L_i(\delta)$ is calculated by using a single-period simulation.

We examine these cases by comparing the mean of each $L_i(\delta)$. For convenience, we evaluated the mean in log-scale by using $E[\log L_i(\delta)]$ as a proxy of $E[L_i(\delta)]$. Here, $E[\log L_i(\delta)]$ is obtained, from equation (9.3), as

$$E[\log L_i(\delta)] = \log L_i(0) + \left\{ \lambda_i \sum_{j=1}^{i} \kappa_j(0) + \lambda_i \varphi - \frac{|\lambda_i|^2}{2} \right\} \delta, \tag{10.6}$$

for the given $L(0)$, λ, and φ.

If we set $\varphi = 0$ and $\mathbf{P}^*$ is the spot LIBOR measure, then $\mathbf{P} = \mathbf{P}^*$ holds from the argument in Section 9.9. As well, $E[\cdot] = E^*[\cdot]$ holds for Case B2, where $E^*[\cdot]$ denotes expectation under $\mathbf{P}^*$. It holds that

$$\begin{aligned} E^*[\log L_i(\delta)] &= E[\log L_i(\delta)]|_{\varphi=0} \\ &= \log L_i(0) + \left\{ \lambda_i \sum_{j=1}^{i} \kappa_j(0) - \frac{|\lambda_i|^2}{2} \right\} \delta. \end{aligned} \tag{10.7}$$

Then, $E[\log L_i(\delta)]$ is obtained for all four cases by the direct calculation of equations (10.6) and (10.7).

Fig. 10.11 shows the mean $E[\log L_i(\delta)]$ against the initial forward LIBOR in log scale for each case. This graph gives interesting properties in the real-world simulation, which are described in the following.

Case B1

This case mostly closely approximates the full-factor model among the four cases. The mean of the simulated forward LIBOR curve at $t = \delta$ shows a bull-steepening trend in Fig. 10.11 (Case B1). It is noteworthy that the mean of the curve at $t = \delta$ is downward-sloping at the short end. Case B1 is the only model that simulates this feature.

Case B2

Case B2 is simulation under the spot LIBOR measure with the same parameters as in Case B1. From Fig. 10.11 (Case B2), the shape of the mean curve $E[\log L_i(\delta)]$ is almost equal to the initial curve after a parallel shift to the left for δ. This feature is typical of the risk-neutral model, as explained in Sections 7.1 and 10.1.2. Namely, it roughly holds that $E[L_i(\delta)] \approx L_i(0)$ for all i. This is quite different from the result in Case B1.

Naturally, $E[\log L_i(\delta)]$ has positive slope at the short end of the curve. We furthermore note that Case B2 has a bear-flattening tendency, which is also different from in Case B1. Hence, the difference between the real-world simulation and the risk-neutral simulation is observed not only in the level of the interest rates but also in the shape of the forward LIBOR curve.

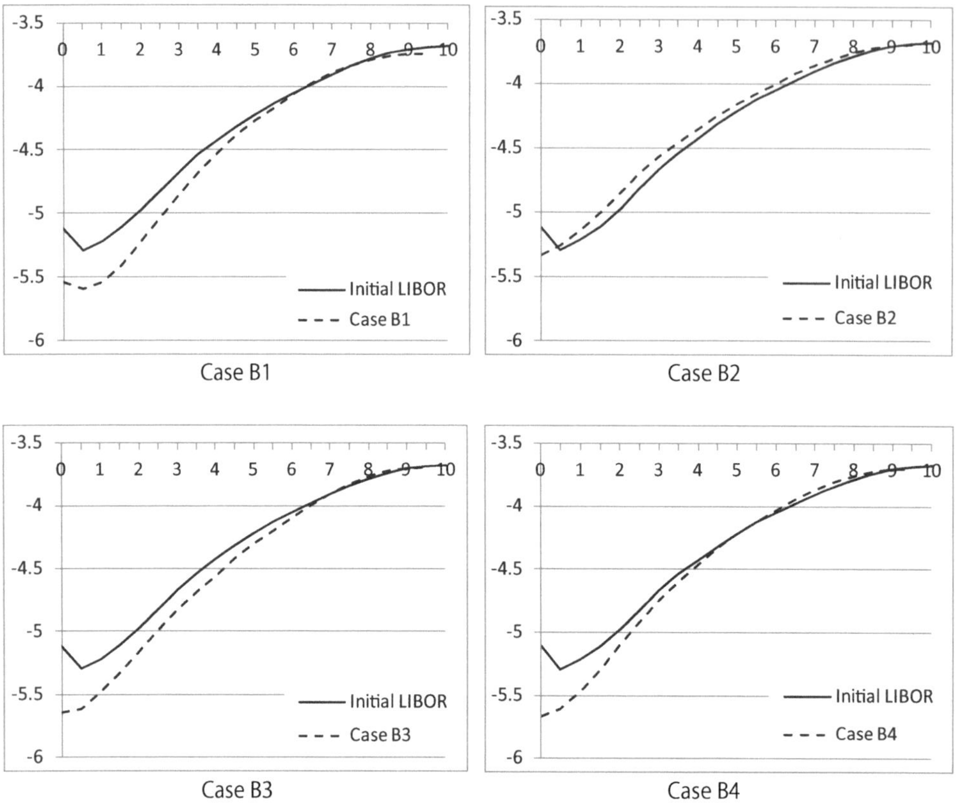

Figure 10.11: Initial forward LIBOR and the mean of simulation. The initial forward LIBOR is shown in log scale, and the dashed line shows the mean of the simulation, $E[\log L_i(\delta)]$.

Case B3

Case B3 is a three-factor simulation in the LMRW. The results shown in Fig. 10.11 (Case B3) are mostly similar to those of Case B1, except at the short end of the forward LIBOR curve. Indeed, $E[\log L_i(\delta)]$ in Case B3 is almost flat at the short end. This means that the three-factor model fails to simulate the short-end dynamics of the forward rate curve. From this, we may take the view that the fourth factor might affect the movement of the short-term forward LIBOR.

Case B4

Case B4 uses $K(t_{k+1}, \delta i)$ instead of $K(t_{k+1}, \delta i - \Delta t)$ without interpolation by equation (9.121). Fig. 10.11 (Case B4) shows that the result seems to be intermediate between Case B1 and Case B2. Specifically, the entire forward LIBOR curve admits a bull-steepening trend like that seen in Case B1, and $E[\log L_i(\delta)]$ is upward sloping at the short-end.

Hence, Case B4 misses both the effect of the fourth factor and the feature of the real-world model. Therefore, we may say that real-world simulation is necessary to properly estimate $K(\Delta t, T_i - \Delta t)$.

Summary of four cases

Consequently, both Case B1 and Case B3 admit plausible results for real-world simulations. However, only Case B1 implies that the negative slope of the forward LIBOR curve at the short end will continue for a half-year (cf. the first footnote in Section 10.1.1). In this respect, Case B1 is suitable for risk management and for profit–loss simulation, where we forecast that the historical behavior of the LIBOR will continue to the future. Accordingly, Case B3 is the second best for this purpose.

Finally, Fig. 10.12 shows 50 simulations of the forward LIBOR at $t = \delta$ in Case B1. Comparing this with Fig. 10.8, the LMRW simulates higher forward rates than the Gaussian HJM model does for the longer term. For valuing the interest-rate-rise risk, this model difference might not be negligible, and this should be studied further in regard to practice.

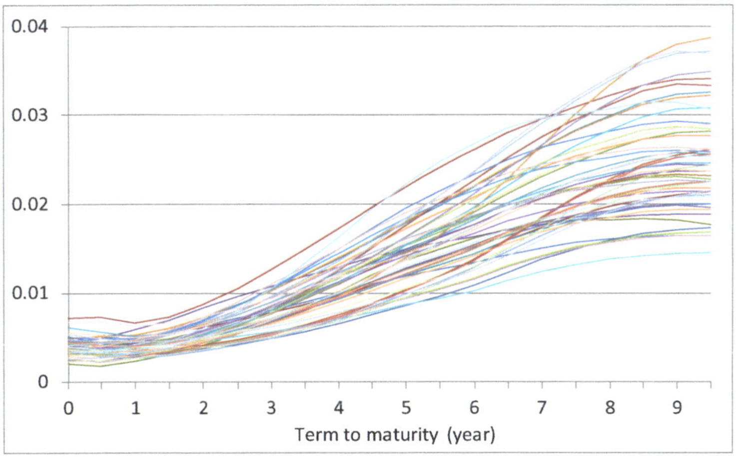

Figure 10.12: Forward LIBOR at $t = 0.5$ years in Case B1, 50 simulations

Remark on dimension reduction

In the Gaussian HJM model, a three-factor model is sufficient to simulate the negative slope of the forward rate curve at the short end, as shown in Fig. 10.7 (Period B). In contrast, to simulate a similar feature in the LMRW, it is necessary to use at least four factors in the model, as shown by Case B1 and Case B3 together. This difference might be due to the complexity of the LMRW, rather than model selection.

Indeed, the drift term in the Gaussian HJM model has a simple form, as $E^H[\Delta F_i/\Delta t]\Delta s$, shown in equation (6.87), which is independent from the dimensionality. In the LMRW, the drift term is given by equation (9.127) as

$$\left\{ \lambda_{0i} \sum_{j=m(t)}^{i} \chi_{0j} + \lambda_{0i}\varphi - \frac{|\lambda_{0i}|^2}{2} \right\} \Delta s, \tag{10.8}$$

and this term depends on the dimensionality.

Let us recall the argument for dimension reduction from Section 9.8.2 and Appendix D.2, where the second term in the above was reduced to $e_i^l \zeta_l$ for each lth component from equation (D.15). Specifically, we have $\lambda_i^l \varphi_l = e_i^l \zeta_l$. Here, ζ_l is the lth MPR score, which is the key to the dimension reduction. Thus, dimension reduction is not trivial in the LMRW, in contrast to the case for the Gaussian HJM model.

10.3 Positive Market Price of Risk

This section presents an actual example, in which the first market price of risk φ_1 takes a positive value. For this objective, we employ the Hull–White model, showing the numerical procedure to construct a real-world model.

As mentioned at the end of Section 7.1, the value of the first market price of risk φ_1 depends on the rolled trend score. From this observation, the market price of risk does not necessarily take a negative value. Indeed, when we use only one-year observation data, it might not be difficult to find a period that admits a positive φ_1. However it turns out to be difficult to do that when the observation period is taken to be longer, which reflects the negative price tendency of the market price of risk.

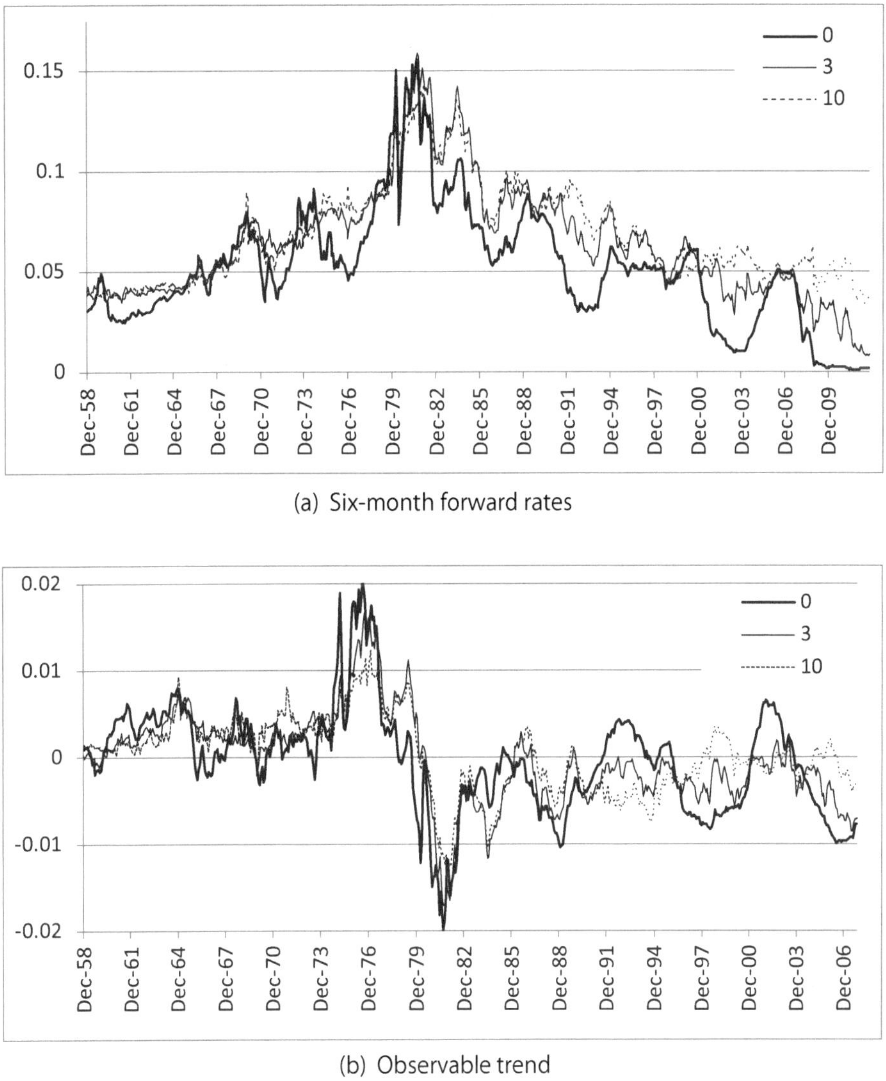

Figure 10.13: Implied forward rates and observable trends in the U.S. Treasury market. 0, 3, and 10 in the figure indicate the forward rates over the intervals [0, 0.5], [3, 3.5], and [10, 10.5] years, respectively. The yield data were retrieved from the Board of Governors of the Federal Reserve System (2014); in those data, monthly yield represents the monthly average of daily yields. The forward rates were calculated by the author.

From the argument for the negative price tendency in Section 7.2, we may view this tendency as not being strongly affected by the choice of model. In this respect, the Hull–White model has been successfully used for studies on the term structure of interest rates, and that model is a special case of the Gaussian HJM model. Along these lines, we employ a one-factor Hull–White model for the examination.

We use monthly U.S. Treasury yields from December 1958 to October 2012 and find the six-month implied forward rates. Fig. 10.13(a) shows a historical chart of the implied forward rates. The forward rates rise remarkably from the late 1970s to the early 1980s, reaching nearly 16% in the early 1980s. Hence, we expect that this period might admit a positive market price of risk. In the following calibration, we regard the six-month forward rate as the instantaneous forward rate for convenience.

Detection of period with positive φ_1

To find a period that admits a positive market price of risk, let us recall Proposition 6.5.1, and specifically that φ_1 is approximately represented by $\varphi_1 \approx R_1/\rho_1$ under certain conditions. Here, R_1 is the first rolled trend score and $(\rho_1)^2$ is the first eigenvalue. Using this approximation, we want to find a five-year period such that $R_1 > 0$. However, it is not feasible to calculate the rolled trend score for each of the multitudinous five-year periods in the sample.

For convenience, we examine the observable trend as a proxy for the rolled trend score. From equation (6.53), the observable trend for a five-year period $[t, t+5]$ is obtained as

$$\frac{F(t+5,x) - F(t,x)}{5} \tag{10.9}$$

for each time t. We calculate this with x fixed at 0, 3, and 10 years for all t.

Fig. 10.13(b) shows the observable trends for the sample period. We find that these trends take a nearly maximal value near March 1975. From this observation, it is expected that the first rolled trend score will take a positive value for the period from March 1975 to March 1980. Thus, we adopt this period for the examination.

Volatility structure

To estimate the market price of risk for the period above, let us begin by determining the volatility structure in the Hull–White model. We set $\delta = 0.5$ years and $x_i = \delta i$ for $i = 1, \cdots, 20$. Calculating $\Delta F(t_k, x_i)$ by the interpola-

Table 10.4: Rolled trend for the sample period (March 1975 to March 1980), and the Hull–White volatility. The interest rate dataset is the same as for Fig. 10.13.

	Rolled trend	Principal component	Hull–White volatility
i	$E^H[\Delta F/\Delta t]$	e_i	$\sigma \exp(\kappa x_i)$
1	-0.0067	0.394	0.0176
2	0.0164	0.423	0.0164
3	0.0236	0.316	0.0152
4	0.0096	0.250	0.0142
5	0.0054	0.249	0.0132
6	0.0066	0.248	0.0122
7	0.0063	0.234	0.0114
8	0.0057	0.216	0.0106
9	0.0054	0.201	0.0098
10	0.0052	0.188	0.0091
11	0.0048	0.175	0.0085
12	0.0046	0.163	0.0079
13	0.0047	0.154	0.0073
14	0.0053	0.147	0.0068
15	0.0061	0.140	0.0063
16	0.0068	0.135	0.0059
17	0.0075	0.130	0.0055
18	0.0079	0.126	0.0051
19	0.0081	0.122	0.0047
20	0.0080	0.119	0.0044

tion (6.93) for all k and i, we find the first principal component e^1 and the eigenvalue ρ_1 by PCA. As a result, we have $(\rho_1)^2 = 0.0022$. Since we are working with a one-factor model, we may omit the "1" superscripts and subscripts (e^1, ρ_1, *etc.*) in this section.

Table 10.4 shows the rolled trend $E^H[\Delta F_i/\Delta t]$, the principal component $(e_1, \cdots, e_{20})^T$, and the Hull–White volatility $\sigma \exp(\kappa x_i)$ for the sample data. Here $e_i, i = 1, \cdots, 20$ shows obvious decaying of the volatility structure, and specifically shows strong mean reversion. Applying the method of Section 8.4, we compute the parameters σ and κ. The results are as follows:

$$\sigma = 0.0190, \qquad \kappa = 0.146. \tag{10.10}$$

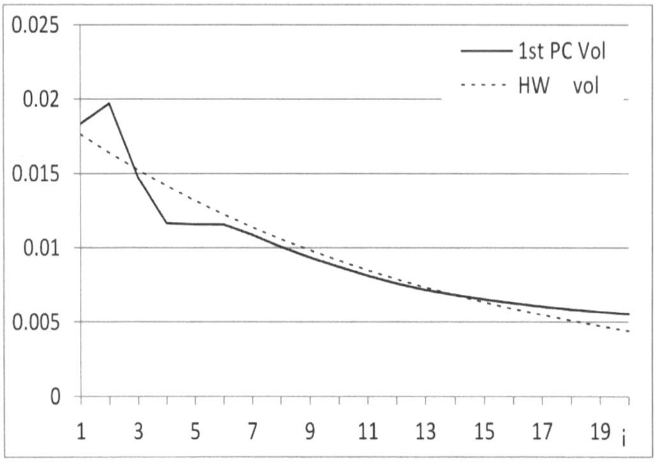

Figure 10.14: The principal component volatility and the Hull–White volatility. The interest rate dataset is the same as for Fig. 10.13.

As expected from the above, the mean reversion coefficient κ is positive.

Fig. 10.14 compares the observed volatility component $(\rho e_1, \cdots, \rho e_{20})^T$ with the Hull–White volatility $\sigma \exp(\kappa x_i), i = 1, \cdots, 20$. We visually see that the Hull–White volatility well approximates the observation volatility. We note that the volatilities of short-term rates are almost all higher than 1.5%, decaying to near 0.5% for the long-term forward rates.

Market price of risk

The second column of Table 10.4 shows the rolled trends, which are positive for almost all i. It is expected that the first rolled trend score R will be positive. And, in fact the calculation of equation (8.30) implies that $R = 0.0304$. From equation (8.25), we obtain that $\beta = -0.0020$.

Theorem 8.5.1 tells that the sign of the market price of risk depends on whether $R > \beta$. From this, the above calculation implies a positive market price of risk. Specifically, this is estimated to be positive as

$$\varphi = \frac{0.0304 - 0.0020}{\sqrt{0.0022}} = 0.609 \tag{10.11}$$

from Theorem 8.5.1. As intended, we have found a period that admits a positive market price of risk.

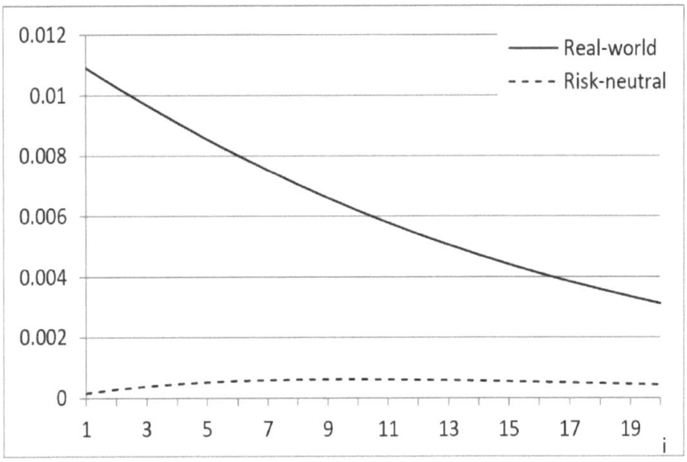

Figure 10.15: Expectation of $\{f(\Delta s, \delta i) - f(0, \delta i)\}$ with $\Delta s = 1$ (year) under $\mathbf{P}$ and $\mathbf{Q}$. "Real-world" indicates the expectation under $\mathbf{P}$, and "Risk-neutral" indicates that under $\mathbf{Q}$. The interest rate dataset is the same as for Fig. 10.13.

Real-world simulation

Finally, we examine the difference between real-world simulation and risk-neutral simulation. For a one-year simulation, by setting $\Delta s = 1$, we calculate the expectations of $f(\Delta s, \delta i)$ in $\mathbf{P}$ and $\mathbf{Q}$ according to Corollary 8.5.2(1). These are compared in Fig. 10.15. The graph shows that the real-world model simulates higher forward rates than the risk-neutral model does. Of particular note, the short-term to middle-term forward rates are considerably higher than the corresponding rates in the risk-neutral model.

This difference is evaluated by equation (8.38) in Corollary 8.5.2 (2) as

$$E[f(\Delta s, \delta i)] - E^{\mathbf{Q}}[f(\Delta s, \delta i)] = \sigma e^{-\kappa \delta i} \varphi \Delta s \;\; ; \;\; i = 1, \cdots, 20. \qquad (10.12)$$

Here, $\delta = 0.5$ (year), $\Delta s = 1$ (year), and the figures in equations (10.10) and (10.11) are substituted into σ, κ, and φ in the right-hand side of equation (10.12). This difference is plotted in Fig. 10.16, in which we see that the real-world model simulates a rate 100 to 25 basis points higher for the forward rates than the risk-neutral model does in expectation. Further, the difference is exponentially decaying in i, which is due to the structure of the right-hand side of equation (10.12).

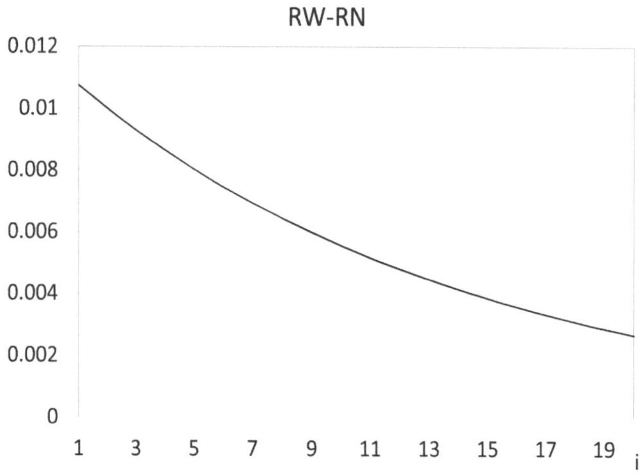

Figure 10.16: Difference between the real-world simulation and the risk-neutral simulation. The graph plots the difference $E[f(\Delta s, \delta i)] - E^{\mathbf{Q}}[f(\Delta s, \delta i)]$ at $\Delta s = 1$ (year). The interest rate dataset is the same as for Fig. 10.13.

10.4 Negative Price Tendency

In the previous section, we estimated the market price of risk in the U.S. Treasury market, from which we found a period so that the first market price of risk takes a positive value. Using the same data, we estimate the market price of risk for a long-period observation and verify the negative price tendency. We refer back to Fig. 10.13(a), the chart of the implied forward rates found from the U.S. Treasury yields. From this dataset, we define three periods of twenty years, as follows.

- Period A: March 1960 to March 1980.
- Period B: March 1970 to March 1990.
- Period C: March 1980 to March 2000.

Period A is a term before the peak in the interest rate at the early 1980s; during this term, the interest rates are rising on average. Period B includes the peak at the middle of the period; during this term, the interest rates are

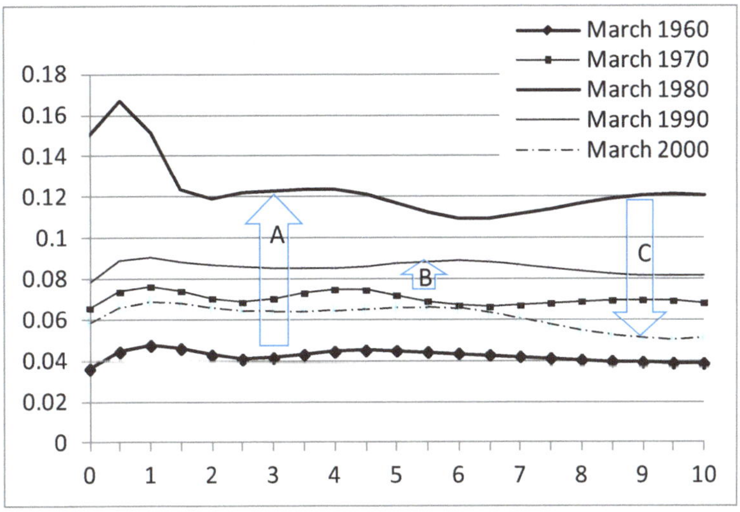

Figure 10.17: Forward rate curves for March of 1960, 1970, 1980, 1990, and 2000. The interest rate dataset is the same as for Fig. 10.13.

mostly rising until 1980 and falling after that. Period C is a term after the peak, during which the interest rates show a tendency to fall.

Fig. 10.17 shows the forward rate curves for March of 1960, 1970, 1980, 1990, and 2000. The changes of the curves during each period are indicated by the labeled arrows.

Estimation by flat yield model

In Fig. 10.17, the graphs show that the forward rates are approximately flat. From this observation, we simply estimate the sign of the market prices of risk, working with a flat yield model to do so. Following the setup in Section 7.2, we set $n = 20, \delta = 0.5$, and $\tau = 20$ for all periods.

We refer back to Fig. 10.14, which shows the volatility structure in connection with the Hull–White volatility for the period from 1975 to 1980. From this view, we assume that the volatility σ is flat, at 1.5%, through the entire period from 1960 to 2000. Referring to Theorem 7.2.1, the right-hand side of equation (7.15a) is calculated as

$$\frac{\delta(n-1)}{2}(\sigma(\tau))^2 = \frac{0.5 \times 19}{2}(0.015)^2 = 0.00107. \tag{10.13}$$

Here, we let $\sigma(\tau)$=0.015. From the assumption of constant volatility over the whole period, we may adopt this value for Period A, Period B, and Period C as the right-hand side of equation (7.15a).

Period A

In Period A, we set, from Fig. 10.17, the values $F(0) = 0.04$, and $F(20) = 0.13$. Hence, it holds that $F(0) < F(20)$, that is, the first rolled trend score is positive. The left-hand side of equation (7.15a) is calculated as

$$\frac{F(20) - F(0)}{20} = \frac{0.13 - 0.04}{20} = 0.0045. \tag{10.14}$$

From these, we have

$$\frac{F(20) - F(0)}{20} = 0.0045 > 0.00107 = \frac{\delta(n-1)}{2}(\sigma(\tau))^2. \tag{10.15}$$

From Theorem 7.2.1, the first market price of risk might be positive.

Period B and C

For Period B, we set $F(0) = 0.07$ and $F(20) = 0.09$. From these, the rolled trend in this period is weakly positive. The same calculation as in equation (10.14) implies that

$$\frac{F(20) - F(0)}{20} = \frac{0.09 - 0.07}{20} = 0.001, \tag{10.16}$$

and this is almost equal to the value from equation (10.13). Hence, Period B might imply a near-zero market price of risk.

For Period C, we set $F(0) = 0.13$ and $F(20) = 0.06$. Accordingly, this period exhibits a negative rolled trend. The same calculation as in equation (10.14) implies that

$$\frac{F(20) - F(0)}{20} = \frac{0.13 - 0.06}{20} = -0.0035, \tag{10.17}$$

which is obviously smaller than the value from equation (10.13). Thus, Period C might imply a negative market price of risk.

Estimation in the Hull–White model

Next, let us calculate the market price of risk for three periods by employing a one-factor Hull–White model. We calibrate the term structure for them in the manner described in Section 10.3. The results are shown in Table 10.5 for the three periods. In this, ρ is the positive square root of the eigenvalue ρ^2, σ is the coefficient for the Hull–White volatility, κ is the mean reversion rate, φ is the market price of risk, and R is the first rolled trend score, and β is a constant given by equation (8.25). We additionally shows the results in Section 10.3 as the last row, in which we calculate the positive market price of risk for the period from March 1975 to March 1980.

The table shows that the mean reversion rate κ is positive for all periods. The first rolled trend score R is positive in Period A, and the market price of risk φ_A is positive, at 0.360, as a rough estimate from the flat yield model (see above).

In Period B, the rolled trend score R is weakly negative, and the market price of risk φ_B is accordingly negative (near-zero), at -0.156. Similarly, the market price of risk φ_C in Period C is negative, at -0.506. As a result, φ_A, φ_B, and φ_C take positive, near-zero and negative values respectively, which roughly agrees with qualitative estimates obtained by using the flat yield model.

Furthermore, the highest of the market prices of risk is that of Period A, followed in descending order by that of Period B and that of Period C. Specifically,

$$\varphi_A > \varphi_B > \varphi_C. \tag{10.18}$$

Comparing the calculations of $\{F(20) - F(0)\}/20$ in equations (10.14), (10.16)

Table 10.5: Market price of risk for Periods A, B and C. The last row exhibits the result of the example in Section 10.3, which shows a positive market price of risk, for comparison. The interest rate dataset is the same as for Fig. 10.13.

Case	Period	ρ	σ	κ	R	β	φ
A	'60-'80	0.033	0.011	0.089	0.0130	-0.0011	0.360
B	'70 '90	0.057	0.019	0.089	-0.0056	-0.0033	-0.156
C	'80-'00	0.055	0.017	0.064	-0.0245	-0.0032	-0.506
Section 10.3	'75-'80	0.047	0.019	0.146	0.0304	-0.0020	0.609

and (10.17) in the flat yield model, the value for Period A is the highest, followed in order by Period B and Period C, which agrees with the order in equation (10.18).

In particular, both Period A and B contain the period from March 1975 to March 1980, in which the market price of risk is larger than that in Period A and B. These relations might be due to long-period observation. From these, we may take the view that the flat yield model is valid for explaining the negative price tendency. A statistical examination of this tendency would be an interesting subject for future research.

Appendix A

BASICS OF NUMERICAL ANALYSIS

This appendix notes some basic tools used for numerical analysis: normal distributions and eigenvectors.

A.1 Normal Distribution

Let $f(x)$ be a real-valued function on $\mathbf{R}$ such that

$$f(x) = \frac{1}{\sqrt{2\pi}\sigma} \exp\left\{-\frac{(x-\mu)^2}{2\sigma^2}\right\}. \tag{A.1}$$

Here, $f(x)$ is called a *normal distribution function* with mean μ and variance σ^2. In particular, when $\mu = 0$ and $\sigma = 1$, $f(x)$ is called the *standard normal distribution*.

Let X be a random variable with a distribution function $f(x)$. If $f(x)$ is a normal distribution, then X is said to be normally distributed. For a positive-valued random variable X, if $\log X$ is normally distributed, then X is said to be *lognormally distributed*. Here, the distribution function of X is given by $g(x) = f(\log x)/x$, which, written in full, is

$$g(x) = \left(\begin{array}{ll} \frac{1}{\sqrt{2\pi}\sigma x} \exp\left\{-\frac{(\log x-\mu)^2}{2\sigma^2}\right\}, & x > 0 \\ 0\,, & x \leq 0. \end{array} \right. \tag{A.2}$$

In this form, $g(x)$ is called a *lognormal distribution function* with parameters μ and σ^2.

Fig. A.1 indicates the graph of a normal distribution function with $\mu = 3$ and $\sigma^2 = 1$ as a solid line, and a lognormal distribution function with $\mu = 1$ and $\sigma^2 = 0.25$ is indicated by a dashed line.

In this book, the normal distribution appears in the distribution of interest rates in the Gaussian HJM model and again in the Hull–White model.

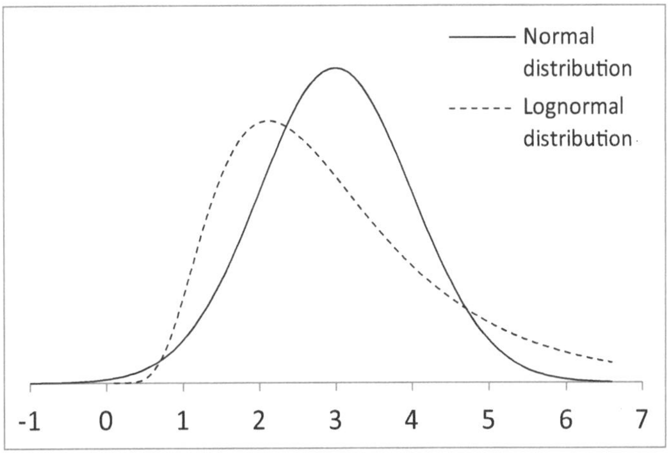

Figure A.1: Examples of a normal distribution function and a lognormal distribution function

For example, it is stated at the end of Section 4.4 that the short rate in the Hull–White model is normally distributed. Additionally, the lognormal distribution appears in the distribution of the asset price, as described in equation (2.48a). The LIBOR in the LIBOR market model, in particular, is lognormally distributed under some measures; for details, see Section 5.5.

A.2 Eigenvalues and Eigenvectors

This section summarizes the basics of the eigenvalues and eigenvectors of a symmetric matrix. In addressing these, the basic results are introduced omitting the proofs. For more details, see, for example, Petersen (2012) or Simon and Blume (1994), among others.

Eigenvalue

Let A be an $n \times n$ real-valued matrix. If $\det A \neq 0$, then we say A is invertible. In this case, the rank of A is naturally equal to n.

Let $x = (x_1, \cdots, x_n)^T$ be an $\mathbf{R}^n$-valued nonzero vector, and let λ be a scalar variable. Let us consider a linear system of equations in the form

$$Ax = \lambda x. \tag{A.3}$$

If λ and x satisfy this equation, then we say that λ is an *eigenvalue* of A, and

x is the *eigenvector* corresponding to λ. In this respect, solving the equation (A.3) is called an eigenvalue problem.

Note that eigenvalues do not uniquely exist, and an eigenvalue λ may not uniquely determine an eigenvector. Indeed, if x is an eigenvector for an eigenvalue λ, then it follows for a constant c that

$$Acx = cAx = c\lambda x = \lambda cx, \tag{A.4}$$

and so cx is also an eigenvector associated with the eigenvalue λ.

In this book, the matrix A for the eigenvalue problem is always assumed to be a symmetric matrix. The next proposition summarizes fundamental results for the eigenvalue problem with a symmetric matrix.

Proposition A.2.1 *(1) A is invertible if and only if zero is not an eigenvalue.*
(2) If A is a symmetric real-valued matrix, then all eigenvalues of A are real, and all eigenvectors are in $\mathbf{R}^n$.
(3) Let A be a symmetric matrix. For two eigenvalues λ_1 and λ_2 of A, let x_1 and x_2 be eigenvectors corresponding to λ_1 and λ_2, respectively. If $\lambda_1 \neq \lambda_2$, then x_1 and x_2 are orthogonal; specifically, $x_1 \cdot x_2 = 0$ in terms of the standard inner product in $\mathbf{R}^n$.

Orthogonal diagonalization

Let E be an $n \times n$ real-valued matrix, and let E^T denote the transpose matrix of E. If E satisfies $EE^T = E^T E = I$, then E is called an *diagonal matrix.*

For an $n \times n$ real-valued matrix A, if there exists an orthogonal matrix E such that EAE^T is a diagonal matrix (i.e., a square matrix with non-zero entries on only the main diagonal), then A is called *orthogonally diagonalizable.* For the diagonalization, the next proposition holds.

Proposition A.2.2 *If A is a symmetric matrix, then A is orthogonally diagonalizable.*

Appendix B

PRINCIPAL COMPONENT ANALYSIS

This appendix briefly presents the fundamental concepts of principal component analysis (PCA) as it is used for volatility construction.

B.1 Principal Component

Diagonalization

Let $S = \{S_{ij}\}$ be an $n \times n$ covariance matrix derived from some sample data. When the rank of S is smaller than n, we reduce the number n of variables of the data so as to be equal to the rank. From this operation, we may assume that S is invertible. Since a covariance matrix is always symmetric, it holds from Proposition A.2.1(2) that all eigenvalues are real values, and all eigenvectors are in $\mathbf{R}^n$. Furthermore, it is known that eigenvalues of covariance matrices are all nonnegative. From Proposition A.2.1(1), no eigenvalues are zero, and so they must all be positive.

We assume that all eigenvalues are distinct and let $(\rho_1)^2 > (\rho_2)^2 > \cdots > (\rho_n)^2 > 0$ be eigenvalues of S and $e^l = (e^l_1, \cdots, e^l_n)^T$ be the corresponding eigenvectors. We assume that $|e^l|^2 = 1$ for all l. Here $(\rho_l)^2$ and e^l are referred to as the *lth eigenvalue* and the *lth eigenvector*, respectively.

The covariance matrix S is orthogonally diagonalizable from Proposition A.2.2. Using this, we can find the orthogonal matrix that will diagonalize S. From the definition of the eigenvector, it holds that $Se^l = (\rho_1)^2 e^l$ for $1 \leq l \leq n$. Regarding $(e^1, \cdots, e^n)$ as an $n \times n$ matrix, we have that

$$\begin{aligned} S\,(e^1, \cdots, e^n) &= ((\rho_1)^2 e^1, \cdots, (\rho_n)^2 e^n) \\ &= (e^1, \cdots, e^n) \begin{pmatrix} (\rho_1)^2 & 0 & 0 \\ 0 & \ddots & 0 \\ 0 & 0 & (\rho_n)^2 \end{pmatrix}. \end{aligned} \tag{B.1}$$

Setting an $n \times n$ matrix E as

$$E = (e^1, \cdots, e^n), \tag{B.2}$$

it follows from Proposition A.2.1(3) that all eigenvectors are pairwise orthogonal. Additionally, from the assumption that $|e^l|^2 = 1$ for all l, the matrix E is an orthogonal matrix, so that $EE^T = E^T E = I$. From this and equation (B.1), we have

$$E^T S E = \begin{pmatrix} (\rho_1)^2 & 0 & 0 \\ 0 & \ddots & 0 \\ 0 & 0 & (\rho_n)^2 \end{pmatrix}. \tag{B.3}$$

Thus, we see that an orthogonal matrix E to diagonalize S is constructed from the set of all eigenvectors.

Principal component

The lth eigenvector e^l is also referred to as the *lth principal component.* In most places, this book uses the term "principal component" rather than "eigenvector."

It holds from $EE^T = I$ that

$$\sum_{i=1}^{n} e_i^l e_i^h = \delta_{lh}, \ 1 \leq l, h, \leq n. \tag{B.4}$$

This means that the principal components are pairwise orthogonal and each have unit length. A set of vectors collectively satisfying equation (B.4) is said to be *orthonormal.*

B.2 Principal Component Space

State space

Under the same assumptions about the covariance matrix S as in the previous subsection, let $e^1, \cdots, e^n$ be the principal components of a covariance matrix S. Since this set is orthonormal, we can define another Euclidean space $\tilde{\mathbf{R}}^n$ spanned by $e^1, \cdots, e^n$. The space $\tilde{\mathbf{R}}^n$ is sometimes referred to as a *principal component space* or a *factor space.* In contrast, $\mathbf{R}^n$ is called a *state space* or an *original space.*

Principal component space

Let $x = (x_1, \cdots, x_n)^T$ be a vector in $\mathbf{R}^n$. The inner product between x and e^l in $\mathbf{R}^n$ is given by $x \cdot e^l = \sum_{i=1}^n x_i e_i^l$, which is called the *lth principal component score* of x. Thus, the vector $(xe^1, \cdots, xe^n)^T$ is regarded as the coordinates of x in $\tilde{\mathbf{R}}^n$. In this context, we say that x is represented by $(xe^1, \cdots, xe^n)^T$ in the principal component space.

Projection to principal component space

Setting $\tilde{a}_l = xe^l$, we have

$$(\tilde{a}_1, \cdots, \tilde{a}_n)^T = (xe^1, \cdots, xe^n)^T. \tag{B.5}$$

We regard the above relation as a linear mapping from $x \in \mathbf{R}^n$ to $(\tilde{a}_1, \cdots, \tilde{a}_n)^T \in \tilde{\mathbf{R}}^n$. Thus, the lth principal component score xe^l is also referred to as the *lth projection.* Since $E = (e^1, \cdots, e^n)$ is an orthogonal matrix, we have

$$\begin{aligned} |x|^2 &= |Ex|^2 = (xe^1, \cdots, xe^n)(xe^1, \cdots, xe^n)^T \\ &= \sum_{l=1}^n (\tilde{a}_l)^2. \end{aligned} \tag{B.6}$$

This means that the norm of $(\tilde{a}_1, \cdots, \tilde{a}_n)^T$ is equal to that of x.

Inverse mapping to state space

Conversely, let us consider an inverse mapping from the principal component space $\tilde{\mathbf{R}}^n$ to the state space $\mathbf{R}^n$. For an element $(\tilde{a}_1, \cdots, \tilde{a}_n)^T \in \tilde{\mathbf{R}}^n$, equation (B.5) is represented by

$$(\tilde{a}_1, \cdots, \tilde{a}_n)^T = (e^1, \cdots, e^n)^T (x_1, \cdots, x_n)^T. \tag{B.7}$$

Left-multiplying both sides by $(e^1, \cdots, e^n)$, we obtain the inverse mapping

$$\begin{aligned} (e^1, \cdots, e^n)(\tilde{a}_1, \cdots, \tilde{a}_n)^T &= (e^1, \cdots, e^n)(e^1, \cdots, e^n)^T (x_1, \cdots, x_n)^T \\ &= I(x_1, \cdots, x_n)^T \\ &= (x_1, \cdots, x_n)^T. \end{aligned} \tag{B.8}$$

Least squares approximation

Let x be an arbitrary vector in $\mathbf{R}^n$. Let us consider the least squares approximation of x by the lth principal component e^l. This is formulated as the problem of finding a constant a that minimizes the sum of squared differences as

$$\sum_{i=1}^{n} |x_i - ae_i^l|^2. \tag{B.9}$$

The next proposition shows that the principal component score gives the solution to this problem.

Proposition B.2.1 *Let $e^1, \cdots, e^n$ be a set of principal components. For an arbitrary $x \in \mathbf{R}^n$, $a = xe^l$ is the unique solution that minimizes equation (B.9) for each l.*

This proposition is applied for the calibration in the Hull–White model in Section 8.4.

B.3 Covariance and Volatility

At the end of this appendix section, we address ourselves to the volatility structure associated with the covariance matrix.

Covariance matrix

In the HJM model, $F(t_k, x_i)$ denotes the instantaneous forward rate with maturity $t_k + x_i$ as empirically observed at t_k. With this, the covariance matrix S is obtained by

$$\begin{aligned} S_{ij} &= \frac{1}{\Delta t} Cov\left(F(t_k + \Delta t, x_i - \Delta t) - F(t_k, x_i),\right. \\ &\qquad \left. F(t_k + \Delta t, x_j - \Delta t) - F(t_k, x_j)\right) \quad ; \quad 1 \le i, j, \le n, \end{aligned} \tag{B.10}$$

as introduced in Section 4.3. From this covariance matrix, we construct a volatility as follows.

As stated at the beginning of Appendix B.1, we may assume that S is invertible. Thus, because S is a covariance matrix, all eigenvalues of S are positive. We assume that all eigenvalues are distinct. Let $(\rho_1)^2 > (\rho_2)^2 > \cdots > (\rho_n)^2 > 0$ be the eigenvalues. From the principal components $e^1, \cdots, e^n$, we define an orthogonal matrix $(e^1, \cdots, e^n)$. It holds from equation (B.1) that

$$\begin{aligned} S_{ij} &= (e^1, \cdots, e^n) \begin{pmatrix} (\rho_1)^2 & 0 & 0 \\ 0 & \ddots & 0 \\ 0 & 0 & (\rho_n)^2 \end{pmatrix} (e^1, \cdots, e^n)^T \\ &= \sum_{l=1}^{n} e_i^l \rho_l^2 e_j^l. \end{aligned} \tag{B.11}$$

Principal volatility component

We determine the volatility structure from the eigenvalues and the associated principal components. Specifically, the lth volatility component is defined by $\sigma^l = \rho_l e^l$. Obviously, this volatility structure captures the covariance S.

Additionally, we always assume in this book that

$$e_1^l > 0, \qquad \rho_l > 0 \;\; ; \;\; l = 1, \cdots, n. \tag{B.12}$$

These assumptions are significant conditions that allow us to obtain the implications of the market price of risk in Sections 6.5 and 9.5.

The argument here is basically the same as that for volatility construction in the LIBOR market model, where the covariance matrix is obtained by equation (9.7).

Appendix C

MAXIMUM LIKELIHOOD ESTIMATION

This appendix introduces maximum likelihood estimation to find the mean of a random variable from sample data. For details of maximum likelihood estimation generally, see, for example, Cramer (1989).

Likelihood function

Let $x_1, \cdots, x_n$ be independent samples from a random variable Y, and let us suppose that the true mean of the variable Y is unknown. Assuming that the mean of Y is equal to θ, let $g(x_i|\theta)$ denote the probability of the outcome x_i. Then, the joint probability of the outcome $(x_1, \cdots, x_n)$ under the condition of θ being the mean is given by

$$g(x_1, \cdots, x_n|\theta) = \prod_{i=1}^{n} g(x_i|\theta). \tag{C.1}$$

Our aim is to estimate the value of θ that maximizes the probability $g(x_1, \cdots, x_n|\theta)$. A *likelihood function* for a fixed $(x_1, \cdots, x_n)$ is a one-variable function of θ defined by

$$\begin{aligned} L(\theta|x_1, \cdots, x_n) &= g(x_1, \cdots, x_n|\theta) \\ &= \prod_{i=1}^{n} g(x_i|\theta). \end{aligned} \tag{C.2}$$

We determine $\bar{\theta}$ such that $\bar{\theta}$ maximizes the likelihood function as

$$L(\bar{\theta}|x_1, \cdots, x_n) = \max_{\theta} L(\theta|x_1, \cdots, x_n). \tag{C.3}$$

Here, the probability of outcome $x_1, \cdots, x_n$ attains the maximum value when $\theta = \bar{\theta}$. From this, we consider that the mean of Y is estimated as $\bar{\theta}$ because $(x_1, \cdots, x_n)$ is most likely to occur when $\theta = \bar{\theta}$. This method of estimating θ

Takashi Yasuoka

is called *maximum likelihood estimation.* We note that the likelihood function is typically defined for other statistical parameters, such as the variance of Y.

Log-likelihood function

A log function of $L(\theta|x_1, \cdots, x_n)$ is represented by

$$\log L(\theta|x_1, \cdots, x_n) = \sum_{i=1}^{n} \log g(x_i|\theta), \tag{C.4}$$

which is called a *log-likelihood function.* Since the log function is strictly increasing, $\log L(\theta|x_1, \cdots, x_n)$ and $L(\theta|x_1, \cdots, x_n)$ take the maximum value at the same value of θ. Furthermore, in terms of form, the log-likelihood function (C.4) is more convenient to work with than the likelihood function (C.2). Thus, we sometimes employ the log-likelihood function in preference to the likelihood function.

Gauss–Markov's theorem

Let us additionally assume that Y has normal distribution with variance σ^2. If the mean of Y is θ, then we see from equation (A.1) that

$$g(x|\theta) = \frac{1}{\sqrt{2\pi}\sigma} \exp\left\{-\frac{(x-\theta)^2}{2\sigma^2}\right\}. \tag{C.5}$$

We have, from equations (C.4) and (C.5), that

$$\begin{aligned} \log L(\theta, x_1, \cdots, x_n) &= \sum_{i=1}^{n} \log g(x_i|\theta) \\ &= \sum_{i=1}^{n} \log \frac{1}{\sqrt{2\pi}\sigma} + \sum_{i=1}^{n} \left\{-\frac{(x_i-\theta)^2}{2\sigma^2}\right\}. \end{aligned} \tag{C.6}$$

This can be reduced to

$$\log L(\theta, x_1, \cdots, x_n) = -n \log \sqrt{2\pi}\sigma - \frac{1}{2\sigma^2} \sum_{i=1}^{n} (x_i - \theta)^2. \tag{C.7}$$

The first term is a constant, and the right-hand side is negative. With this, the log-likelihood function attains its maximum when

$$\sum_{i=1}^{n} (x_i - \theta)^2 \tag{C.8}$$

attains its minimum. Therefore, maximum likelihood estimation solves the least squares problem, equation (C.8). Then, we have the following proposition, known as the Gauss–Markov theorem.

Proposition C.0.1 *Let Y and $x_1, \cdots, x_n$ be as defined above. If a random variable Y has a normal distribution, then the maximum likelihood estimate of the mean θ of Y is given by the solution that minimizes equation (C.8).*

In practice, we sometimes need to estimate some parameters for financial data assumed to have a normal distribution. Proposition C.0.1 makes it convenient to estimate various type of parameters in practice.

Time-series data

As an application of Proposition C.0.1, we present a simple example. Let $X_i, i = 1, \cdots, J+1$ be sample data observed at times $t_i, i = 1, \cdots, J+1$, respectively, with $t_{i+1} - t_i = \Delta t$. We assume that the dynamical behavior of X_i follows the equation

$$dX = (A + B\varphi)dt + CdW. \tag{C.9}$$

Here, we suppose that A, B, and C are known constants, but φ is unknown.

By the Euler approximation of the above, we have a discretization as

$$X_{i+1} - X_i = (A + B\varphi)\Delta t + C\sqrt{\Delta t}W_1 \quad ; \quad , i = 1, \cdots, J, \tag{C.10}$$

where W_1 is regarded as a random variable with standard normal distribution. This equation then becomes

$$\frac{X_{i+1} - X_i}{\Delta t B} - \frac{A}{B} = \varphi + \frac{C}{\sqrt{\Delta t}B}W_1 \quad ; \quad , i = 1, \cdots, J. \tag{C.11}$$

Here, the left hand-side is obtained from observation, and normally distributed with mean φ. According to Proposition C.0.1, the maximum likelihood estimate is the solution to the least squares problem for φ such that

$$\sum_{i=1}^{J} \left\{ \frac{X_{i+1} - X_i}{\Delta t B} - \frac{A}{B} - \varphi \right\}^2 . \tag{C.12}$$

Since Δt, A, and B are nonzero constants, this expression is reduced to the following least squares problem:

$$\sum_{i=1}^{J} \{X_{i+1} - X_i - (A + B\varphi)\Delta t\}^2 . \tag{C.13}$$

Similar equations appear in the proofs of Theorem 6.2.1 and Theorem 9.2.1 for the maximum likelihood estimation of the market price of risk.

Appendix D

PROOFS FOR DIMENSION REDUCTION

D.1 Proof of Proposition 9.8.1

The market price of risk in the full-factor model is given by Theorem 9.3.1 as

$$\begin{aligned} \varphi_l &= \frac{1}{\rho_l}\sum_{i=1}^{n}\left\{E^H\left[\frac{\Delta\tilde{K}_i}{\Delta t}\right] - \lambda_{0i}E^H\left[\sum_{j=1}^{i}\kappa_j\right] + \frac{|\lambda_{0i}|^2}{2}\right\}e_i^l \\ &= \frac{1}{\rho_l}\sum_{i=1}^{n}E^H\left[\frac{\Delta\tilde{K}_i}{\Delta t}\right]e_i^l - \frac{1}{\rho_l}\sum_{i=1}^{n}\lambda_{0i}E^H\left[\sum_{j=1}^{i}\kappa_j\right]e_i^l \\ &\quad + \frac{1}{2\rho_l}\sum_{i=1}^{n}\sum_{k=1}^{n}(\lambda_{0i}^k)^2 e_i^l \ ; \ l = 1, \cdots, n. \end{aligned} \tag{D.1}$$

We remark that Theorem 9.3.1 is also valid for a d-factor model. Then, $\breve{\varphi}_l$ in the d-factor model is represented by

$$\begin{aligned} \breve{\varphi}_l &= \frac{1}{\rho_l}\sum_{i=1}^{n}E^H\left[\frac{\Delta\tilde{K}_i}{\Delta t}\right]e_i^l - \frac{1}{\rho_l}\sum_{i=1}^{n}\lambda_{0i}E^H\left[\sum_{j=1}^{i}\kappa_j\right]e_i^l \\ &\quad + \frac{1}{2\rho_l}\sum_{i=1}^{n}\sum_{k=1}^{d}(\lambda_{0i}^k)^2 e_i^l \ ; \ l = 1, \cdots, d. \end{aligned} \tag{D.2}$$

Let us examine the convergence[1] of the three terms in the right-hand side of equation (D.2) to the respective terms in equation (D.1). We see that $E^H[\Delta\tilde{K}_i/\Delta t]$ does not depend on d because this term is determined by the sample of the forward LIBOR. From this, the first term in equation (D.1) is independent from d.

Using this assumption, we see

$$C_d = \frac{\sum_{l=1}^{d}(\rho_l)^2}{\sum_{l=1}^{n}(\rho_l)^2} \approx 1. \tag{D.3}$$

[1]Here the convergence is measured in the engineering sense of equation (9.108), as described in Section 9.8.1.

With this and from equation (9.108), we have $\sum_{l=1}^{d}(\rho_l)^2 \approx \sum_{l=1}^{n}(\rho_l)^2$. Since the volatility is constructed by PCA as $\lambda_{0i}^l = \rho_l e_i^l$, it holds that

$$\sum_{l=1}^{d}(\lambda_{0i}^l)^2 \approx \sum_{l=1}^{n}(\lambda_{0i}^l)^2. \tag{D.4}$$

Accordingly, the third terms in equations (D.1) and (D.2) each satisfy

$$\frac{1}{2\rho_l}\sum_{i=1}^{n}\sum_{k=1}^{d}(\lambda_{0i}^k)^2 e_i^l \approx \frac{1}{2\rho_l}\sum_{i=1}^{n}\sum_{k=1}^{n}(\lambda_{0i}^k)^2 e_i^l \;\; ; \;\; l = 1, \cdots, d \tag{D.5}$$

The second term in equation (D.1) is specified from equation (9.5) as

$$\frac{1}{\rho_l}\sum_{i=1}^{n}\lambda_{0i}E^H\left[\sum_{j=1}^{i}\kappa_j\right]e_i^l = \frac{1}{\rho_l}\sum_{i=1}^{n}\sum_{k=1}^{n}\lambda_{0i}^k E^H\left[\sum_{j=1}^{i}\frac{\lambda_{0j}^k\delta K(t_k,\delta j)}{1+\delta K(t_k,\delta j)}\right]e_i^l. \tag{D.6}$$

Also, the second term in equation (D.2) is represented by

$$\frac{1}{\rho_l}\sum_{i=1}^{n}\lambda_{0i}E^H\left[\sum_{j=1}^{i}\kappa_j\right]e_i^l = \frac{1}{\rho_l}\sum_{i=1}^{n}\sum_{k=1}^{d}\lambda_{0i}^k E^H\left[\sum_{j=1}^{i}\frac{\lambda_{0j}^k\delta K(t_k,\delta j)}{1+\delta K(t_k,\delta j)}\right]e_i^l. \tag{D.7}$$

It holds from equation (D.4) that equation (D.7) approximates equation (D.6) when $C_d \approx 1$. This completes the proof. □

D.2 Proof of Theorem 9.8.2

We assume that we have already obtained all of the market prices of risk $\varphi_1, \cdots, \varphi_n$ in the full-factor model. Next, we examine the approximation of each term in the right-hand side of equation (9.110) by the corresponding term in equation (9.111) for different values of d.

The first term in equation (9.111) is initially given as a constant, and so we may ignore this term for the proof. The second terms of equations (9.110) and (9.111) are represented as

$$\sum_{l=1}^{n}\lambda_{0i}^l\sum_{j=1}^{i}\frac{\delta\lambda_{0j}^l L_j(0)}{1+\delta L_j(0)}\Delta s \tag{D.8}$$

and

$$\sum_{l=1}^{d} \lambda_{0i}^{l} \sum_{j=1}^{i} \frac{\delta \lambda_{0j}^{l} L_j(0)}{1+\delta L_j(0)} \Delta s, \tag{D.9}$$

respectively. It holds from the assumption and the approximation (D.4) that

$$\sum_{l=1}^{n} \lambda_{0i}^{l} \sum_{j=1}^{i} \frac{\delta \lambda_{0j}^{l} L_j(0)}{1+\delta L_j(0)} \Delta s \approx \sum_{l=1}^{d} \lambda_{0i}^{l} \sum_{j=1}^{i} \frac{\delta \lambda_{0j}^{l} L_j(0)}{1+\delta L_j(0)} \Delta s. \tag{D.10}$$

The third terms of equations (9.110) and (9.111) are written as $\sum_{l=1}^{n} (\lambda_{0i}^{l})^2 \Delta s/2$ and $\sum_{l=1}^{d} (\lambda_{0i}^{l})^2 \Delta s/2$, respectively. For the same reason as in the above approximation, we have

$$\sum_{l=1}^{n} \frac{(\lambda_{0i}^{l})^2}{2} \Delta s \approx \sum_{l=1}^{d} \frac{(\lambda_{0i}^{l})^2}{2} \Delta s \quad ; \quad i = 1, \cdots, n. \tag{D.11}$$

Thus, by the same argument as above, it holds that

$$\breve{\gamma}_i \approx \gamma_i \quad ; \quad i = 1, \cdots, n. \tag{D.12}$$

This approximation will be used at the end of this proof.

For the last terms of equations (9.110) and (9.111), it follows from equation (D.4) that

$$\sum_{l=1}^{n} \lambda_{0i}^{l} \sqrt{\Delta s} W_1^l \approx \sum_{l=1}^{d} \lambda_{0i}^{l} \sqrt{\Delta s} W_1^l \quad ; \quad i = 1, \cdots, n \tag{D.13}$$

in the sense of convergence in probability when $C_d \approx 1$.

From these, it remains to show when the fourth term in equation (9.111) approximates that in equation (9.110); specifically,

$$\sum_{l=1}^{d} \lambda_{0i}^{l} \breve{\varphi}_l \approx \sum_{l=1}^{n} \lambda_{0i}^{l} \varphi_l \quad ; \quad i = 1, \cdots, n. \tag{D.14}$$

Here, we note that $\breve{\varphi}_l$ depends on d for each $l = 1, \cdots, n$. From equations (9.43), (9.51), and (9.113), it holds in the full-factor model that

$$\begin{aligned} \lambda_i^l \varphi_l &= \rho_l e_i^l \varphi_l = e_i^l \sum_{k=1}^{n} \gamma_k e_k^l \\ &= e_i^l \zeta_l \quad ; \quad l = 1, \cdots, n. \end{aligned} \tag{D.15}$$

Similarly, for the d-dimensional model, equations (9.114), (9.115), and (9.116) imply that

$$\begin{aligned}\breve{\lambda}_i^l \breve{\varphi}_l &= \rho_l e_i^l \breve{\varphi}_l = e_i^l \sum_{k=1}^{n} \breve{\gamma}_k e_k^l \\ &= e_i^l \breve{\zeta}_l \;\; ; \;\; l = 1, \cdots, d. \end{aligned} \tag{D.16}$$

From these, we have

$$\left| \sum_{l=1}^{n} \lambda_{0i}^l \varphi_l - \sum_{l=1}^{d} \lambda_{0i}^l \breve{\varphi}_l \right| \leq \left| \sum_{l=d+1}^{n} e_i^l \zeta_l \right| + \left| \sum_{l=1}^{d} (\zeta_l - \breve{\zeta}_l) e_i^l \right| . \tag{D.17}$$

From equations (D.12), (9.113), and (9.115), we then see that $\breve{\zeta}_l \approx \zeta_l$ for all $l \leq d$. Because of these, when $|\zeta_l|$ is sufficiently small for all l with $d < l \leq n$, it hold that

$$\sum_{l=1}^{d} \lambda_{0i}^l \varphi_l \approx \sum_{l=1}^{n} \lambda_{0i}^l \varphi_l \;\; ; \;\; i = 1, \cdots, n. \tag{D.18}$$

This completes the proof. □

Remark

In Section 10.2.2, the numerical example shows that the magnitude of the market price of risk $|\varphi_l|$ is not monotonically decreasing in l. From this, the convergence $\lim_{l \to n} \lambda_{0i}^l \varphi_l = 0$ holds independently from the convergence of the accumulated contribution rate as $\lim_{d \to n} C_d = 1$. Hence, the approximation (D.14) is not implied by the measurement of C_d alone.

References

Ahn, D., & Gao, B. (1999). A parametric nonlinear model of term structure dynamics. *Review of Financial Studies, 12*(4), 721-762.

Alexander, C. (2001). *Market Models: A Guide to Financial Data Analysis.* Chichester: John Wiley & Sons.

Artzner, P., Delbaen, F., Eber, J., & Heath, D. (1999). Coherent measures of risk. *Mathematical Finance, 9*(3), 203-228.

Basak, S., & Shapiro, A. (2001). Value-at-risk-based risk management: Optimal policies and asset prices. *Review of Financial Studies, 14*(2), 371-405.

Basel Committee on Banking Supervision. (2004). *Principles for the Management and Supervision of Interest Rate Risk.* Bank for International Settlements. Available from: http://www.bis.org/publ/bcbs108.pdf.

Basel Committee on Banking Supervision. (2006). *International Convergence of Capital Measurement and Capital Standards, A Revised Framework - Comprehensive Version.* Bank for International Settlements.
Available from: http://www.bis.org/publ/bcbs128.htm.

Baxter, M., & Rennie, A. (1996). *Financial Calculus an Introduction to Derivative Pricing.* Cambridge: Cambridge University Press.

Björk, T. (2004). *Arbitrage Theory in Continuous Time.* New York: Oxford University Press.

Bhar, R., Chiarella, C., & To, T. D. (2002). *A Maximum Likelihood Approach to Estimation of Heath-Jarrow-Morton Models*, Research Paper Series: University of Technology Sydney, Sydney, *80.*

Board of Governors of the Federal Reserve System (2014), Economic Research, Available from: http://www.federalreserve.gov/releases/h15/data.htm [Accessed 20 Dec. 2014].

Brace, A., Gatarek, D., & Musiela, M. (1997). The market model of interest rate dynamics. *Mathematical Finance, 7*(2), 127-155.

Brace, A., & Musiela, M. (1994). A multifactor Gauss Markov implementation of Heath, Jarrow, and Morton. *Mathematical Finance, 4*(3), 259-283.

Brennan, M. J., & Schwartz, E. S. (1977). Savings bonds, retractable bonds and callable bonds. *Journal of Financial Economics, 5*(1), 67-88.

Brennan, M. J., & Schwartz, E. S. (1979). A continuous time approach to the pricing of bonds. *Journal of Banking & Finance, 3*(2), 133-155.

Brigo, D., & Mercurio, F. (2007). *Interest Rate Models-Theory and Practice: With Smile, Inflation and Credit.* Berlin: Springer.

Cairns, A. J. (2004). *Interest Rate Models: An Introduction.* Princeton: Princeton University Press.

Chan, K. C., Karolyi, G. A., Longstaff, F. A., & Sanders, A. B. (1992). An empirical comparison of alternative models of the short-term interest rate. *The Journal of Finance, 47*(3), 1209-1227.

Cheridito, P., Filipovic, D., & Kimmel, R. L. (2007). Market price of risk specifications for affine models: Theory and evidence. *Journal of Financial Economics, 83*(1), 123-170.

Choudhry, M. (2004). *Analyzing and Interpreting the Yield Curve.* Singapore: John Wiley & Sons.

Chung, K. L., & Williams, R. J. (1990). *Introduction to Stochastic Integration (2nd ed.).* An Arbor: Springer.

Cochrane, J., & Piazzesi, M. (2009). Decomposing the yield curve. *Working paper, University of Chicago.*

Cox, J. C., Ingersoll, E., & Ross, S. A. (1985). A theory of the term structure of interest rates. *Econometrica, 53*(2), 385-407.

Cramer, J. S. (1989). *Econometric Applications of Maximum Likelihood Methods.* Cambridge: Cambridge University Press.

Dai, Q., & Singleton, K. J. (2000). Specification analysis of affine term structure models. *Journal of Finance, 55*(5), 1943-1978.

De Jong F. (2000). Time series and cross-section information in affine term-structure models. *Journal of Business & Economic Statistics, 18*(3), 300-314.

De Jong, F., & Santa-Clara, P. (1999). The dynamics of the forward interest rate curve: A formulation with state variables. *Journal of Financial and Quantitative Analysis, 34*(01), 131-157.

Dempster, M. A., Medova, E. A., & Villaverde, M. (2010). Long-term interest rates and consol bond valuation. *Journal of Asset Management, 11*(2), 113-135.

Devineau, L., & Loisel, S. (2009). Risk aggregation in solvency II: How to converge the approaches of the internal models and those of the standard formula? *Bulletin Franais dÁctuariat, 9*(18), 107-145.

Dothan, L. U. (1978). On the term structure of interest rates. *Journal of Financial Economics, 6*(1), 59-69.

Duffee, G. R. (2002). Term premia and interest rate forecasts in affine models. *Journal of Finance, 57*(1), 405-443.

Duffie, D., & Kan, R. (1996). A yield-factor model of interest rates. *Mathematical Finance, 6*(4), 379-406.

Filipovic, D. (2009). *Term Structure Models, A Graduate Course.* Berlin: Springer.

Gatarek, D., Bachert, P., & Maksymiuk, R. (2007). *The LIBOR Market Model in Practice.* Chichester: John Wiley & Sons.

Geiger, F. (2011). *The Yield Curve and Financial Risk Premia: Implications for Monetary Policy.* Berlin: Springer.

Glasserman, P. (2004). *Monte Carlo Methods in Financial Engineering.* New York: Springer.

Gordy, M. B., & Juneja, S. (2010). Nested simulation in portfolio risk measurement. *Management Science, 56*(10), 1833-1848.

Gupta, A. (2013). *Risk Management and Simulation.* Boca Raton: CRC Press.

Hardy, M. R., & Wirch, J. L. (2004). The iterated CTE: A dynamic risk measure. *North American Actuarial Journal, 8*(4), 62-75.

Harrison, J. M., & Kreps, D. M. (1979). Martingales and arbitrage in multiperiod securities markets. *Journal of Economic Theory, 20*(3), 381-408.

Harrison, J. M., & Pliska, S. R. (1981). Martingales and stochastic integrals in the theory of continuous trading. *Stochastic Processes and their Applications, 11*(3), 215-260.

Heath, D., Jarrow, R., & Morton, A. (1992). Bond pricing and the term structure of interest rates: A new methodology for contingent claims valuation. *Econometrica: Journal of the Econometric Society, 60*(1), 77-105.

Ho, T. S., & Lee, S. (1986). Term structure movements and pricing interest rate contingent claims. *Journal of Finance, 41*(5), 1011-1029.

Hull, J. C. (2000). *Options, Futures, and Other Derivatives.* Upper Saddle River: Prentice Hall.

Hull, J. C., & White, A. D. (1990). Pricing interest-rate-derivative securities. *Review of Financial Studies, 3*(4), 573-592.

Hull, J. C., & White, A. D. (1994). Numerical procedures for implementing term structure models I: Single-factor models. *The Journal of Derivatives, 2*(1), 7-16.

Hunt, P., & Kennedy, J. (2004). *Financial Derivatives in Theory and Practice.* Chichester: John Wiley & Sons.

Ingersoll, J. E. (1987). *Theory of Financial Decision Making.* Totowa: Rowman & Littlefield.

Jacod, J., & Protter, P. E. (2003). *Probability Essentials.* Berlin: Springer.

James, J., & Webber, N. (2000). *Interest Rate Modelling.* Chichester : Wiley-Blackwell Publishing Ltd.

Jamshidian, F. (1997). LIBOR and swap market models and measures. *Finance and Stochastics, 1*(4), 293-330.

Jha, S. (2011). *Interest Rate Markets: A Practical Approach to Fixed Income.* Hoboken: John Wiley & Sons.

Jorion, P. (2007). *Value at Risk: The New Benchmark for Managing Financial Risk.* New York: McGraw-Hill.

Karatzas, I., & Shreve, S. E. (1998). *Methods of Mathematical Finance.* New York: Springer.

Kriele, M., & Wolf, J. (2014). *Value-oriented Risk Management of Insurance Companies.* London: Springer.

Litterman, R. B., & Scheinkman, J. (1991). Common factors affecting bond returns. *Journal of Fixed Income, 1*(1), 54-61.

Longstaff, F. A., Santa-Clara, P., & Schwartz, E. S. (2002). The relative valuation of caps and swaptions: Theory and empirical evidence. *Journal of Finance, 56*(6), 2067-2109.

Medova, E., Rietbergen, M., Villaverde, M., & Yong, Y. (2005). Modelling the long-term dynamics of the yield curve. *Working Paper, Judge Business School,*

University of Cambridge.
Mercurio, F., & Moraleda, J. M. (2000). An analytically tractable interest rate model with humped volatility. *European Journal of Operational Research, 120*(1), 205-214.
Merton, R. C. (1973). Theory of rational option pricing. *Bell Journal of Economics and Management Science, 4*(1), 141-183.
Miltersen, K. R., Sandmann, K., & Sondermann, D. (1997). Closed form solutions for term structure derivatives with log-normal interest rates. *The Journal of Finance, 52*(1), 409-430.
Moraleda, J. M., & Vorst, T. C. (1997). Pricing American interest rate claims with humped volatility models. *Journal of Banking & Finance, 21*(8), 1131-1157.
Munk, C. (2011). *Fixed Income Modelling.* Oxford: Oxford University Press.
Musiela, M., & Rutkowski, M. (1997). Continuous-time term structure models: Forward measure approach. *Finance and Stochastics, 1*(4), 261-291.
Musiela, M., & Rutkowski, M. (2011). *Martingale Methods in Financial Modelling.* Berlin: Springer.
Nawalkha, S. K., Soto, G. M., & Beliaeva, N. A. (2005). *Interest Rate Risk Modeling: The Fixed Income Valuation Course.* Hoboken: John Wiley & Sons.
Nawalkha, S. K., Beliaeva, N. A., & Soto, G. M. (2007). *Dynamic Term Structure Modeling: The Fixed Income Valuation Course.* Hoboken: John Wiley & Sons.
Nelson, C. R., & Siegel, A. F. (1987). Parsimonious modeling of yield curves. *Journal of Business, 60*(4), 473-489.
Norman, J. (2009). Real world interest rate modelling with the BGM model. SSRN working paper, 1480174,
Available from: http://papers.ssrn.com/sol3/papers.cfm?abstract_id=1480174.t
Øksendal, B. (2003). *Stochastic Differential Equations.* Berlin: Springer.
Petersen, P. (2012). *Linear Algebra.* New York: Springer.
Pliska, S. (1997). *Introduction to Mathematical Finance.* Malden: Blackwell Publishers.
Poon, S., & Granger, C. W. (2003). Forecasting volatility in financial markets: A review. *Journal of Economic Literature, 41*(2), 478-539.
Rao, C. R., Toutenburg, H., Shalabh, H. C., & Schomaker, M. (2008). *Linear Models and Generalizations. Least Squares and Alternatives (3rd ed.).* Berlin: Springer.
Rebonato, R. (1996). *Interest-rate Option Models.* Chichester: John Wiley & Sons.
Rebonato, R., Mahal, S., Joshi, M., Bucholz, L. D., & Nyholm, K. (2005). Evolving yield curves in the real-world measures: A semi-parametric approach. *Journal of Risk, 7*(3), 29-61.
Riskmatrix. (2014). BBA LIBOR: Historical Market Rates,
Available from: http://66.84.43.120/TF/bba-libor-historical-market-rates.html [Accessed 20 Dec. 2014].
Ritchken, P., & Sankarasubramanian, L. (1995). Volatility structures of forward rates and the dynamics of the term structure. *Mathematical Finance, 5*(1),

55-72.

Sadr, A. (2009). *Interest Rate Swaps and Their Derivatives: A Practitioner's Guide.* Hoboken: John Wiley & Sons.

Schoenmakers, J., & Coffey, B. (1999). LIBOR rate models, related derivatives and model calibration. *WIAS working paper.*

Shreve, S. E. (2004). *Stochastic Calculus for Finance II: Continuous-time Models.* New York: Springer.

Simon, C. P., & Blume, L. (1994). *Mathematics for Economists.* New York: W. W. Norton & Company.

Stanton, R. (1997). A nonparametric model of term structure dynamics and the market price of interest rate risk. *Journal of Finance, 52*(5), 1973-2002.

Tavella, D. (2003). *Quantitative Methods in Derivatives Pricing: An Introduction to Computational Finance.* Hoboken: John Wiley & Sons.

Vasicek, O. (1977). An equilibrium characterization of the term structure. *Journal of Financial Economics, 5*(2), 177-188.

Wu, L. (2009). *Interest Rate Modeling: Theory and Practice.* Boca Ration: CRC Press.

Yamai, Y., & Yoshiba, T. (2002). On the validity of value-at-risk: Comparative analyses with expected shortfall. *Monetary and Economic Studies, 20*(1), 57-85.

Yamai, Y., & Yoshiba, T. (2005). Value-at-risk versus expected shortfall: A practical perspective. *Journal of Banking & Finance, 29*(4), 997-1015.

Yasuoka, T. (2001). Mathematical pseudo-completion of the BGM model. *International Journal of Theoretical and Applied Finance, 4*(03), 375-401.

Yasuoka, T. (2012). LIBOR market model under the real-world measure, and real-world simulation. *Shibaura MOT Discussion Paper*, 2012-2.
Available from: http://mot-innovation.shibaura-it.ac.jp/wp-content/uploads/2013/07/d_p_2012-02.pdf.

Yasuoka, T. (2013a). LIBOR market model under the real-world measure. *International Journal of Theoretical and Applied Finance, 16*(04), 1350024.

Yasuoka, T. (2013b). L^2-theoretical study of the relation between the LIBOR market model and the HJM model. *Journal of Math-for-Industry, 5*(2), 11-16.

Yasuoka, T. (2015). Interest-rate simulation under the real-world measure within a Gaussian HJM framework. *Quantitative Finance Letters, 3*(1), 10-16.
Available from: http://www.tandfonline.com/doi/full/10.1080/21649502.2014.995213#.VNfX6-asWCk.

Author Index

Subject Index

Takashi Yasuoka

www.ingramcontent.com/pod-product-compliance
Lightning Source LLC
LaVergne TN
LVHW070947210926
848482LV00002B/129